BLACK FIRE

BLACK FIRE

*The Making of
an American Revolutionary*

NELSON PEERY

THE NEW PRESS · NEW YORK

PUBLISHED IN THE UNITED STATES BY THE NEW PRESS, NEW YORK
DISTRIBUTED BY W.W. NORTON & COMPANY, INC.,
500 FIFTH AVENUE, NEW YORK, NY 10110

FRONTISPIECE:
THE AUTHOR AS AN INFANTRYMAN IN THE 93RD DIVISION,
MOJAVE DESERT, CALIFORNIA, 1942.

LIBRARY OF CONGRESS CATALOGING-IN-PUBLICATION DATA

PEERY, NELSON, 1925–
BLACK FIRE.
P. CM.
ISBN 1–56584–158–1
1. PEERY, NELSON, 1925– . 2. AFRO-AMERICANS—BIOGRAPHY.
3. RACISM—UNITED STATES. 4. AFRO-AMERICANS—CIVIL RIGHTS.
5. UNITED STATES—RACE RELATIONS. I. TITLE.
E185.97.P44A3 1994
973'.0496073'0092—DC20
(B)
93–46901
CIP

ESTABLISHED IN 1990 AS A MAJOR ALTERNATIVE TO THE LARGE, COMMERCIAL
PUBLISHING HOUSES, THE NEW PRESS IS THE FIRST FULL-SCALE NONPROFIT
AMERICAN BOOK PUBLISHER OUTSIDE OF THE UNIVERSITY PRESSES. THE PRESS
IS OPERATED EDITORIALLY IN THE PUBLIC INTEREST, RATHER THAN FOR PRIVATE
GAIN; IT IS COMMITTED TO PUBLISHING IN INNOVATIVE WAYS WORKS OF EDUCA-
TIONAL, CULTURAL, AND COMMUNITY VALUE THAT, DESPITE THEIR INTELLECTUAL
MERITS, MIGHT NOT NORMALLY BE "COMMERCIALLY" VIABLE. THE NEW PRESS'S
EDITORIAL OFFICES ARE LOCATED AT THE CITY UNIVERSITY OF NEW YORK.

PRINTED IN THE UNITED STATES OF AMERICA.

94 95 96 97   9 8 7 6 5 4 3 2 1

It is a peculiar sensation, this double consciousness, this sense of always look-ing at one's self through the eyes of others. . . . One feels his two-ness—an American, a Negro; two souls, two thoughts, two unreconciled strivings; two warring ideals in one dark body, whose dogged strength alone keeps it from being torn asunder.

—W. E. B. DU BOIS, *Souls of Black Folk*

(

CONTENTS

PREFACE

THIS BOOK WAS started shortly after World War II. I was twenty-four and could still remember. When I became old enough to be honest with myself and the typewriter, I finished the work.

The story is true. Sometimes an event had to be put in a different time frame to maintain continuity. At times, various experiences were consolidated to maintain a background for the story. All the characters are true. Some, especially in the army, become a little bigger than life as I gave them a bit of other soldiers' personalities to round them out.

Most of the names are true. I changed a few to avoid a scene, sometimes to protect a person's well-being.

Because it's a true story, I kept the language as it was spoken then. During the period covered by the book, we forced America to capitalize the word "Negro." It identified us, it set us apart and held us together. We were very proud of it. Sometimes we used the term "Afro-American" but hardly ever "black" or "African American." This would come later, with changed circumstances.

I'll not make a dedication. So many people contributed to this story and to this book that it would be impossible. The dedications are in these pages. To avoid a physical confrontation, I'll mention my mom, Caroline; my brothers, Ben, Al, Carroll, Ross, Norman, and Richard; and my sons, Steve and Patrice.

ACKNOWLEDGMENTS

THIS BOOK WOULD not have been written were it not for Meridel Le Sueur. She instilled in me a dialectic, a sense of history that led me to love America and her diverse people enough to write about them, to fight them, to fight with them—and to fight for them. Her confidence in me as a revolutionary and a writer sustained me during difficult times when I lost confidence in myself.

I am grateful for the comradely support from that prolific poet of the world's people, Jack Hirschman, and the fighting bard of the San Francisco Bay Area, Sarah Menefee.

A special thanks to Chris Mahin, whose professionalism as a proofreader and our close comradeship over the decades gave him the courage to wade through and straighten out the morass of misspelled words and garbled sentences.

A special medal and thanks to Sue Ying, who let me remain husband and comrade as I relived other loves and fought other battles while writing this book.

For factual material, I leaned especially heavily on four outstanding works. First of these is the prodigious history of the *U.S. Army in World War II: The Employment of Negro Troops*, by Ulysses Lee, issued by the office of the Chief of Military History, United States Army.

Col. Bernard C. Naty's *Strength for the Fight* (New York: Free Press, 1986) gives an unparalleled historical continuity to the struggle of the Negro soldier against his segregation and oppression.

Lee Finkle's excellent study, *Forum for Protest: The Black Press during World War II* (Cranbury, N. J.: Associated University Presses, 1975) is a rare, courageous, and indispensable historical analysis.

I took most of the background material concerning the Philippines from *The Philippines Reader*, edited by Dabuek B. Schirmer and Stephen Rosskamm Shalom (Boston: South End Press, 1987).

Whenever my personal observations conflicted with these works, I relied on my observations or experiences. This is a biography, not a history, and I am solely responsible for its content.

Part One

RAISING HELL IN MINNESOTA

1

"HOLY COW!"

Hank whistled through his teeth. I stretched my neck above the weeds to get a better look.

The bull missed his mark. The force of the lunge knocked the cow to her knees. Now the target was in line. The bull mounted her again, front hooves lightly touching the sides of her spine for balance, head tilted upward, lips curled back as if to say, "Goddamnit, I got you now!" Another thrust and the monstrous pink organ slid into her body.

"Holy smokes!" Hank whistled again.

★

I hiccupped because my diaphragm and lungs began going in different directions. Then I saw the engineer and the brakeman walking toward the corral.

"Let's scram," I said in the best tough-guy tone I could muster.

Hank didn't have to worry. He was sixteen and nobody cared whether he went to school or not. We were both in the sixth grade, but I was only twelve and my old man promised to whip me with the gun belt if I skipped school again. Besides, I finally figured out that being a member of the only black family in Wabasha meant it was the same as caught if I were seen.

It was springtime and the farmers brought their livestock to the corral beside the railroad for shipment up to the packing plant in South Saint Paul. Hank kept track of all those things.

Earlier that day, during the morning recess, he had walked over to me. "They got some more cattle in the corral over at the railroad. Let's go up and watch 'em fuck."

Nothing on earth could have stopped me. I knew that if I left school I was going to get a beating from Pop or the teacher or maybe both. I went anyway. I got the beating. We went back again and watched the rams and hogs and horses. I got some more beatings, but I never forgot any of it.

★

3

If a kid had to grow up during the Depression, Wabasha, Minnesota, was as good a place as any. The town nestled between the Mississippi River and a semicircle of bluffs to the west. The hunting and fishing were perhaps the best in the southern part of the state. With twenty-three hundred inhabitants, Wabasha was little more than a railroad junction where the dirt-poor dirt farmers brought their cattle and wool and cabbages for sale or shipment to Minneapolis and Saint Paul, eighty-five miles upriver.

Like many small towns during the 1920s and 1930s, Wabasha was geographically divided between rich and poor. The east side of town contained the business section, the churches, and the high school. The teachers, the doctor, the lawyer, and the manager of the flour mill and the John Dill Company lived there. Those who worked at the mill, the Dill Company, and the railroad, and those who had no jobs at all, lived on the west side.

In 1928, when we moved to Wabasha, I was five years old. That move was another of the prolonged battles, and for me, an important battle, in our people's and our family's long struggle for equality.

When my father came back from France at the end of World War I, his mind was made up to get his equal share of American life as he had gotten his equal share of the war. Intelligent, egotistical, argumentative, prone to violence, he decided to become a lawyer. Working on construction during the day and studying at night ended with marriage and two babies in two years.

My father did get something from studying the law books. He understood that despite the tightening segregation and discrimination, if he passed a civil service examination they would have to give him a job. He took an examination for the Railway Mail Service and passed, along with another black veteran. Until then, this lily-white cream of the Postal Service had successfully barred blacks from employment. The furious district supervisor got rid of him by immediately assigning him to a division in Minneapolis, Minnesota. We moved from Saint Joe, Missouri, to our new home. The first time my father complained about the crude discrimination on the job, they transferred him to Wabasha. It was, in its isolation and winters, somewhat akin to Siberia.

Like most blacks, he was used to moving. Since the end of slavery, those not held on the plantations by force constantly moved outward. Fleeing the violence and poverty, they searched for employment and a place to be free.

My mother told me how Great-great-grandma Elisa's Cherokee parents were driven westward through Kentucky along the Trail of Tears toward Oklahoma. Uprooted, their life force strangled and died. This was the real meaning of the Trail of Tears. Tears for their ancestral home preceded those spilled by starvation and rape, disease and brutality.

With broken hearts they wrapped their baby in a blanket and secured her to a tree limb. Perhaps they thought Cherokees who had escaped the dragnet would find her and raise her close to her earth and rivers. A slave trader found the infant and sold her to the Hazard family of Scott County, Kentucky. They enslaved the child and handed her over to a slave family, which raised her as one of their own.

Great-grandma Caroline, Elisa's daughter, stayed close to her mother in all things. The stories of these women came down to us, generation by generation, from fireside to fireside—stories of their hatred of slavery, a hatred that spilled over into a burning hate for the master class.

Kentucky, a slave state loyal to the Union, was exempt from the Emancipation Proclamation. While blacks in Mississippi were free, the slaves in Kentucky labored under the lash for another two years.

Finally emancipated by the Thirteenth Amendment after the ending of the Civil War, the mother and daughter left "the damned ol' Missy." They left the big farm and its legacy of labor and whips and chains and the sale of their children. These former slave women hand-built a covered wagon and with their five children set out, they said, for "the land where John Brown fought for them."

They worked and walked their way across the hills and mountains. They forded the streams and rivers. They survived the bitter winters on the plains. Finally, they arrived at Junction City, Kansas. The two ex-slaves became frontier women. They hired themselves out as field hands and day laborers until they accumulated enough money to purchase a little plot of land of their own.

That was one of the first of an unending series of moves toward freedom.

★

The morning following our move to Wabasha, my older brother, Ben, and I walked to what must have been everyone's notion of the country school. The two-story, box-shaped, red brick building held all eight classes of elementary school. There was one row of chairs for each grade. The first floor held the first through the fourth grade; the other four classes were upstairs.

The thin body of our teacher, Miss De Witt, looked even thinner because her thick glasses made her eyes look larger and more knowing than they were. She showed me a seat. I took it and sat down. In a few moments a chubby girl with long blond hair sat next to me. She would glance at me and then look straight ahead. I was going to ask her what she was looking at, when she turned to me.

"My name's Shirley. What's yours?"

"Nelson."

Miss De Witt rolled her big stern eyes in the direction of the whispers.

"My mama said you ain't no different from nobody else, 'cept God kept you in the oven too long."

I wanted to tell her that she wasn't in long enough, but Miss De Witt was glaring at me. Later, Shirley and I became close friends.

As Ben and I walked home after school, Richard, who lived across the street, waited for us. As we passed him, he said, "My Dad says you're a black nigger."

I didn't know what all that meant, and didn't respond. I'm sure Richard didn't know either. Ben knew, so he hit him in the mouth, knocking him down, and sat astride him, hitting him until his nose bled. Richard's little brother, David, ran over. He was my size, and when he tried to help his brother, I grabbed him and threw him down and hit him as hard as I could. Ben let Richard get up and the two of them ran home.

I told Mom about the fight and how we won. She became very worried and said if they called us that, we should call them poor white trash and come home. Pop entered the room and when he found out what had happened, he said we should try to kill anybody who said that. Mom nodded toward us and Pop sent us upstairs to bed.

Ben and I lay still, trying to understand the measured, low-voiced discussion downstairs. Mom said that real strength and courage lay in not paying attention to such name-calling. Pop sneered at that. Then Mom spoke of how we were alone and isolated and how we would have to give these people time to know us. Then I heard Pop interrupt.

"I don't care how right you are." His voice lower and more intense, he added, "I'll not have these kids grow up afraid to defend themselves."

"Ben, it only has to happen one time." Her voice took on a pleading tone. "Who's to defend us if you are on the road? Who's to defend us if you are here?"

"I don't believe it will come to that. These people are not animals, and we're far enough away from the saloons so there is no need to fear the drunks."

"But what if it should happen?"

"Then Goddamnit, it happens." There was a sudden anger in his voice, and we all knew he was thinking of his .30–06 rifle and the .38 caliber service revolver he carried on the railroad. Pop had been out of the infantry and combat for nearly ten years, but even at our early ages we knew that he could not get it out of him.

"If any of these pecks put a hand on my kids I'll kill him."

"Hush, Ben, the children will hear you."

The voices downstairs became too low to hear and, as she often did, my grandmother came into the bedroom to help us with our prayers. She was a treasure-house of stories and folktales. We learned all about Horse Cave, Kentucky, from her. We knew by heart every cyclone and every struggle of the black farmers in that area. When she sat down on the bed, we knew we would hear another story.

She looked at us for a moment, her long, braided hair making her resemble an ancient squaw more than ever.

"Do you remember your great-grandfather?"

Ben nodded. Great-grandpa died at ninety-five, when I was three. I knew this stooped old man with the kindly black face only through our photographs.

The family story was that he came to the hospital to see me the day I was born. He held me for a few moments and gave me back to my mother, saying, "Carrie, that's a sorry baby."

She promptly named me after him.

"Do you remember that my father was a slave?"

We nodded our heads.

"I was born the year the Civil War started. Your great-grandfather wanted our freedom more than anything else. When President Lincoln declared that all the slaves who take arms for the Union would be free, Father refused to go. He said that the Union would have to go some better than that. It wasn't long before Lincoln said that if a slave would bear arms for the Union, then their families would be free. Your great-grandfather slipped away that night and joined the Ninth Colored Heavy Artillery. He became a sergeant major."

She paused for a moment and then asked, "Do you know why I told you that story?"

Ben nodded his head.

"Why?"

"So we won't fight for nothin' again."

"Now say your prayers and go to sleep."

We knelt beside her, our heads in her lap, and recited the children's prayer, "Now I Lay Me Down to Sleep."

I knew we had had another session of "fireside" training. After she left the room, I listened to the wind rising as it swept over the bluff toward the river.

★

That summer and fall were the best time of my life. There was money for clothes and toys. Ben and I made friends with all the kids on the west side of town.

Later that year the good times ended. Neighbors would come to the house and speak in whispers to Pop. We knew they came to borrow money. Young as we were, we knew something terrible had happened and only a few of our neighbors were working. The Dill Company closed down. The Big Joe Flour Mill went on part-time. A few people still worked on the farms and on the railroad section crews. Pop was one of the lucky ones. Every other week he would shake our hands good-bye and enter the big railroad car marked United States Mail for the ten-day trip to Walla Walla, Washington, and back.

As the new year wore on, things seemed to get worse. A hobo jungle appeared in the big gully across the tracks. The freight trains going west, crowded with men looking for work, passed freight trains going east, crowded with men looking for work. Our house, only a block from the tracks, seemed to attract every hungry hobo in the area. One of them took some chalk and marked a big E on the side of the house. When I started to scrub it off, Mom said to leave it on since it meant the men could get something to eat here. The big E stayed on the side of the house for several years.

All kinds of fellows came to our house from the freight trains.

The guys from the West wore big country hats, and men from the East wore city hats. Farm boys wanted to work for their food, and fellows with guitars would sing for their supper. Old men came to our door, and young men came. Now and then, Negroes, guys our color who talked with funny accents, knocked at our door. They made us laugh when they said "you all" and meant only one. Mom treated everyone well. Those who were brown like me she treated best of all. They could wash in our bathtub and they didn't have to eat from the plate with which she always fed the hoboes. These men ate with us, and Mom always gave them a quarter or something to take with them so they could eat the next day. She always told us that all people are equal and that everyone should be treated the same. Then she would treat some of the guys better just because they were our color. When I asked her why, she just said they were our people, that she loved them all and we had to make up for what had been taken from them. I didn't understand because Howie and Shirley and Bert and Dick were my people too, and they were white.

Conditions worsened during 1933 and 1934. One day, men from the government came to town and purchased almost half the cattle in the area. They herded the cattle into a ditch and shot them. The government agents poured lime over the carcasses and covered them with dirt so people wouldn't eat them. When the people cursed at them, the government people said it was necessary to do this in order to come out of the Depression. People starved because there were too many cattle.

Pop got another wage cut and, for the first time, I saw him come home drunk. He tried hard to walk straight and to talk normally, but he didn't fool us. Even though we laughed about it, deep down it hurt. Somehow we understood that our Pop wasn't as strong as we had believed.

We fished in earnest now. We would bring the fish live from the river and keep them in the big rain barrel. Hardly a day went by without our eating fish. We feasted on the big, slimy walleyed pike and snakelike pickerels, crappies, sunfish, and bass, with the catfish or river trout on the side. A sack of sweet corn cost a nickel and when the railroad dicks left to have coffee, it was easy to break the seal on a boxcar and loot enough cabbage to fill the sauerkraut crocks for the winter. Stealing cabbage and apples and corn wasn't stealing. A person had to eat, and if we didn't take the food, the government agents would buy it and pour oil on it.

Three more brothers were born in Wabasha. A nun at the hospital, seeing a brown-skinned newborn baby in the bassinet, ran down the hall screaming for the doctor to come save the baby who was turning black.

My youngest brother, born during the worst of the Depression, had rickets. Even at eleven I understood that a lack of milk, vegetables, and fruit caused rickets. I also understood that the government shot cows, fed milk to pigs, and buried fruit to end the Depression that caused rickets.

After saying "good morning," our next-door neighbor would always add, "The world's going to hell in a handbasket." We accepted this as a fact of life and went about our business of growing up. Over the years, the kids in the immediate neighborhood formed a little gang. Bert wanted to be a postman like his father. (He made the grade.) Don wanted to be a doctor. (He became a famous surgeon.) I don't think Richard's family ever felt at ease with blacks living across the street. Richard and I fought a lot, but we were good friends. He wanted to become a fireman. (His head was blown off in the fire of Omaha Beach during the invasion of Normandy.)

The Civilian Conservation Corps came to Wabasha. Part of Roosevelt's plan for economic recovery, the CCC was under the direction of the Army Corps of Engineers. In another eight years, the young men from the CCC would become the backbone of the army. My parents' hope that some blacks would come with them never materialized. The CCC, like the army, was segregated. The 3C boys, as we called them, set about planting trees and building roads and small dams. In the evenings they would roam the streets looking for women, or just someone to be friendly with.

Sometimes, a truckload of the 3C boys would pass us on some back road on their way to work. We would shout, "Hooray for the CCC!" They would always wave back. One day when they passed us we yelled out our greeting according to the plan. When they waved back we shouted, "You cross-country cocksuckers!" and ran into the woods. Two days later, while playing baseball by the tracks, two of the 3C boys approached us.

"You the kids that cussed us?"

"I ain't cussed nobody," Richard said defiantly.

"I ain't never saw you before," Bert said.

One of the guys looked at me. "That little black bastard's one of them." He grabbed my arm. Terrified, I tried not to show it.

"You're the one's calling me names. I ain't called you nothin'."

"There ain't no other colored kids in this town." He looked at the rest of the gang. "I can't identify the rest of you—but I know this one." He jerked my arm, nearly yanking me off my feet. "You dumb kids don't know what that word means—but I ain't no cocksucker, and I'll beat hell out of anybody calls me that." He gave me a shove and kicked his army work boot sideways against my butt. I half fell, recovered my balance, and ran a little ways from them.

"Go home and tell your pappy what I did, an' I'll tell him what you said." He turned to the gang. "You kids want some of it?"

The guys moved away. From a safe distance Bert mumbled, "I ain't no kid."

"If I'm a kid, you're a goat—an' all the slop runs down your throat!" Richard yelled. The gang scattered in all directions. I didn't run because I hadn't said anything. It finally sank in: I'm a black boy in a white man's town, and I can't get away with anything, so I'd better not do anything.

★

Ben entered ninth grade and started high school on the east side of town. He was on the football team and growing up. One evening at the supper table he sat looking at his food. Finally Pop asked him what was the trouble. He answered matter-of-factly that he was going to tell him something. Then he announced that he had a girlfriend. My grandmother snickered; Mom looked at Pop. He was in the middle of guiding a forkful of food to his mouth. It missed and spilled on his shirt. Cleaning up the spilled food gave Pop time to think, and when he composed himself he merely said, "Well, that's fine, Ben. I guess you're a man now." But he gave Mom one of those I-want-to-talk-about-this looks.

All the rest of Ben's crowd had girlfriends and I thought it was only natural. I knew by the glance exchanged between Mom and Pop that something was amiss. His girlfriend, Joy, lived within shouting distance of our house. Her mother thought that the puppy love between Ben and her daughter was "cute." They said no more about it, but I knew that both Mom and Pop were disturbed by our growing up isolated from our people, in a rural, all-white town.

In 1935, Pop got another wage cut. It seemed that almost no one was working on our side of town. More men than ever rode the freight trains. More of them came to our house asking for food. Mom still fed them but there was less than before on their plate and ours. Their mood changed from belief that prosperity was "just around the corner" to sullen anger. People would speak of how the bankers and monopolies took everything from them. Now and then, discussing the Depression with Pop, some would say there needed to be a revolution in the country.

One afternoon there was a soft rap on the front door. Mom shouted "Come in" from the kitchen. Again the soft knock. She got up and opened the door. An elderly black man bowed slightly toward Mom and said, "I assume this is the Peery household."

Mom smiled at the obvious and invited him in.

"My name is Ned Sparks," he said. "I am faring through this country and I was told of the lovely colored family that lived here. I was determined to meet you."

Mom thanked him and offered him a seat. Mr. Sparks, dressed in faded but immaculately clean blue-denim jumper and coveralls, must have been in his sixties. A slender five foot seven with thick white mustache and neatly brushed gray hair, he was a picture of the southern "colored gentleman."

Mr. Sparks had just got in from New Orleans. Mom listened eagerly as he told of the difficulties "our people" faced in the South. We listened to the soft cultured drawl for a while, then left to play with the gang.

We came home as the darkness settled into the valley. Mom, Pop, Gran, and Mr. Sparks were still sitting around the table.

"We are facing a dangerous thing because of this case. You know, the youngest of the Scottsboro boys was about the same age as this youngster." He nodded at me. "If they lynch or execute these boys, none of us will be safe. Negroes will become fair game for any bunch of drunken whites. We will become bird free—outside the protection of the law—like our brothers in South Africa."

Mr. Sparks looked over to me. Aside from a tiny suggestion of crow's-feet at the corners of his eyes, the dark chocolate skin of his face was smooth.

"Do you know about the Scottsboro boys?"

Everybody knew something about the nine black youths accused of raping a white prostitute on a freight train near Scottsboro, Alabama. A Klan-like jury of up-country whites, in a kanga-

roo court surrounded by a lynch mob, had sentenced them—
including the thirteen-year-old—to death.

I, too, was frightened by what had happened in Scottsboro. I
could not understand more than that's the way things were in the
South, and that's why all colored people should leave.

"I know a little about them."

"We all have to help them. It could just as well have been
you." Then he turned back to Pop and continued. "We're still like
crabs in a barrel, pulling each other down. We can't even get
together for something like this. I'm a good Catholic, but I tell
you, if not for the Communists, those boys would be dead."

There was a moment's silence. The grown-ups pondered the
contradiction of black folks being at the mercy of whites unless
they stuck together, and they couldn't.

Mr. Sparks spoke again.

"Such a fine set of youngsters. It's a pity that you're stuck out
here."

Pop looked over his brood of seven and said, "Yes, I've got to
find some way of getting out of here before something happens."

This was my first glimmer of understanding why my grandfa-
ther's generation was so gentle and good to children, and why
Mom treated the Negro hoboes in a special way. Something—
something terrible—could happen to any of them at any time. It
frightened me—but that was another country or another world. I
couldn't visualize anything bad happening to me in our little
town.

Mr. Sparks declined to spend the night with us. Bowing
slightly, he thanked Mom and Pop for the supper and the conversation.

As he stood to leave he said, "I'll be heading back to New
Orleans after early morning Mass. I'll be seeing you again. God
bless you all."

I could see that Pop was too embarrassed to offer him
money.

"You're going to be all right? Can we help you out?"

"Oh, no thank you. I'll be all right. The side-door Pullman
will be just fine."

Mr. Sparks chuckled at his description of the boxcar and
turned to leave. We all stood on the porch and watched him as he
disappeared into the night, walking toward the freight yards a
block away.

★

Fred and Mary lived in the last house before the cemetery, where their father was the caretaker. Fred was one grade behind me, and Mary was in my class. They became part of a turning point in my life.

It began like any other day in school. The late spring sunshine made us more interested in looking out the open windows than paying attention to the teacher. Mrs. De Witt spent an hour with each grade. When the hour was up, students were given study material and she would move to the next class, which was the next row of students.

I felt a sting on my cheek, and from the corner of my eye, I could see that Richard had shot a spitball at me. I made one and sent it whizzing toward him. We soon got tired of that, and Richard looked at Mrs. De Witt. I missed her on purpose. Richard hit her. She turned angrily toward us.

"Who did that?"

Snickers, and behind books, laughter.

"We're going to sit here until I find out who did it. Now, for the last time, who was it?"

"Nelson and Richard did it." Mary pressed her lips together making it seem even more factual.

"We did not," Richard said.

"You did so. I saw you."

Mrs. De Witt made us stand before the class and apologize. Then she took me into the cloakroom and told me to clench my hands into a fist. She whacked each fist three times with a ruler and sent me back to my seat. When I sat down blood was oozing from a knuckle and there were tears in my eyes. She then took Richard to the cloakroom. He screamed as she gave him the same punishment, and came to his seat crying. He leaned over toward Mary and whispered, "Boy, we're going to get you for this."

After school was out, Richard came over to me.

"Let's get her for snitching on us."

"Aw, heck. It's all over with. Let it go."

"Well, she'll just go and do it again sometime. We won't hurt her."

I hung back. If there was one thing I had learned, it was never to hit a girl, no matter what she did. Richard argued and argued, and finally, when he called me chicken, I agreed to go with him. We settled on a plan. We would hide in the wheat field along the road near her house. When she came down the road we would scare her and make her run home.

The next day after school, we ran down the tracks and through the wheat field to the road. We could see Mary and her younger brother coming toward us. As they neared us Richard jumped out at her.

"What'd ya snitch on us for?"

Mary started to cry and ran toward her house. Richard walked back to me. We threw our arms over each other's shoulder and walked back home.

I opened the door of the house and saw Mom crying and Pop looking angry and worried.

"Where have you been?"

"Out with Richard."

"Mr. Fredrickson called about you jumping on his daughter."

My heart began pounding in my throat and ears and I suddenly understood the implications of what we had done.

"We didn't hurt her. She snitched on us in school and we were just going to scare her."

"My God, child, aren't you ever going to learn? *You are a Negro!*"

Pop reached for the heavy leather gun belt. Mom looked pleadingly at him for a moment and left the room.

"I'll beat you half to death before I let you make another Scottsboro case here."

I received my first real beating. My father whipped me until the sweat ran from his face—until my legs and back felt unreal and my body burned as if scalded by hot water.

Finally he stopped and called Mr. Fredrickson. They talked for a bit and then Pop said, "Yes, I gave him the worst whipping he ever received. . . . I'd appreciate it if this didn't get any farther than us. No . . . I'm sure he didn't mean her any harm. No, no—he'll be all right. He has to learn or some day he'll get killed. Sure . . . he'd like to apologize."

He handed the phone to me.

"Beg her pardon." There was a terrible threat and something akin to fear in his voice more frightening than the beating. I took the phone.

"I'm sorry, Mary," I sobbed and sat back on the floor crying.

Pop talked for a moment, thanked him for calling, and hung up.

"My God, boy," he said. "I know you didn't mean anything, but you've got to learn some time. You just don't do things like that."

"But I didn't . . ."

"I don't give a Goddamn what you didn't. We're outnumbered a thousand to one. All it would have taken was for Fred to call a couple of those peckerwoods and there is no telling where it would end. It was decent of Fred not to call the sheriff."

Pop left the room. Mom came in, her eyes swollen and red. I knew no matter what happened, I was her son. She pressed me close to her and said, "Honey, I'm sorry that you got such a whipping, but we've tried to tell you a thousand times to stay away from these white girls. Leave them alone. I don't care what else you do, stay away from them. There's not another Negro within a hundred miles, and anything you do you're going to get caught. White boys can do lots of things that you can't. I want you to listen to me. You have to learn to conduct yourself so that everyone else forgets you're Negro. But don't you ever forget it. Now don't forget what I've told you."

Pop stood in the doorway and nodded to Mom. He looked at me for just a second and I could see the hurt and pain in his face. I knew that he had hurt something in himself far more than he had hurt me. I went upstairs to the room I shared with Ben.

"I'm colored. I ain't just a kid in Wabasha—I'm a colored kid." I clenched my fist and made the muscles ripple in my arm. They were brown arms—different from Richard's, different from Don's, different . . . different . . . different. I lay back on the bed trying not to cry anymore. I knew crying wouldn't help. The trouble wasn't inside me.

The five o'clock fast freight for Kansas City was approaching. I went to the window and looked out as the big Eighteen Hundred engine let off a blast of steam and highballed for the right-of-way. The engine and its big coal tender shot past, jerking the rattling, swaying boxcars toward the bend in the river, toward a whole new world.

Where you going, freight train? Your big black engine pullin' all those cars. What you hauling, freight train? Pig iron, and potatoes and wheat and hoboes. You goin' to Kansas City and on to Topeka and Salina and all points west. When the prairie becomes foothills you're going to howl "get out the Goddamned way!" and you'll laugh at the mountains and blow steam and cinders to show a big black engine ain't afraid of no mountain. In Denver they're going to couple you up with another big black engine. You'll head up a mile of freight cars hooked together with a big black engine pushing at the end. You'll be a mountain jumper then. I've heard the hoboes talk about you. You're gonna jerk all those boxcars up into the mountains where the snow gets ten feet deep. You gonna shake the ground and make the fir trees tremble when you blow your whistle and pull that train across the hump. You're a big black Eighteen Hundred, with eight drivin' wheels, and everybody got to get out of your way. You're not like me, you're not a black boy in a white man's country. Someday I'm going to grab ahold of you, freight train, and we're going to highball on out of here. I know that somewhere it's different. You're going to take me there.

The rattle of the train faded away. The dust and scraps of paper following in its wake settled back along the tracks. I turned to my bed.

★

I don't know if our minister heard about my troubles, but he seemed to know that I was going through a terrible period. He went out of his way to talk to me after church and let me know that whatever was wrong, I should "take it to the Lord in prayer." Childless, he was sincerely fond of Ben and me. Unaware of racial barriers, he was one of the most decent men I've ever known. When the local chamber of commerce held its annual Fathers and Sons banquet, Father Calhoun asked Mom if we could go with him.

Scrubbed, brushed, and dressed in new suits, we went to the downtown hotel. After the dinner, the leading citizens of the town rose and introduced their sons. Father Calhoun introduced Ben and me as his own children. After that, I believed anything he said and was sure that someday I would see the brotherhood of man under the Fatherhood of God. I got religion and became an acolyte. I knew Mom was proud of me when I would approach the altar, genuflect, and light the candles. I studied the Bible and prayer book until I knew the services by heart.

Everybody on the west side thought I would become a minister and treated me with just a little deference. Even so, when Peggy, the freckled-faced redhead in my class, told me she wanted me to be her boyfriend, I shuddered and lied that I didn't want a girlfriend. I was miserable.

I spent my idle time to myself, away from our little gang, lost in a world of daydreams. I walked through the woods, off the trails, dreaming of life in this valley before the white man came. On one such journey I found a moccasin flower, the most beautiful thing I'd ever seen. Afraid of losing it, I drove a branch into the ground near it. Every week I came to visit my flower and daydream with it until it shriveled and disappeared beneath the oak and maple leaves that carpeted the forest in September.

★

As he had every year, Pop wrote the division supervisor a letter requesting a transfer to Minneapolis. This time he clipped a letter to it that was to go up through channels to the postmaster general. Using all the big words he had learned from the law books, Pop explained how the oldest of his seven sons were reaching puberty and as members of the only colored family in town, they were beginning to associate with white girls. He wrote that he was sure that the postmaster general was as opposed to this as he was. Moving his family where the children could associate with girls of their own color benefited everyone.

Within a month the transfer was approved.

The day that Pop rented the truck, most of the men in the neighborhood came over to give a hand loading up. The women cooked lunch and dinner. The doctor who had brought three of my brothers into the world, the sheriff, and the minister came to say good-bye. Our gang stood around, sadly making our final handshakes and saying good-bye for the tenth time. At last, the truck was loaded and the family taken to the bus station. Ben and I stayed behind and rode the truck to Minneapolis with Pop.

As we left Wabasha, my heart hurt. I would never again live this kind of life, and I did not know what lay ahead.

2

THE TEN OF us moved into a five-room frame house a few steps from the "corner." The "corner" was the center of all social and political activity in the neighborhood. Two short, quiet, introverted Jews, Mr. Spiegel and Mr. Crane, owned the drugstore. They made more money in bootleg whiskey than in prescriptions.

The Dreamland Cafe, which sold 3.2 beer and served short-order dinners, was owned by Anthony Brutus Cassius. Everyone liked this barrel-chested, pockmarked, light-brown-skinned bull of a man. Cheerful and honest, he always conducted himself as if he were responsible to and for the people in our neighborhood. Concerned about the Negro people, always contributing to some cause, Mr. Cassius was the first "race man" I met. Long before we came of age, the Dreamland—at least the cafe side—was our only social center. Sam Pantell owned the grocery. He overcharged everyone to make up for what he lost giving credit to his destitute customers. After he found out there were ten in our family, Mr. Knutsen of Karl Knutsen's Fine Meats always left some meat on the bones he would give us for the dog. Chris Christensen's shoe shop always hired a black kid as an apprentice shoemaker. Elmer, who ran the used magazine shop, was paraplegic. We always helped him across the street and over the curb. One day I heard him tell one of his white friends he would rather be the way he was than be one of "them." We never helped him again and I hoped he'd get hit by a car. Brownie, the brown-skinned lady barber, sold policy slips and her shop was the gossip center of the community. She charged twenty-five cents for a haircut and pressed her big breasts against my shoulder when she cut my hair. Curtis, a young Negro guy, ran the dry cleaners. Everyone called him "Sporty-Orty." It was a good name. He took in policy, sold whiskey, and rented rooms upstairs by the hour.

We were barely settled in our crowded little house when a white lady and her little girl knocked at our door. Mom opened it, inviting them in. We kids sold papers in Wabasha, but I had never seen a grown woman selling papers. She talked with Mom and Pop for a while, laughing cheerfully about all these boys crammed into such a little house. Pop gave her a nickel for the *Daily Worker*, shaking hands before she left.

Having belonged to the Episcopal Church in Wabasha, we joined it in Minneapolis. The pastor, whose brown parchment skin stretched tautly across his face and bald head, was from Trinidad. Stooped and monklike, this little old man barely held his little flock together with dry, low-order services.

Most of my parents' friends belonged to the African Methodist Episcopal Church. We soon joined them.

I never heard a spiritual except the bits and pieces my mother would sing or on the radio, when "Wings over Jordan" came on

for an hour every Sunday morning. Mom considered our going to
church, hearing the spirituals, and participating in the worship as
part of our education. She never tired of telling us about the
churches in the South. She loved the deep faith of the Negroes of
Mississippi and Georgia, where she taught school before marry-
ing. Although she never shared that faith, it was an expression of
something she wanted us to have.

That first Sunday at the A.M.E. was very different from anything I had ever known. Everything in the Episcopal Church was
as dignified as the altar candles I used to light. At the A.M.E.,
each person chose his or her own emotional path to God. The
minister entered the pulpit, hushing the congregation by beginning his sermon in a barely audible voice. At first embarrassed, I
joined in as, over the next ten minutes, he slowly raised his voice
and us to a shouting, arm-waving crescendo. As he cajoled and
urged us along the rocky road to heaven, the singing began. Joining in, I was swept, for an hour, to heretofore unknown emotional
heights. The minister held up an open hand to end the singing
and shouting. The church was silent as he turned to the choir and
nodded for them to begin.

A buxom woman stepped forward. The pianist struck a few
melancholy chords to give her the key, and the woman began to
sing a cappella:

> *Sometimes I feel like a motherless child,*
> *Sometimes I feel like a motherless child,*
> *Sometimes I feel like a motherless child,*
> *A long wa—ay from home.*

The soft, low voices of the choir joined in. Their singing added to
the mood of unreality that set in with the ending of the congregation's singing and the sudden silence. I wasn't a motherless slave
child, but for that moment I felt like one.

I knew at once that these songs, rooted in the slave pens and
shacks of the Delta, were mine. They made me feel a deep sadness, but I also had a feeling of pride and warmth. As far as I
knew, aside from the discrimination, these songs were all we
Negroes had in common. They held us together and formed a
kinship wherever we found one another.

I knew we had to fight against the white man's forcing us

together. I learned, conversely, that the internal bonding with song and stories and love was something to cherish.

★

There was a trio of Negro lads in my class. They were at once the bullies of the school, protection for the handful of black students, and a terror to the principal and the teachers.

Chuck, a thin, brown-skinned youth with sometimes asthmatic breathing, was the leader of the trio. He was sensitive about his big nose, which his father told him was "Roman." We were quick to point out it was roamin' all over his face. A superb athlete despite his asthma, his wiry, coordinated body was hard as nails. In short-distance running and basketball, he was the best in our junior high school. Chuck was the smartest of the group. His cunning mind, lacking direction, drifted toward the criminal. No one encouraged or directed his remarkable artistic talent. His quickly drawn, often beautiful pencil-sketched pornography made him popular with the guys in school—black and white. His father, a mail carrier, was an old friend of Pop's.

Mac and Mort were big dark-skinned guys. My grandmother told me more than once that Mac's clean-looking, shiny black skin was preferable and showed more character than Mort's dull ashen black. Mac was almost as ungainly as he was big. More likely just to threaten, he generally stepped aside and let the other two do the fighting.

Mort, the biggest of the three, was a good-natured fellow but tough in every sense of the word. Unless egged on by Chuck, he would laugh off almost anything. Mort was sensitive about his color. Any snide remark about the color black got you a bloody nose. When he did fight, he became a wild animal closing in for the kill.

I was at once attracted to and afraid of this tight little group. Each day after school they would eye me as I hurried home to my chores and my brothers. Friendly enough, they let me know I had to reckon with them when they were ready.

That time came one Friday after school. The three of them approached me.

"Where ya goin'?" Chuck flared his nostrils for a more dangerous look.

"Home."

"Why?" Roosterlike, he pushed his chest against mine.

"I reckon that's my business."

Chuck shoved the other two out of the way.

"Who ya gettin' smart with?" His fists doubled, his head jutted forward like some game cock. At first I wasn't afraid of them, but I knew I couldn't whip the three of them and I couldn't back down. The more Chuck hollered and cursed, the more aggressive he became. "We been watchin' you, nigger."

"I don't take that word off nobody."

He looked coldly at me, raised his fists, and began to dance toward me like a person who knew how to box. I only knew how to fight, to get in close and slug it out until one or the other was down. I closed with him—swinging both fists. He went down. I stepped back and let him up. Now I had the scent of blood. He went down again. This time he got up and said simply, "I quit."

As was the custom in Wabasha, I stuck out my hand. He looked at it for a moment and then shook hands. "You sure fight crazy."

"I never learned how to box," I answered.

The four of us became fast friends after that. I soon learned that among our people, "nigger" could be a word of affection. We never used it between us, and as we began listening to the race men on the corner, we never used it at all.

By the time summer came to Minneapolis, the new city had truly become our home. Our little gang roamed the neighborhood looking for something to take up the time. There was never fifteen cents among us. Having a Coke with one of the girls destroyed our weekly budget. We spent our evenings on the corner listening to the men, soaking up the back alley philosophy and tales of sex, politics, and war. It was our schoolroom.

★

Living in the five-room frame house finally became unbearable for the ten of us. We moved to a much larger house on Fifth Avenue, a block away. Socially, we moved a hundred miles. The street was quiet and the corner, with its tavern, drugstore, and streetcar lines, was a block away. The "better class" of black folk lived on Fifth Avenue.

There were only a few skilled workers among the thousand blacks in the state. Only a few more had what could be called good jobs. Nonetheless, the tiny Negro community in Minneapo-

lis was "color struck." The light-skinned section was better educated and had better jobs, such as waiters in the big hotels. They
socialized and banded together against the lower-class, darker-
hued folk. They openly resented the growing trickle of black-
skinned immigrants, the "field Negroes" coming up from the
South.

My father, very light-skinned, was sometimes mistaken for
white, and my mother was a rich coffee brown. My brothers were
alternately light- and brown-skinned. Our family never discussed
the role of color.

The largest and nicest house on the block belonged to a very
light-skinned family. At first glance I knew they were the social
leaders of the community. Their well-dressed children kept aloof
from those of us who played tackle football in the street or had
rock fights and swore when other people could hear us.

We heard that a party for "fair-skinned" people was going to
be held on the weekend. I remembered hearing about parties
where they nailed a tan grocery bag to the door. If you were
blacker than that bag, you couldn't get in. I also heard stories
about the Haitian revolutionaries who killed anybody lighter-
skinned than that bag.

That Saturday night, Mort, blacker than the night itself,
Chuck, and I walked past the house where the party was being
held. There was a break in the dancing and the young people were
sitting on the porch or standing on the lawn talking. Chuck's asthmatic breathing was worse than ever. Mort stopped and looked
them over. In a loud, contemptuous voice as if talking to himself,
he said, "Guess anybody's mammy can fuck a white man."

A few of the guests stepped forward, but the do-or-die look on
Mort's face and Chuck holding his switchblade in his pocket were
enough to turn them around.

I soon learned about an entire social set of light-skinned
Negroes who didn't mix with their dark-skinned brethren. We
were only seventy years out of slavery. The light-skinned children
of the slave owners generally had a monopoly on what little education a slave had. They were closer to the ways of whites, understood their values, and tried to conform to them. Therefore, after
slavery, they moved ahead educationally and into the better jobs.
This grouping controlled the entire Negro people. The dark-
skinned ones countered by quoting Dr. W. E. B. Du Bois on how
black is beautiful. More often, they talked about Marcus Garvey

and the coming race war. Like everyone else, I soon learned the ditty:

> *If you're white, you're right,*
> *If you're yellow, you're mellow,*
> *If you're brown, stick around,*
> *And if you're black—get back.*

We moved to a poorer part of town a few miles away from my gang and the corner. It was like starting a new life. I registered in the junior high school as the only black kid. A black student, Ann, had attended the school some three years ahead of me. She was loved by the teachers. Pretty and talented, a brilliant, straight-A student, she graduated from junior high at thirteen, high school at sixteen, and the university at nineteen. I knew about her. Black and female, this lovely, brilliant young woman had no place. The best job she could get was at the post office. America forced her frustration inward until it turned to bitter, morose self-doubt and ended in a general nervous breakdown.

Within a week, the teachers were asking me why I didn't apply myself as Ann did. Since Ann was black and a straight-A student, they couldn't understand why I wasn't making straight A's.

There at Fowell Junior High, I came to the conclusion that whites are strange folk. If the first black they met was a scholar, then all blacks were scholars. If the first was a criminal, then all were criminals. Anyone different from the first was an exception. I began to understand why my parents kept reminding us of the importance of putting "our best foot forward" when dealing with whites. It wasn't, as I assumed, to get along with them, but a good impression made it easier for the next black that came along.

At an early age I learned the game that becomes a serious part of every black person's social personality. We learned roles. One person with our peers, we became a totally different person around whites. It was impossible for them to know us, and this was our defense. I didn't know how our race could stay out of the schizophrenic ward, considering the split personalities they forced upon us.

★

If the economy of the nation was slowly improving, it was getting worse for our family. What we didn't eat up, Pop drank up. White

America had no use for a black man's intelligence. America wouldn't acknowledge it and couldn't respect it. My father's search for prestige and respect finally carried him down to the skid row, where the winos and whiskey heads doted on his every word. They respected him there. I often heard them say, "Old Ben sure is a smart fella."

That winter I learned the art of putting enough paper in my shoes to keep my feet off the ground, but not enough to hurt or cramp. I began going to the dime store and taking things from there I needed. The rubber soles and heels were for the family's shoes. I never considered it stealing; I felt no guilt and never got caught.

★

I forgot that Tuesday was my gym class. Because I didn't have my gym shoes, the coach said I would have to go in my socks. We never had more than one pair of socks apiece and it was impossible to keep them mended. Taking off my shoes would be too embarrassing. I was wearing what we called "spats" since the toes and heels were missing.

I finally sat down in the locker room and began pulling off my shoes. Across from me sat the school's prize athlete. I didn't like this guy. From the first day of school he made it clear that he didn't like me. Almost six feet tall, he lived on the richer side of the school district and showed it. I slipped one shoe off and a brown toe emerged through the hole. He started to laugh.

"What the heck's so funny?"

"Don't they sell socks anymore?"

I stood up. He stood up in front of me. My head barely came past his shoulder. "I'm going to get a lickin' now" I thought. The big guy in front of me had a contemptuous grin. I knew I had to hit him or I wouldn't be able to stay in the school. I doubled up my fist, he pushed me hard, and I fell backward over the bench behind me and ended up wedged between the bench and the footlockers. I had to roll over to free myself, but I was angry and ready to fight. When I got to my feet, the big guy was sitting in the corner holding his jaw. Behind me was the biggest guy in the school. At sixteen, this broad-chested, sandy-haired Norwegian was over six feet tall. Everybody called James Peterson "Six." He wasn't paying any attention to me. Fists doubled up, long sandy hair in front of his eyes, he glared at the bully.

"Why don't you pick on somebody your own size—like me. If you don't like gettin' punched in the jaw, I'll meet you after school."

Someone shouted "fight" and a group of students rushed over to see. The bully got up from the corner and said with face-saving bravado, "I'll see you after school." We knew he wouldn't.

I wasn't part of this long-standing feud. The students who had gathered around to see the fight dispersed toward the gym.

"Thanks, Six."

His grin showed a row of big, even, white teeth. He pushed the hair from in front of his eyes. "There's some little guys around here you can punch for me."

We shook hands. It was the beginning of a deep friendship.

★

Athletics, an important part of the school, was the basis of the feud going on between Six and the bully, Harold Mosley. Mosley was a natural athlete. Still in ninth grade, he competed in high school tournaments. He had already tied or broken high school records in the shot put, discus, and hammer throw. Six was not a natural athlete but powerful and full of determination to beat Mosley. I read training books and kept up with the sports magazines until I acquired a sense of form and motion in competition. I became Six's trainer. Often during those fall evenings I would kneel beside Six criticizing his form and urging him on. No matter how hard he tried, Six would lose to Mosley in the discus and shot put.

It was a different story in boxing and football. Six was a champion boxer because no one dared get in the ring with him. In football, I would run interference if Six got the ball, and it was a touchdown for sure. It wasn't long before the guys in the neighborhood and school treated me with respect because they knew Six would fight.

His widowed mother, a devout Christian, made me welcome in their house. What I knew about the church and the Bible came in handy. Six wouldn't go to church, while I "feared the Lord." She believed I was a good influence on him and paid no attention to the gossip about her "letting her son run around with that nigger."

★

Heidi, Six's girlfriend, more cute than beautiful, kept her fine brown hair in place with a cow ear clip. When she talked of how she and Six were going to get married when they grew up, her greenish gray eyes would sparkle. The tiny lines around her mouth would dance and the shy half-smile showed healthy, even teeth.

Her immigrant father loved Germany with near fanaticism. A member of the German-American Bund, he supported Hitler, because "Hitler was for Germany." Heidi carefully told me that her father did not believe in any of the other things the Nazi's were doing. She changed her mind when she told her parents I was her friend and Six's friend. Her father slapped her and her mother wailed that she was going to "marry a nigger."

Although she was crying when she told me about it, I didn't have a chance to comfort her—I was arguing with Six that it wouldn't do any good to go over there and bust the bastard's nose.

Our last days in junior high were happy ones. Sometimes, I hiked with Six and Heidi to the falls or the home the army provided for destitute old soldiers. Down at the Ford Bridge we sat for hours talking about the hard times and the rotten deal the Negroes got. Six and I would draw dirty pictures on the white concrete while Heidi looked on, ashamed to join us and too excited to turn away. Six would laugh, showing his big white teeth and push the hair out of his eyes. Heidi would blush, look at the ground, and say, "You guys are awful."

3

SUMMER VACATION BEGAN, and I longed for the gang and the corner.

Our little gang was growing slowly. Carl, Don, and Sonny fought Chuck and came in. We spent most of our time just sitting on the curb talking about sex and race. None of us had girlfriends, so sex was an abstract discussion. Race wasn't, and took most of our time. Young lions, we began to slip under the influence of a group of men who talked of race war. There didn't seem to be any other solution. A solid white resistance kept us in the ditch of poverty and discrimination. It didn't make sense to keep searching for powerful white allies. We would have to stick together and fight them. In the spirit of this race war, our gang clinched its fist against the world. A lynching, or if one of us was discriminated against, would send us down to the parks to beat every white face we could find. We knew it was wrong. We all had white friends and knew that all white people weren't our enemy. But we had to strike back—or we'd lose what little self-respect we had.

At the beginning of the summer we figured out that a canvas *Minneapolis Journal* delivery bag was the best piece of equipment a colored kid in Minneapolis could have. If the cops saw us in a white neighborhood, they assumed we were delivering papers. It was big enough to carry the milk bottles we swiped off back porches and sold for three cents each. With that bag as a cover, we could steal a bundle of papers at the delivery point and sell them to passing motorists. Most of all, it was good for carrying rocks.

A rock was our artillery. Anybody chasing us would stop if hit by one. A few rocks would send a white gang scattering for cover. If need be, it was the silent, perfect weapon for ambush. The good rocks we found were hard to carry in pockets. The delivery bag was perfect and a few papers covered the evidence.

★

The White Castle hamburger house was a concentration of everything we hated. They refused service to blacks, and that miniature white castle was, to us, the symbol of white supremacy. We declared war on the one located at Lake and Eleventh Avenue.

We planned our attack carefully. Waiting until evening covered us, we positioned ourselves across the street. Since Chuck was the fastest runner, he went in to buy a hamburger. They refused to serve him and ordered him out of the shop. The manager stood in the doorway to make sure he didn't try to get back in. Chuck screamed it loud as he could, "You Paddy son of a bitch. You fuckin' peckerwood."

The manager rushed forward and Chuck hit him in the face with a rock. He went down like a sack of wheat—blood everywhere. We ran to the middle of the street and threw ours. First, the big bay windows went, and when the customers ran out we pelted them. It was over in fifteen seconds. Running through the alleys and side streets, we made the half mile to Fourth Avenue and were on a streetcar heading for the corner when we heard the sirens of the police cars. It was a total victory.

Chuck and Mort were laughing. I was physically and emotionally exhausted. So were the other guys. We knew what would happen if the cops caught us. They never did. We went back once a year for the next two years. We never again gave a warning. We would smash the windows with a volley of rocks and pelt whoever ran out. White Castle wouldn't integrate, and I have never eaten one of their hamburgers.

★

There was nothing approaching healthy, organized activities. The Boys Club and the Police Athletic League didn't exist for us. They did not allow us to poke our black noses inside the YMCA. Fun cost money and we never had much of that. We spent our time on long bike rides, frisking cars, or leaning against the drugstore listening to the older fellows talk. The corner was our major classroom. What we learned there sank in over the years and saturated our whole outlook on life without our knowing it.

During that year one of the national Negro papers started a campaign to instill race pride and give us an understanding of our history and culture. "Be a Race Man!" headlined the front page. Inside there were cartoons on how and how not to advance the race in daily living. Chief among these was the advice to trade with Negro establishments. The slogan "Don't buy where you can't work!" was a powerful idea.

The one black-owned grocery store in the city had bigger and greener flies than any other store in our neighborhood. The owner was more ruthless with those who couldn't pay their bills on time than Sam Pantell. Seemed to us that race pride meant something different to the unemployed than to a grocer.

★

The Negro slum on the north side of town was the most destitute part of Minneapolis. Hundreds of ragged, unemployed black men stood up and down Sixth Avenue and Lyndale looking for a drink, to talk, to joke, and to laugh away the hunger cramps.

A white kid told me, "God made the world, a Jew bought it, hired an Italian to run it, and a Negro came along and enjoyed it." White people believed in the "happy Negro." It relieved them of any responsibility for the misery they caused us. White people might fool themselves, but the Negroes couldn't fool themselves. A middle-aged black guy told me, "Yep, I liked Hoover. He set the men down and put the women to work." His sarcasm didn't make the joke any funnier, nor did it hide his humiliation.

Early in the morning the women lined up at the "slave mar-

ket." Selected and taken out to white people's homes, they
scrubbed, cleaned, and cooked for ten or fifteen cents an hour.
More often than not, the gracious lady of the house turned back
the clock at least forty-five minutes before paying off her
exhausted "day workers." At home the exertion began again.
Cheap, coarse food bought with day work was cleaned and
cooked; the children were fed and washed and put to bed. Then
came the hardest part of the day—propping up her disheart-
ened man.

The men, too, were miserable, beating their wives because the
world beat them, cruel to their fellow men because only the cruel
survived, searching for some temporary haven in a bottle of bootleg corn, lost in thought listening to the jukebox moan its sorrow,
searching for peace of mind between the full brown breasts of
some sporting woman.

We referred to the area as simply "the North side." Whorehouses, broken whiskey bottles, mean cops who fleeced the
whores who had money and beat those who didn't, ashes in the
streets, rats that walked boldly in front of the skinny alley cats,
houses without running water, a drunk urinating against a lamp-
post, black streetwalkers cursing the white ones for cutting in on
their trade. The Keystone bar, where no one bothered to mop up
the vomit. The Bucket of Blood, where a drunk snored loudly in
one of the ramshackle booths . . . coke and hemp peddlers who
employed the few Negro youths who found work . . . the Clef
Club, where Benny Goodman, Artie Shaw, Chick Webb, Lionel
Hampton and others who were or became great musicians drank,
smoked "gage" (marijuana), and held jam sessions far into Sunday mornings. (I heard it was in the Clef Club that the beautiful
and democratic singer Peggy Lee convinced Benny Goodman to
hire Lionel Hampton as the first black musician in a major white
big band.)

Along Sixth Avenue, it was chili and beans and death and flies
and pneumonia in the winter; it was the white man who came
looking for a "clean young colored girl," the yellow-toothed Uncle
Tom who helped him, and the young race man who whipped out
a switchblade knife, cut him, and took his wallet. It all mixed with
jackleg preachers, the crippled old woman dancing at the revival,
and "Honey, please go to church" and "Hey, baby! You can get
this fine brown frame for fifty cents."

I hated this wretched poverty. It seemed part of being Negro.

We listened to the older fellows expressing this idea. "Man, your people's a bitch."

"Don't blame 'em on me, man. I'm Indian."

"An' you so black it don't make no difference."

And perhaps one of them would toss his woolly head as if to throw hair out of his eyes. Everyone on the corner would fall against the drugstore screaming with laughter. Laughing and joking against ourselves was all we had.

★

I made many firm friendships in my new neighborhood, but I was never allowed to forget my color. Scuffling and fist fighting were almost daily occurrences. I took my share of whippings from older boys who would call me names. Sometimes, I would come home with a nosebleed or a puffed-up eye. Pop would seem almost happy, and when I confessed I had lost the fight he would declare that I would have to go out and fight the guy the next day. He believed this would keep me from being afraid of anyone. I don't remember having to fight anyone twice. The cause of the fight was too soon forgotten.

My younger brothers had their share of fights. If someone older picked on them, one of the brothers would take care of it. That was a rule Pop insisted on. We were not to be beaten. We liked the idea because as our reputation for defending one another spread, people were not so quick to pick on us.

Our family was a little island set off in a vast sea of blue eyes and blonde hair. Isolation kept us tightly knit. Mother, in her total devotion to each and all of us, engendered a warm love between us. If it were up to Pop, he'd have sent us to a Roman army at age fifteen.

Even so, I could see the inevitable breakup of the family as each brother formed his own personality and struggled to develop and direct his individual talents.

How deeply the feeling of inner dependence and responsibility ran was brutally brought home when Pop received a long, sad letter from his mother. My Uncle George—Pop's younger brother—had been murdered. When assigned a white man's job in the stockyards in Saint Joe, the white man shot him down in cold blood.

Pop read snatches of the letter aloud. When he finished reading, he dropped the letter to the floor, buried his face in his hands, and wept from his guts. "Oh, God," he moaned over and over. "I'd rather it had been me. My poor brother—my baby brother."

Mom comforted him for hours and then slowly packed his clothes so he could go and return to the earth that which had been so brutally taken from him.

White man's justice declared the murderer insane at the moment he pulled the trigger and released him. Pop knew the law of the Missouri hills. He carefully disassembled his .38, cleaned it, oiled it, cleaned the fat lead bullets, loaded the pistol, and laid the extra bullets in the suitcase beside the gun. Horrified, Mom watched him. When he closed the suitcase she said, "Ben, if you go and avenge this one death, who is to avenge yours? Who's to care for the eight you leave behind?"

Pop looked at her. He knew she was right. He turned and looked at me as if he hadn't known I was there. We looked at each other for a moment. I moved my eyes to meet his and said, "Go kill him."

Mom pressed the back of her hand against her open mouth. Tears welled up again in Pop's eyes. When the moment had passed, she simply said, "Are you proud of your son?"

Pop slowly took the pistol from the suitcase, shook the bullets from the cylinder, and laid them on the dresser. By that time four or five of my brothers had entered the room. I could see in their eyes the words that were in my heart: if any person hurts mine— I'll hurt him. I'll avenge mine blow for blow. By then I knew that the cohesion of not simply our family but also our race was our only protection.

Pop buried his murdered brother, and we were all relieved when he returned home safely.

4

THE FINAL SEMESTER at junior high drew to a close. We chose to have a class picnic rather than the traditional graduation. Since the murder of Uncle George, my race consciousness had deepened. I did not look forward to spending the day where I would be the only Negro and among people who, I felt, weren't my friends.

I had to go, and it wasn't long before I was teamed up with Six in a tug-of-war and having a great time. When the picnic ended and most of the students had gone home, I sat in front of a camp-fire with Six and Heidi. We were going to split up. Six, living at the edge of the upper-class neighborhood, would go to Roosevelt. Heidi would go to solid working-class Central and my neighbor-hood put me in South High, one of the roughest and poorest schools in the city.

Six pushed his long, sandy hair from his eyes. "I'm sure going to miss you, Nels."

"Yeah, I'm going to miss you too, Six."

"S'funny, me white and you colored and you're the best friend I ever had—I guess you're the only friend I ever had."

I felt embarrassed.

"I just want you to know that when the rest of these white guys grow up, they'll turn on you—I won't."

"I know. Thanks, Six."

Heidi leaned on Six's big shoulder. Silence. I poked the fire with my stick until a little blue flame came from the embers. "It's funny, isn't it," Heidi said turning to me. "We're all going to differ-ent schools. I love Six and I love you."

I felt alone, yet very much with them in the gathering dark-ness. I was looking at the fire and didn't notice Heidi as she bent over toward me. I turned toward her and her lips pressed against the corner of my mouth. Her face was soft in the glow of the dying fire. The cow ear clip shone and reflected the red embers. The electricity of manhood shot through me. I knew she felt some-thing, too. The moment staggered awkwardly by. Six looked at us, laughing and pushing the long hair out of his eyes. "Never been kissed before?"

I laughed too. The world righted itself.

"Gimme your hand, Six."

He extended a big paw over to me. I took out my pocket knife, opened it, and squeezed his thumb until it was tight with blood.

"What the hell you doin'?"

"I'm going to make an Indian pledge."

He didn't understand. I made a small cut and squeezed the blood out. Then I cut my thumb and held the two together so the blood would mix. "In the old Indian world, this makes us broth-ers. From now on we stick together and be friends and look out for one another."

Heidi smiled. Six looked at me, his blue eyes shining in the firelight. He opened his big paw and held it out to me.

"In the old Norskie world, this means I promise."

With the seriousness and faith of sixteen years, we shook hands and pledged our friendship, one for the other.

5

FATHER THOMPSON CAME to Minneapolis to take charge of the Episcopal Church. A handsome, copper-colored man with a neat bristly moustache, he graduated from Fisk and the seminary in North Carolina. His Southern accent was soft and pleasant. In his early thirties, he had the zeal and confidence to tackle the monumental job before him. The little wooden church was down to twenty-five members—not one under forty-five—and a huge mortgage.

He set about his task with the vigor of someone who knows he is going to accomplish his goals. He visited every black family on the south side of town. With the few young couples he recruited, he started a social program that set tongues wagging. With a few of us teenagers he started a youth club, opening the church basement and kitchen to us. He would not tolerate adult supervision of our activities, and often told me of the criticism he was getting because of it. Father Thompson understood very well that putting us on our honor was a more certain discipline than all the supervision in the world.

The weekly dances held at the church were the first real social contact I had with young women my age. We all were friends and had always grouped together because of color, but there was precious little socializing. That cost money—and we didn't have any.

During these Sunday evening youth socials, I developed a long-lasting friendship with Ernestine. She was different from the rest of these young women. She could talk about more than boys and dates and showed an interest in what was going on in the city and the world. She was the first sixteen-year-old I ever knew to use the word *revolution*. When she was sure of me she told me her father was a Communist and asked if I was one. I had no idea what Communists were. I told her I wasn't and asked why she asked. She told me she thought I talked like her dad sometimes, and she was sure he was with the party.

The Communists? They fought for the Scottsboro Boys. They fought for the working class of people. They led the Soviet Union. Everybody and everything I hated, hated them. They were against the government, and that was fine with me.

At sixteen, Ernestine seldom stood still. She danced as she walked, danced little dances while she waited for the bus. Sometimes she would catch me watching her and tried to teach me, but I was too awkward and embarrassed. I wanted to know her better. Velvet soft, brown-colored skin, dancing black eyes, grown-up body, and pretty face, she was sought after by every guy in the city. I knew better than to try.

During the political campaign for governor, Father Thompson announced that this Sunday he was not going to preach a sermon. Instead he introduced Sam Davis, who was running for governor on the Communist Party ticket. The intense Jewish fellow spoke for nearly two hours on Negro-white unity, jobs for Negroes, and the program of the Communist Party.

I came away from church with two thoughts. The first was that Sam Davis couldn't have spoken there unless Father Thompson wanted him to. He must have believed at least part of what that guy said, which made it easier for me to believe in it. Second, that Father Thompson was going to get into a lot of trouble with the bishop. I don't know what happened with the bishop, but the next edition of the local Negro newspaper, which was Republican, took a blast at Father Thompson. He laughed at them and told me that Republicans could walk under a snake's belly with a top hat on, just like a Democrat.

If I had any doubts about Father Thompson's thinking, he cleared them up a few weeks later. While walking home, he looked across the park where two apartment buildings were being constructed. "I'll be glad when they finish those apartments," he said.

"Why, Father?"

"Because when the Communists take over, they're going to put colored people in them."

I believed in the Communists.

★

We rejoined the church. In a short time it had grown to over a hundred and fifty people. I went back to my old duties as an acolyte.

Part of those duties was to take the sacraments last. Very often there would be quite a bit of wine left in the chalice. I would kneel in front of Father Thompson, his back to the parishioners. He would make the sign of the cross with a wafer and say, "This is my body which was broken for you. Take, eat this in remembrance of Me."

Then, making the sign of the cross with the chalice, he would continue, "This is my blood which was shed for you. Take, drink this in remembrance of Me." And in a hushed whisper, "If you stagger when you get up I'm going to belt you."

I thought to myself, "This is an OK guy."

★

Neither admiration for Father Thompson nor work in the church could stop the doubts about God and religion that were creeping into my consciousness. The contradictions in my life began to find intellectual expressions. I hesitated to talk them over with anyone. I wanted to approach my brother Ben. Although we never had a relationship of serious talking, he was always ready to give his opinion and leave the rest up to me. Liberated by courses in science, he already loudly proclaimed he didn't believe in God.

"Why do you continue this foolishness?" he asked. "One semester of science would make you forget all that rot. Why doesn't the earth stop? Why don't you fall up? Science, my boy, science." When he saw the desired expression on my face, he added, "Curses on your God."

I finally took my troubles to Father Thompson. "Father, what do you think about God—not when you're preaching, when you're just thinking?"

He reached for his sack of Golden Grain. When he didn't have money for regular pipe tobacco, he used the stuff people rolled cigarettes with. "There's a God, Nelson. I work for Him."

"I was just wonderin' . . . "

"I know. I used to wonder. The meanness of the world . . . but men made a bad world out of the good things God put here. I also know that a bad world makes bad men." He puffed his pipe for a moment.

"Yesterday, there wasn't a bite of food in this house. I didn't know how in the world I was going to feed my family. I went into the bedroom and got down on my knees and prayed. It wasn't for much. I needed twelve dollars. It wasn't fifteen minutes later when Mr. Cary walked in and said, 'I was just passing by and thought I'd drop in. Do you need anything?' I told him I needed twelve dollars, and he said he had brought that much. He said something told him to bring some money with him. I know that it isn't the best illustration—but I think that I got that money because I never doubted that the Lord would remember me when I needed Him. That's the secret—faith. That's what we all need. I don't think there's a great man above us that records in a book every time we do right or wrong, but I do believe there is a God and He is the whole spirit of charity and love and kindness. I think that this is the spirit in which the world was created. Man is of God, and God is in man. You remember the first two commandments. You do both of them together and then you can't be wrong. Someday you'll understand."

He sat puffing his pipe. I sat beside him for a long time, desperately wanting to believe as he did, knowing that I never would.

★

At home, the money problems worsened. Pop drank heavily, arguing and cursing throughout the house. We stayed out of his way. Mom did the best she could, walking long distances to the bakery that sold day-old goods or to a store where the beans or potatoes were a few cents cheaper than elsewhere. We were not alone in our struggle against poverty. At that time, in 1938, 92 percent of black America was in poverty. The day finally came when there was nothing left—no food, no money. Mom had struggled hard to stay at home and raise her children. She lost her battle with the "system" and took a job as a chambermaid at the auditorium. It was the only job she could find.

Negro mothers of America! How I love you saviors of a people. You who never knew sanctuary or retreat, you guardians of the race are made of better grit and guts. For grit and guts is what it takes to scrub another's floors, cook others' meals, wash another's clothes, conjure strength and time and love to hold the little ones when day is done, to gather them in communion: "The Lord is my shepherd."

Tired, worn black mother is my shepherd. She who worked and begged and sold her body; she who held our race together with sweat, prepared this table, and stilled the waters.

★

From servitude to servitude was a long trail to the beginnings for my mother's family. My great-grandfather Nelson, decorated with sergeant-major chevrons and a medal for bravery at Lookout Mountain, hurried back to his place of slavery in Kentucky to reclaim his family. His Shawnee wife and their children were still enslaved on the neighboring farm. Grampa claimed them under Lincoln's declaration that the families of the soldier slaves would be free. Since slavery was still legal in Kentucky, the government paid the ransom.

His former master, seeing the farm beyond repair and his human chattel gone, left for the frontier. Grampa wrestled to reclaim the farm from the wilderness that had taken it. He rebuilt the forge and this time became a free craftsman, his smith serving blacks and whites—but now, for money.

The hostility of the slaveholding neighbors, the night riders, and the poverty were too much to overcome. As he began thinking of moving on, a letter from his former master, postmarked Salina, Kansas, arrived. There was no blacksmith in this booming frontier town. There were horses to shod, wagons to repair, plows to face with iron, but no one knew the trade. There was an offer of financial help and the urging to come, "posthaste!"

Grampa built his wagon, loaded up the anvils, hammers, tongs, bellows, and all the other tools of the trade, loaded up his wife and children, and struck out for Salina.

At the turn of the century, Kansas had still not reconciled itself to social equality. There was no school for black children in the county. The law required twenty black children to live in the county before it would build a segregated school. Mom did not attend school until she was fourteen. Then, her extended family raised the money to send her to relatives in Kansas City. Graduating from high school, she went to Chicago to ask that great benefactor, Madam Walker, for a scholarship.

Madam Walker, a black woman, was the first self-made woman millionaire in this country. A chemist, she developed beauty products for the dark skin, tightly curled hair, and full lips of black women. Her fabled wealth never stood between her and her duties to her sisters of color. Before my mother knocked at her door, hundreds of other bright but poor young Negro women came to her for help. All Madam Walker asked from any of them was their word of honor that they would spend five years teaching in the Deep South. Mother gave this lovely woman her word and through her help, graduated from the Drake University Teachers College at age twenty-four.

Her teaching time in Atlanta, Georgia, and Greenwood, Cleveland, and Mound Bayou, Mississippi became the foundation for her social consciousness and faith in education. She carefully passed these things on to her children.

When Mom left for the auditorium to wipe out lavatories and clean toilets after the white ladies, these lessons died in me. Education? We needed a gun! We needed education on how to use a gun! The men on the corner were right. Any people without a flag and an army were going to be slaves! Love and Charity were going to save the world? It's never going to happen between the races. I hated them for what they were doing to us, whoever "they" were. The black Uncle Toms, the white cops, the black fronts for the white exploiters—how were we to tell them apart? There seemed to be no real answer. I was lost and so was everyone I knew. Heidi was lost—her parents were Hitlerites, while she believed in equality. Six was lost, flat broke, no direction, not even an answer to "what is life?" Chuck and Mac and Mort and the gang were lost. Having a goal in life of outsmarting cops isn't a life. The men on the corner were lost. No job, no money, no self-respect—no nothing. Every day deepened the urge to get away and find a place where a black youth could build a future. I had to get away before I surrendered to the demoralization that was stifling the lives of everyone I knew.

6

SOUTH HIGH WAS so old and the floors so warped it was dangerous to run in the halls. The school must have been a hundred years old and we believed that some of the teachers helped build it.

A statue of Oglethorpe guarded the huge main stairway at the entrance to the school. Someone stuck a huge clay penis on the old gentleman. He didn't seem to mind a bit. He stood there with his plumed hat and magnificent sword majestically exposing himself. Girls giggled and boys guffawed. A teacher saw it and screamed. The janitor removed it, attempting to look stern. The next day, they expelled two guys in the senior class.

South was the high school designated for most of the small, scattered black communities on the south side of town. A large number of black youth went to school there. We formed a tight circle, partly because we knew one another over a long period of time and partly for protection. Unconsciously, we began to fall into the typical social patterns of American adults. The fellowship between the blacks and whites who had grown up together became more and more formal. Neither side was angry about it. Somehow we understood. The paths were tangent now and beginning to separate. They were on their way to the trades, to business and respectability in a white man's country. We were on our way to the mop pails, the coal yards, the pick and shovel. This separation was so slow, so natural, so much a part of America that no one noticed.

I had been in high school about a month when I saw Six coming out of the school office. I waited until he saw me.

"Hey, fella!" I shouted. "What are you doing over here?"

Six grinned, pushing the hair out of his eyes. "I can't stand Roosevelt. I already been expelled once for knocking one of those rich bastards out. I just lied about my address, thought I'd come over where the rest of the bastards are."

Glad to see each other, we traded slaps on the back.

★

South High continued my indoctrination. Coach Bernard was well known and respected throughout the state as an outstanding coach. Although black players sparked his best teams, he didn't try to hide his hate for the black kids.

Four of us generally went to the gym early to work out on the bars. When the gym period started we were still at it. Coach Bernard sauntered over to us and said, "You black crows get out of here."

Before I could even think, one of the guys jumped off the bars and knocked Bernard into a set of barbells. As he staggered to his feet another guy caught him in the stomach, doubling him over. Since they would punish me with the rest, I stepped forward and got my blow in. He staggered to his feet, ran to the office, and locked the door. One of the guys was still sitting on the bar.

"What the hell's wrong with you? You Tommin' now?"

He slid off the bar. "I ain't no black crow."

I suggested we go to the office and get our story in before Bernard did. We told the principal that Bernard had called us "nigger bastards." Since his attitude was well known, we got off without a reprimand. Bernard turned sweet as sugar with us.

★

Six knew a group of daredevils in the senior class. They would spend the weekends hopping freights to nearby towns or catching cattle trucks to the stockyards, where sometimes they could pick up a day's work.

One Saturday we joined them, hopping a truck to the yards in South Saint Paul. There were plenty of exciting things to do. We climbed the high water towers, tried to ride the bucking steers, or measured our strength by bulldozing a big calf. The biggest excitement, though, was catching the big trucks on the run. The danger provided the thrill. From catching trucks we graduated to grabbing our first freight train and rode it to Montevideo nearly a hundred miles away. We slept in the jungle overnight and caught another train back to Minneapolis in the morning. I got a great satisfaction from riding that train. I felt free sitting atop the boxcar, rolling with the sway and finding words to fit the clickety-clack of the wheels. I felt a peaceful quiet in the countryside, letting the train do the rumbling and traveling and searching. By the time I got back to Minneapolis I knew I was not simply running from something; I was searching for something. Perhaps I could find it far from here—perhaps out to the west, over the horizon.

★

During the summer of 1939, we moved back to Fourth Avenue, a half block from the corner and my gang. The neighbors got up a petition to prevent us from moving into the neighborhood. Instead of renting, Pop used his last ten dollars as a down payment on the house. Avoiding the glares of the neighbors, the ten members of our family and the ragged, broken furniture moved in.

I transferred to Central High. Six got expelled for fighting and went back to Roosevelt.

I was lonesome for the corner and began making up for lost time. The little gang had grown into a real force. We developed goals, not simply getting into mischief as we had done before. Our first project was to force Mr. Spiegel and Mr. Crane, who owned the drugstore on the corner, to give one of us a job. They swore they couldn't afford it. We weren't asking to become a clerk or work in the stockroom. We asked only for a part-time job cleaning the place up. We knew they could afford five bucks a week. They made more than that every day selling bootleg liquor at thirty-five cents a shot.

Each week we would ask them to hire one of us. They would say no. We would wait a few days and then raid the store. We knew they couldn't call the cops. We'd ransack the candy and notions counter and run outside. After a few weeks of this war, Spiegel and Crane surrendered. Chuck got the job mopping the store at closing time. We stopped our raids. The five-dollar-a-week pay was more than he'd ever earned. The week before our victory, Chuck won first prize in the National Scholastic art contest. We didn't speak about it, but we were all aware of the senseless contradiction. But after all, art was for art classes and contests. Mopping floors was the way colored people made a living.

★

Second only to those on the North Side, our area got the meanest cops on the force. They were the major influence forcing us along a predetermined path.

Whenever the cops saw more than three of us together, they would stop, frisk, and question us. If money had been taken out of milk bottles, if a car battery was missing in the adjacent white neighborhood—things we stopped doing a year ago—they would accuse us.

Chuck had just received his five-dollar pay when they stopped us. When he pulled out his five dollars, they wanted to know where he stole it.

"I got a job. This is my pay," Chuck told them.

The cop said he was going to check it out and Chuck better not be lying. They got back into the squad car. Chuck mumbled "white motherfuckers" under his breath.

The cops leaped out of the car like attack dogs. A backhand slap and Chuck was on the sidewalk. They turned to us. "You want some of it?"

We didn't answer for fear they'd kill Chuck. As they drove off, we helped him up and turned back toward home. The cold-blooded violence of the cops frightened us. Although we were barely seventeen and no match for them, they fingered us and intended to stop us before we got started.

An unpredictable Italian gang dominated one of the nearby parks. Overnight, their attitude toward us could change from indifference to hostility. An Irish gang dominated the other park. To be caught in either park after dark was dangerous. We tried again to organize some activity, but there was only the rock-strewn lot in front of Bryant Junior High for a playground.

Sometimes we climbed the fence at Central High and used the football field. Too often the cops would chase us out. We weren't allowed inside the Young Men's Christian Association. It never occurred to us to challenge their Christianity. That's the way white people were.

One day we finally saw what should have been obvious. Why not use the gym at Bryant Junior High? It was right in the middle of our neighborhood. There was a swimming pool, weights, everything.

The next day we put on our best clothes and went to the principal, Mr. Markham, and asked to use the gym after school hours. He smiled as if it were the most amusing thing he'd heard that day. "How can I turn this school over to three teenagers? There is thousands of dollars worth of equipment here."

"We can get an adult to be responsible."

"That will never do."

"Maybe you could get an adult to be responsible."

"Every other neighborhood takes care of its needs. You are talking to the wrong person. You should talk to your parents."

We could see this guy was laughing at us. We turned and left.

That night we talked it over and decided it was time to get our canvas delivery bags. Over the next several days we collected rocks and stored them in our bags. A week passed and in the evening we met and walked down the alley to the school yard. There we split up. First we knocked out the streetlights and then smashed over half the windows in the school before we ran down the alley to the safety of our homes.

The next day the evening papers had the story of the "senseless vandalism" on the front page. The cops knew who did it. For weeks they hid out in unmarked cars or cruised the neighborhood looking for an excuse to run somebody in. The principal knew who did it. He also knew that if six hundred dollars' worth of windows were broken out in his school again, he might not have a job. He called representatives of the Juvenile Division and the YMCA to a conference. They decided that they would have to make a move, but the cops made their move first. They picked up Mort and Sonny for questioning. Down at the Juvenile Division the cops made them hold a telephone book on their heads and hit the book with their blackjacks. Before releasing them, the cops shoved them around and threatened to "beat their ass" if they caught them breaking the law. The guys had headaches for a week.

Coming home from fishing Saturday afternoon, I turned into the alley on our block. I saw the squad car and knew they were looking for me. My first impulse was to run, but that would give them the opportunity to shoot or arrest me. I walked toward them. As I neared the car, three cops got out. I suddenly realized what a beautiful day it was. Summer was still in its splendor and everything was still green. A few cotton balls of clouds drifted across the bright blue sky.

"Come 'ere, boy."

I turned toward them.

"Yes?"

"Don't you know how to say 'sir'?" One of them snarled.

I remembered how Pop used to tell us to die on our feet rather than live on our knees.

"No, I never say 'sir.'"

I almost flinched as one of them put his hand on my shoulder—friendlylike—frighteningly friendly.

"Gene, you're always getting rough with these colored boys. They act all right if you give 'em a chance—don't you, boy?"

"I try to stay out of trouble." I kept looking at the ground so they wouldn't see how afraid I was.

" . . . all I want to know is who was the rest of the guys who threw the rocks?"

"I don't . . . "

"Listen, you little nigger . . . "

"Now, Gene, let me talk with the boy."

"Look, boy . . . "

I was in for a beating. The rest of them didn't talk and neither would I.

"Who . . . "

"I'm telling you the truth. I don't know anything about breaking any windows."

"Where you been, boy?"

"Fishing."

"Sir!"

A small breeze blew across the vacant lot. How did the old man say it? A hero or on your shield.

Whack!

Stars, red flashes, and whirligigs ruined the sky.

"You coward son of a bitch!"

A cop grabbed each arm, jerking me to my tiptoes. Get their numbers—no badges—the bastards had taken them off.

Whack! His gloved hand spun my face halfway around, a backhand spun it the other way. Blood and mucus ran into my mouth. Whack! The world spun and then righted itself. They loosened their hold and I fell, sitting in the dirt. I got up with what dignity I could.

"You damned niggers think you're so smart. When you talk to an officer, say 'sir.'"

It was the nice guy talking.

"I said I didn't know. Goddamnit, you're going to pay for this." I wasn't afraid anymore.

"Let's go. This little bastard don't have enough sense to talk."

They got into the car. Gene pushed his fat face out of the window. "Maybe if we kill a couple of you crazy niggers, you'll learn some sense."

"Go ahead. You got three guns."

"You want some more of it?" He started to open the door of the car, thought better of it, slammed the door, and drove off.

I hadn't crawled; I hadn't squealed. I won the victory. They knew it, too. I picked up my tackle and walked the half block home. Pop was furious. He grabbed his .38 and walked the alleys for half an hour. It was no use. We had no badge numbers and could prove nothing.

Our little gang changed after that run-in with the cops. Most of all, it changed Chuck. He was by nature a gentle and talented artist. Cops and segregated slums were strangling him and turning him into his opposite. A sensitivity that the rest of us didn't have was replaced by a brutality that the rest of us didn't have. He needed it to live.

The little white boy couldn't have been more than seven. As we passed him, he giggled,

Nigger, nigger never die
Black face and shinny eye
Crooked nose and crooked toes
That's the way the nigger grows.

He probably learned that ditty from his dad that morning. Chuck calmly walked over to him so as not to frighten him and kicked him in the stomach. The kid fell back, kicking the air, struggling to breathe. We scattered through the yards and down the alley.

"You shouldn't have done that, Chuck."

"Might grow up to be a cop. Besides, he has to learn sometime."

A few of the guys bought switchblade knives. I didn't. I was sure that if I carried one, I eventually would have to use it.

The cops were the stick, the YMCA was the carrot. A few days later, two white men came to the corner. Al, with rimless glasses and receding hairline, had the look of an official in the YMCA. A smiling, sharp-faced, athletic twenty-year-old who introduced himself as Chuck Cline accompanied him. They told us how they had been trying to get recreational facilities for the "colored kids" in the neighborhood for a long time. The "incident" had convinced everyone that we weren't getting a fair deal.

Bryant Junior High agreed to open the gym on Monday and Wednesday nights. Chuck Cline was going to be in charge. A few weeks later they added a Thursday night tap dance instructor who was white. It sure seemed funny, having a white guy teaching black youth how to dance. He won us over when he held his guitar behind his back, playing it while he tap-danced. It sure was something we couldn't do.

He taught us, and it was the only dance I ever learned.

7

THAT SUMMER SIX got a job in the stockyards. Well known and liked, he would amuse the workers there by jumping into a corral and bulldozing a fully grown steer. Sometimes I would go with him to the yards. He would beg the foreman to give me a job. There was never an opening.

Trying to land one's first job is the most formative experience of youth. If you hadn't learned about class and class relations before, trying to get your first job would teach you. In 1939 there wasn't much hope of finding a job, but I had to get one. I couldn't live any longer with the feeling of utter dependency, without pocket money or decent clothes.

The only way to find a job was to pick a street and go to every business establishment—up one side and down the other. I would walk every day from seven-thirty in the morning until five at night. I stopped at every shop and store and factory. Sometimes the answer was gentle and understanding. Sometimes it was harsh and rude. Often it was hostile. It was always the same: "I'm sorry, boy." "You know there's family men out of work." "I can't use you."

I became painfully aware that I was not going to find a job while white men willing to work were unemployed. Hungry families forced many black men into the groveling, shuffling, hat-in-hand begging for work. I never did it. The alternative, though, was to look for a "Negro" job.

First, I went to all the restaurants and drugstores in hopes of finding a job washing dishes or cleaning up. These were choice jobs to the hundreds of black unemployed family men, and there were no openings for a youth without a family.

I finally faced it. I wasn't going to get a job unless I shined shoes like the older guys on the corner. I started making the rounds of the barber shops. I finally landed a job in a small one on Bloomington and Lake. When I asked for the job, the barber told me the terms in a gruff, offensive voice: "No wages—I get the dime, you keep the tips. That make you work good."

I wanted to tell him to shove it, but the older black guy who worked there nodded his head ever so slightly. I took the job. I would work only on Saturday when the traffic was too heavy for Joe, the other bootblack, to handle by himself. This was a second job to Joe. His wife was in the tubercular sanatorium, and his two children ate up every cent he could get. Every penny counted with him, so I thought there might be a few nickels to be made.

I went to work hating that job, and after a few weekends I loathed it. I averaged three dollars a Saturday. That was enough to give Mom a buck and still have pocket change for the week. I had to grin and laugh to hold the job. Nobody wanted a "surly" Negro around, and a shoeshine boy who didn't grin at white folks' jokes about colored people was surly. Joe hated the job, too. He was so desperate they could make him come crawling anytime they needed him.

I knew from the first day's work that I would not be able to hold on. After a few weeks went by I accidentally smeared a bit of maroon shoe polish on a white silk sock. The man held up his foot examining the smear and muttered to himself, "Damned clumsy niggers."

Joe jerked him from the chair and smashed him in the face. We left him lying on the floor unconscious.

Walking toward our neighborhood, Joe turned to me. "You got to draw a line when you dealing with these crackers. I know I got to take low sometime—an' I do. But I draw a line. They got to know that it's a man takin' low, not a dog. Natural for a dog to take low. It ain't natural for a man. You got to draw a line. Part of that line is don't low-talk my race. Fuckin' hunkey do that—I knock him out. I got to, 'cause if I don't, I'm a dog takin' low 'cause it natural with dogs. I'm a man who's forced to take low now and then—but I ain't no dog."

I told Joe I understood and agreed with him, and I did. I made him take the little money I had. He went to beg for another job. I went home.

Uncle Ed was at the house when I got home. I hadn't seen him since he visited us in Wabasha some five years back. I always liked this warm, easygoing Filipino and could sit for hours listening to him. He knew something about everything.

He and Pop were arguing politics. "Now that Spain is lost, world war is inevitable."

"Well, I don't agree with appeasement," Pop said, "but it wasn't just Roosevelt. You know there's not a government in Europe that would allow Spain to go Communist."

"That's not the issue. Communism was never the issue. It was whether to stop the Hitler alliance or build them up to attack the Soviet Union." He stopped for breath, raising his hand in a hello to me.

Uncle Ed looked handsome as ever, hair slicked straight back, nut-brown face, piercing Chinese-looking eyes. Just divorced from my father's sister, he dropped by on his way back to his home in Iowa.

"Don't you agree?" he jokingly asked me.

"I don't know much about that war. What was it actually about?"

Uncle Ed thought for a moment, rubbing his knuckles against his chin. "Just suppose the Negroes in Mississippi got the right to vote. Then they elected a state government that was going to be for them instead of for the plantation owners. What do you think would happen?"

"I guess the Klan would lynch them. I think that's what happened after the Civil War."

Uncle Ed pursed his lips. "That's exactly what happened in Spain. Only the Klan was the Fascists, the landlords, and army around Franco. If they could have whipped the Klan after the Civil War, we'd have a democratic country. If we could have whipped Franco, Europe would change and we'd have peace. If I was a few years younger, I'd have gone over with the Lincoln Battalion and fought. It was that important."

Pop looked a bit perturbed. He didn't like anybody telling us anything. He felt that was his job.

"You still a Communist, Ed?"

Uncle Ed opened his wallet and pulled out his party dues book. The "paid" stamps were up-to-date. It was book number eleven.

"You know I am. It's the future."

"Number eleven! Gee whiz, Uncle Ed, you must have been in for a long time."

"Since the beginning."

"Well, Ed," Pop said. "Let's walk up to the corner. Some of the boys from home will want to see you."

I watched them leave, thinking, "It's the same all over the world—people like the Klan fighting people like us."

★

Sometimes on a Saturday, Six would grab the Thirty-Eighth Street bus and come up to spend the day. I introduced him to the young women around the corner. He would blush and push the hair out of his eyes when they said, "Hey, Nels—where did you get this fine thing?"

We never forgot our pledge and we never mentioned it.

I saw Heidi often. Some Saturday afternoons she would hang around with the teenagers from Central High in the candy and soda shop next to the theater on Chicago Avenue. Just on the edge of our little segregated community, it wasn't a dangerous area for me. I would make up reasons to go there in hopes of seeing her. When I did, I would feel embarrassed and guilty. At those times, I couldn't look into her eyes. She lived a few blocks from the park, and sometimes I would find her there. We would sit on the grass and talk. Her first year of high school was an introduction to Shelley, Keats, and Byron. A gentle part of her loved poetry. She would memorize bits and pieces of verse and we spent hours understanding what it meant. That way I learned, too.

She thoroughly enjoyed whatever she was doing at the moment. That was part of her charm. She didn't seem to be reaching for anything, didn't seem to have any goals. Perhaps she didn't need any. Maybe at sixteen, a white woman doesn't have to have goals. But all the young black women I knew, by that age, committed themselves to something.

I admired her commitment to democracy. She would speak bitterly against her parents, who were becoming even more anti-Negro, anti-Semitic, and anti-Communist. In 1939, if a person had one of those prejudices, that person would have the others. At that time they came as a package.

"I'm proud to have you for a friend, and if somebody don't like it, I'll . . ."

"Sic Six on 'em," I added. We laughed.

I never felt embarrassed with any other young woman. I felt it with her because in a secret and, I felt, treacherous way, I was falling in love.

8

SEPTEMBER 1, 1939. Hitler invaded Poland. Summer vacation ended. Central High opened its doors to a class of suddenly serious youth flung out of the frying pan of the Depression into the fire of total war.

Walking to school that first day, I felt that the explosions shaking the world were thrust back into the shadows by the heart-quickening knowledge that I would be in school with Heidi.

★

Miss Setterberg, the youngest teacher in the school, was an excellent instructor. We soon forgot about her stylish blue sweaters and blond hair when she began talking about Shakespeare. Her enthusiastic discussions about national cultures and how they were blending into an American culture captured our imagination. People like Miss Setterberg fought the national chauvinism pouring out of Germany and the rising race-baiting fascism here the best they could.

"America is a melting pot of culture and heritage, but it is more, because the American culture grows from and takes strength from the many cultures and national heritages of the people who today make up this country. In two weeks, I want each of you to write a theme paper that examines your own heritage and how it contributes to present-day America."

I left the class without the slightest idea of what to present as the Negro's contribution to American heritage. I sure wasn't going to say it was the spirituals. I wanted to present something hard-hitting—something nobody talked about.

I had more to think about than an assignment for the following week. The school paper announced the competition to select the school swimming team. In Wabasha, I used to swim across the Mississippi to Wisconsin. I knew I was a good swimmer and was sure I could make the team.

On the way home, I mentioned it to Chuck.

He laughed. "How come there has never been a Negro on the team before?"

"I don't know. Maybe nobody tried out before."

"Well, maybe. I think old man Webber don't want any colored on the team."

"What are you talkin' about? Webber told me to try out. Besides, the competition is going to be held at Bryant. Old man Anderson is going to choose the team—you know how fair he is."

"Only thing I know is that there ain't never been a Negro on the team."

We didn't discuss it anymore. I knew I'd make the team, and it would mean breaking down another barrier—that's how we progressed, a step at a time. If we didn't try, we couldn't win. I didn't say these things to Chuck. But that is what I believed. I would show them that the heritage Miss Setterberg spoke of was more than relief lines and being hurt in everything we try.

At the supper table that night, Mom asked me why I wasn't eating much. I told her that since I was going to try out for the swimming team, I didn't want a full stomach.

"Oh," she said. "You didn't tell me that you were going to try it."

"I thought I'd surprise you—I was going to wait until I knew what position I would get . . . "

I noticed the all-too-familiar shadow of worry cross her face as she glanced up at Pop.

He scowled at Mom and turned to me. "Go out there and get on the team. When you hit that water, just remember that you are swimming for the whole race, not for fun."

I smiled. How often and in how many ways had he drilled it into our heads: " . . . a hero or on your shield." We didn't have shields in athletic contests, but I'd make the team and come back a hero.

I stopped by the corner on my way to the tryouts. I glanced into the Dreamland. The usual crowd was standing at the bar. Chuck and Mac were over in the corner that Mr. Cassius tactfully reserved for those of us who were underage but wanted to drink soft drinks in the tavern. I went inside.

"What say, Nelson?"

"Fine, Mr. Cassius. How's the family?"

"OK. They tell me that you're going to try out for the swimming team."

"Yeah. Tonight." Sure aren't any secrets around here.

"Good. Good. We have a couple on the football team, a couple on the basketball team; if you make the swimming team, it'll be good for the race."

I smiled at Mr. Cassius. He sure was a race man. He kept up on everything that happened in the neighborhood, too. I turned to Chuck and Mac.

"Hey, now. What you cats talking about?"

"Nothin' happenin'. You going over there now?"

"Yeah."

Mac looked at me, his head cocked to one side. "Hope you make out."

I was sorry I had stopped in there. Too many people knew about it already. If I should fail, there would be no way to cover it up. Now, I'd have to win.

It was only a short walk to the school. Some of the fellows were already in the showers; others were in the locker room taking off their clothes.

"Hello, Nels. Glad you came out. What are you going to try out for?" Ward stuck out his big hand. He was one of the school's top athletes and a good guy. Others I knew shouted "hello." This was the upper crust of the school—good students, from upper-middle-class families. They never fought, never made enemies.

They seemed so clean-cut and innocent compared with our gang. I wished I knew these white boys better.

After the showers we went naked into the big cool room that contained the pool. I hadn't seen Mr. Anderson, the coach, for over three years. He made a point of remembering me and asked about my brothers.

Finally it was time to start the races. Mr. Anderson blew the whistle for silence and shouted, "Everyone for the underwater swim for distance—over here."

A group formed and the blast of the whistle sent sheets of water gushing into the air. I watched their white bodies, distorted by the water, wiggling above the white tile floor of the pool. One by one, flushed and out of breath, they surfaced. Mr. Anderson chose the two who had made the longest swim and called for those who would try out for the backstroke. Another whistle—the water splashed to the walls of the room. Arms flailed the greenish water, outstretched fingers touched the opposite end of the pool, and heads submerged for the sprint back. Mr. Anderson formed the backstroke team from the winners.

"All right," he shouted. "Now for the freestyle endurance. Five times up and back. Winners will also form the relay team."

I stepped to the edge of the pool. Ward, to my right, whispered, "Good luck." My toes grasped the edge of the pool.

"Swimmers ready." Arms arched back, bodies leaned forward, leg muscles tensed for the all-important first leap.

"Get set. Go!"

I sensed the bodies near me. I knew I had gotten off well—a long, shallow dive. As my face and arm came out of the water, I could see Ward swimming a stroke ahead of me. Kick, stroke, stroke, exhale. Ward was in his first turn when I reached the end of the pool. We stroked the length of the pool, back and forth. He maintained his stroke lead over me. I knew we far outdistanced the rest of the swimmers. I also knew that I could not overtake Ward. On the final turn I tried with all my might to make up that one-stroke lead. Ward was just as determined to keep it. He reached the end first. I was less than a yard behind him. Arms reached down to help Ward out of the pool. He turned and thrust his hand to me. Hands grasped each other's wrists and I climbed out of the water.

"Good going, Nels."

"Thanks, Ward. I couldn't catch you, though."

Mr. Anderson blew the whistle. "Free style—Ward Satter-field."

"Relay team—Satterfield, Nels Peery, Howie Marshall, Jim Grantz."

We congratulated one another and went to the showers. Happy I made it, I didn't have to come back on my shield.

★

At home they accepted my making the team as a matter of course. Up on the corner, though, Mr. Cassius was happy. He drew a small glass of draft beer and handed it to me. I took it back to the booth where the gang was drinking Coke. I upheld the race and I deserved the beer.

The next day Coach Webber called me into his office. A bit apprehensive, I knocked and opened the door. Perhaps the gang was right. Maybe Webber didn't want Negroes on his team. Maybe he was going to give me the white-man-to-colored-boy talk that we get in such situations.

Webber swiveled around in his chair and motioned to me to take a seat. "Glad to see that you made the team, Peery."

"Thanks, Coach." I knew he had more to say.

"Far as I know, you're the first colored boy to make the team. You know that we practice at the downtown YMCA—hold our meets there, too. They've got a regulation-size pool."

I couldn't understand what he was hinting at. I knew the Y didn't allow black kids inside—but this was a high school team . . .

"Well, I just wanted to tell you—they have their own regula-tions covering the use of the pool; the board of education just rents it from them." The coach pursed his lips and then nodded. That was all he had to say.

"Oh, by the way, Peery."

"Yes, Coach?"

"A good athlete fights all the way—don't forget that. Perhaps a lot depends on the way you fight."

"I'll fight all the way, Mr. Webber. I wouldn't have tried out if I thought that I might let the team down." I knew that wasn't what he was talking about. Webber smiled. I picked up my books and left the office. I knew he didn't give that lecture to the rest of the team.

Outside the gym I ran into Mort. "Hey, man. Have you started that assignment for the English class? Darned if I know what to write about. What the heck kind of a heritage do we have here? I ain't going to write about slavery, and I don't know anything about Africa."

"Man, I haven't given it much thought. I don't know what to write about either," I said.

"These Swedes know what they are—I guess we don't. Well, if you think of something, let me know."

"OK, Mort."

I watched him walk away. Strange thing, "heritage." Everybody got one—I don't think anybody knows what it is.

★

I had never been in the YMCA before. Black folk develop a danger sensor that tells them where they aren't welcome. They don't go alone to places if they think they're going to get thrown out. It was an impressive building, red brick and big windows. From inside there came the sounds of youth at play. I swung open one of the big oak doors and walked in. I've never gotten used to the split second of silence when a Negro walks unexpectedly into a room full of whites. I walked to the desk. Over to my right some young men played Ping-Pong. To my left, a few boys glanced over the latest periodicals. Looking over this lush playroom, I thought of the miserable corner that was our recreation area.

The clerk gave me a blank stare.

"Where is the team from Central High practicing?"

"The swimming team?"

"Yes."

"Go to the right all the way to the end of the hall. That's where the pool is."

"Thanks."

I knew he was still looking at me, but I didn't turn around.

"Hi, Nels." Ward and Howie came in, pushing the door closed behind them. They were protection for me, and I was glad to see them. Things didn't seem so hostile now.

After the showers, the team lined up against the wall, waiting for Webber to call us to practice. After a few moments, someone asked, "What happened to the coach?"

"I don't know. He went into the office with the Y director."

One of the teammates glanced at me, adding to my discomfort. In a few moments Webber and a tall thin man wearing rimless glasses entered the pool room. I recognized the guy immedi-

ately. It was Al, the guy who brought Chuck Cline to the corner to
talk to us. He didn't seem to recognize me. Webber glanced about
the room. I had already taken a step forward when he motioned
me over to him. I wished I had some clothes on. I felt more than
naked before this man in his suit and tie.

"Yes, Coach?"

"Ah—Peery, I—uh—"

I wanted to shout at them—what's wrong? Instead, I looked
at my nakedness and said nothing. I knew what was wrong.

"Peery, believe me. I didn't know—I wasn't sure—I wouldn't
have put you through this—I'd have told you."

Webber clasped his hands as if to pray, then held the open
palms toward me.

"I don't understand, Mr. Webber. I don't know what you're
trying to tell me."

"It's some rule here. Something I wasn't sure of. They don't
allow Negroes to swim in the pool." He blurted it out as if saying it
was more painful than holding it in.

I turned with a sneer to Al, the Y director.

"I'm a Christian young man—that's what YMCA stands for."
I was terribly aware of my nakedness—I felt defenseless.

"It's not me," Al was saying. "The board; the men who make
the donations—we have to run this organization according to
some rules; they make the rules."

Webber would not look at me. There was a moment of awkward silence.

"It's OK. I understand. You people never did mean Christian—you meant white. You meant that hanging out on Thirty-
Eighth Street is good enough for us." I recalled what Webber said
about "fight to the end." There was nothing to fight with.

"You know, Mister," I turned to Al. "I'm not going to let this
die here. I'm going to tell my minister; he'll know what to do. I'm
going to tell the teachers in school about it. I'm going to make you
stop saying Christian when you mean white." The slap of my bare
feet on the wet tile echoed in the silence of the pool room. I
dressed and almost ran from the building.

The gang was still hanging around the corner. Mac looked up
at me from the evening paper and put it back on the counter.
"Thought you were at the Y. Done already?"

"Yeah. All done."

I started to say something about what had happened. Mort

looked up at me from his Coke. "What about that English assignment?"

"Huh?"

"The assignment to write about our heritage. We have to hand it in day after tomorrow."

"Guess I'd better get home and start on it."

I left the drugstore and waved to Mr. Cassius behind the bar in the Dreamland. I knew my heritage and knew what to write for the class assignment.

9

INSULATED IN THEIR neat neighborhoods, viewing the world through their blue eyes, my teachers never imagined that one of "their" colored boys would be humiliated by race prejudice. For the moment, Hitler was on our side. He said democracy was decadent and the YMCA proved it. Some people couldn't live with the contradiction.

Miss Setterberg raised it at the teachers' meeting and asked that the team be withdrawn from the Y. Pop was furious. He wrote a long article for the local Negro press. Father Thompson said he was going to raise it with the bishop. Mr. Cassius refused his beer delivery until assured the beer company would make no further donations to the Y.

In a few days, Al Hensen, the director of YMCA work in the area, and Chuck Cline came to the house. We had grown fond of Chuck. A great basketball player, he could laugh and joke with anyone. His sharp facial structure hadn't left enough room for his teeth to expand. Jutting outward, his two front teeth were slightly crossed, pushing his lip outward in a perpetual grin—but it suited him.

They talked first with Mom and Pop and then with me. They wanted us to form an all-Negro Hi-Y club as a beginning to break down the discrimination. Ben immediately objected, saying it would justify Jim Crow. I wanted to talk to the guys at the corner. They had mixed reactions. One group said the hell with the YMCA. They didn't mean us any good yesterday and they don't mean us any good today. Tell that guy to take his Jim Crow Hi-Y and ram it up his ass. There were other thoughts. Our gang was

already a Jim Crow organization. We didn't want to be broken
up. They had what we wanted and we would have to get near
them to get it. The athletic facilities available to the white youth
was the persuading argument. We realized the danger of our position but decided to give their Jim Crow organization a try.

Belonging to the Y didn't change our gang. It just gave us a
name, The Cavaliers. Our Y club took citywide championships in
nearly everything. Most important, we were thrown into a new
level of relationships with the guys at school. Most of them had
never held a serious discussion with a Negro. Fundamentally they
were democratic-minded young men and women but unbeliev-
ably ignorant of the world in which they lived. First, we competed
against one another, but afterward we talked. During the retreats
to the campgrounds, the question "What does the Negro want?"
meant bull sessions lasting until dawn. They learned from us; we
learned from them. I learned that, in their ignorance, they were
afraid of us. When they found out that we didn't fit their stereo-
types, they went to the opposite extreme. They then thought there
was no such thing as black, antisocial criminals. This stereotype
was harder to fight than the other.

I began to understand how important segregation was to controlling both blacks and whites. As long as one group didn't even
know who the other was or thought or wanted, there was no hope
of solving the "race problem."

I spoke at meetings of different Hi-Ys and even at the girls'
Blue Triangle. During one of the bull sessions on religion, I raised
some point of religious dogma Father Thompson had pointed out
to me. I became little less than a saint. They asked me to lead
school prayers calling for peace and the brotherhood of humanity.
In my heart I prayed for the Almighty to open the floodgates of
war and catastrophe and pay the white people back for what they
had done to us.

I knew the YMCA and some of the teachers used me to show
how "democratic" they were. I knew it was an old tactic, not far
removed from the "head nigger" role under slavery. Things came
to a crisis when one of the older fellows on the corner said to me,
"I hear you're pullin' the man's coattail and grinnin' in his face."

I knew I wasn't playing the role of an Uncle Tom, yet I couldn't
deny that they were using me apart from the rest of the Negro
youth at school.

I resigned my position as president of the Hi-Y Club and

drifted back to spending more time on the corner, soaking in the philosophy of race war. Race war? We didn't have any organization, and no weapons. We couldn't even agree on the most unimportant things. I knew that the road I was traveling now was wrong, but I would not go back to being the representative of a Jim Crow organization. I was at the end of the road. Maybe there was no way out. The overwhelming numerical superiority of white people hemmed us in. Our disunity magnified our impotence.

I stopped going to the corner; I stopped studying. I would spend hours sitting on the front steps. One of those evenings I heard the long, lonesome howl of a freight train as it left the Western Division and pulled out for the Rockies. I had to hit the road.

Report cards came out. I got As in Shakespeare, history, and civics and failed the other three subjects. As was the procedure, the principal called me into his office.

After the preliminary admonition to study in order to get ahead was over, he motioned for me to sit down. "What seems to be the trouble, Nelson? You are not even trying. A in three subjects and three fails? What's the problem?"

"I don't know. I guess I haven't been studying."

"Well, you have to study. You have to prepare for your future."

"I don't need to prepare for a mop pail."

The principal narrowed his eyes, flushing red with anger.

"Get out of my office. You prepare for a mop pail—that's what you're going to get. Get out of here."

I left knowing I'd made a mistake but glad I'd angered him.

A few days later, leaving for school, I heard the wail of the engine. I left my books on the porch and headed for the yards. A train was pulling out of the division. I ran for it, sliding over the concrete embankment, jumping across the empty tracks. Running alongside the freight, I grabbed one of the rungs, paced the car, feeling the speed and motion—then leaped aboard. Up ahead, the engine howled and gathered speed. We cleared the city, the engine spitting hot cinders. I turned my back, wondering when I'd have a chance to get inside a boxcar. All that day we raced across the rich Minnesota plains and gently rolling hills. I did not eat that day. The only time I got off the train was to climb into one of the boxcars. We roared through western Minnesota into the wheatlands of the Dakotas. The only sound in the world was the unending clickety-clack of steel on steel.

Jumping off the train at Mobridge, South Dakota, I went into the little town to find food. "Ma'am, can I do some work for a bite to eat?"

With the yard raked and the trash burned, I sat down to a plain but huge meal of meat and vegetables. Back at the yards, I was overcome by sleep. I woke up, prodded by the boot of the railroad dick. The sentence was three days for "sleeping." The sheriff's wife nearly cried when she saw me being led to the two-by-four jail behind their house. She yelled at him until he bought me food from their table rather than having me eat the regulation chow. I left the jail rested and stuffed.

Clickety-clackety-clack—the Little Big Horn. The nights were becoming bitterly cold. A hobo shared his beans and bacon butts with me. At Bozeman the only human voice I heard snarled, "Goddamnyou—get of'n my land!"

I pushed on—Butte, Helena. I had to get a coat. Following a hobo's advice I asked for work at the Salvation Army. I got the coat—ragged and too big—for four hours' work. I no longer had a reason to keep going; moving onward was the reason and the goal.

Fewer and fewer men headed west. Those drifting to the east and south warned me, "You must be crazier than hell, boy. You can't get over the Great Divide. It's already forty below in those mountains. Go back East!"

"Boy, in the name of God, if'n you got a home or a mama, go back. Men are dying out there. There ain't no work."

There was other talk in the jungles—the hobo hangouts near the tracks—snarling, bitter talk I heard hints of before.

"Yeah? Well, maybe Roosevelt's all right, but I think he's going to try playing Hitler."

"Them Social Security numbers ain't nothin' but a way to keep tab on the workers. They're registering workers, that's all— just like in Germany, so they'll know where to come and get you when they want you."

"Sure there's gonna be a war. They tried everything else to get out of the Depression. It ain't no worker's war. Stay out of it."

And there was cruel talk and heartbreaking talk on the corners and vacant lots of the towns: "Don't let the moon shine on ya in this town, black boy."

"Boy, kin I have a drag on your cigarette?"

"If'n you're hongry, boy, have some of my stew. Don't be scared 'cause ah'm from the South. We both bums."

The bitter October cold and the constant hunger kept forcing me to the east. Back through Billings, through Butte, past the Missouri. I jumped off the train at the Little Big Horn and walked down where the river bends away from the railroad. There, I took off the ragged coat. The schoolboy clothes were crawling with lice. After the fire was leaping from the bed of embers, I bathed in the cold, clean water of the river.

This wasn't far from the battle site. As the fiery autumn sun sank below the horizon, I thought about the Indians making their final stand. "This red dirt ain't much to die for," I thought. "But it was theirs." After rolling and lighting up another cigarette, I knew why I jumped off the freight. I had to make a decision, and I had to be alone to do it. I was going back home. There was no choice. What was I going to do after I got home? I came here to make that decision. The decision about getting along in the white man's world had already been made. I wasn't going to get along. The problem was, how to resist. Two men on the corner long ago took one of the paths. Half drunk most of the time, one of them kept a pistol inside his shirt. The cops didn't bother them and neither did anyone else. Nobody messed with them while they destroyed themselves. It was the one thing America allowed them.

Another role was simply stated and quietly carried out—do the best you can. The "best you can" advocates provided the core of stable Negro leadership and middle-class success. They also provided the stool pigeons, the informers and betrayers.

There was another path, that of fighting back. You had to be more cunning than the strong. You had to have the courage of the rebellious slave. You had to have the tenacity of the dirt farmer who struggles with obsolete instruments against the burnt-out land but gathers in the harvest.

The second section of the freight was approaching.

We're like that big old engine. Pulling the load with a white man at the throttle. We got to get hold of the throttle. We got to get the driving wheels working together. We have that much power, if only we can put it together. The question was, how? As for that crap about love being the way, what are you supposed to feel for a person who hurts what you love? Love him, too? They teach us that shit. But they hate us; that's why they come out on top. Hate sure got them further than love got us. That talk sounds good. It'd go over good on the corner. How do you hate some poor white bum? Or even the dumb kids at school? There's a way to do this. I'm seventeen. I'm going to learn who I have to fight and I'm going to learn how to fight. If love and the church can't do it, who can? Maybe Father Thompson was telling me something and didn't know it. Maybe the Communists got the answer. I think I'll look them up when I go home.

The train sped past, taking my jumbled thoughts with it. I heaped more wood on the fire, wrapped the coat around me, and slept.

The next morning I grabbed the blinds of a passenger. It was an exhausting and dangerous way to ride. I stood between two cars, one foot on the ledge of each, holding on to the grab rail of each car. The train roared along at a seventy-mile-an-hour clip. On a sharp curve to the south, the cars nearly touched, squeezing me against the blinds. A curve to the north and they would separate, while I would stretch out, barely hanging on. To lose my footing or my grip was a sure and immediate death. The train wouldn't even slow down.

It was faster than the freights. In eight hours we covered the distance into Minneapolis. The sharp curve in the tracks forced the train to brake near Fourth Avenue. As it did, I jumped off and made it through the alleys to our house.

It was good to be home again. I bathed, burned my clothes and the lice, and basked in the love reserved for a prodigal son. Pop regarded me as a man now. He bought me a beer and cussed without apologizing.

A few lies and a lot of pleading got me back into school. Before long I caught up with the rest of the class. Hard work was easy. I had to learn. I didn't have the answers, but I did have understanding and with that, determination.

10

WINTER FASTENED ITS grip on Minnesota. The long, cold evenings lent themselves to staying home, studying and reading, if the other nine people who lived there allowed it. I was sitting on the radiator reading when I heard the loud and steady knock. As always, all six of my brothers yelled "Come in" simultaneously. It was enough to scare anyone away.

Stamping the snow off his feet, Six opened the door, grinned and yelled, "Hi ya, Nels!"

After we had traded slaps on the back and had shaken hands for the fourth time, I set a pot of tea to simmering and we sat down to catch up. Six had to quit his job at the stockyards when school started. He had gotten it back on weekends. Work was beginning to open up in meat packing, and he thought he could get me on, too. So much had happened, so much lay ahead. We talked about Heidi, about our mutual friends from school, and we laid plans to take to the road the coming summer. All the time he kept smiling, brushing his hair from his eyes, and saying, "I'm glad to see ya, ya bastard."

Suddenly it was morning. We had talked the night away. He should have gone to work, but we were both groggy from the night-long powwow. Having missed the one bus to the stockyards, he decided to go home and get some rest. When he left the house the sun was shining brilliantly on the sparkling snow that blanketed our city.

I slept until four o'clock that afternoon. Half awake, I forced myself to get up to read the afternoon paper. Halfway down the stairs I stopped. The house was strangely quiet. Normally my brothers would be wrestling and arguing over the funnies. The paper lay unopened on the coffee table.

My younger brother looked at me with soft, protective eyes. I knew that something was wrong. Mother picked up the paper and handed it to me. "I'm terribly sorry, son."

I opened the paper. One glance at the headline, and—Oh God! No!—I read it again: "Youth Crushed Beneath Truck." A smiling picture of Six, his hair partly in front of his eyes, shone beneath the banner headline. I glanced down the column of type. He had decided to go to the yards. Since there was no other transportation, he tried to catch a truck on the run, slipped, and fell between the cab and the trailer, and was crushed beneath the wheels. I sat down on the stairs pretending to read the article, grappling with the finality of the headline. My true friend—my blood brother—why you? Just a few hours ago he had been here, so strong and bold—the plans we made—and now, suddenly—. I could not think the word, so terrible in its finality.

I did not cry. I could not express the hurt. Mom watched me

for a moment and turned to the kitchen. My brothers would not look at me, afraid to make it worse. My first impulse was to call his mother, then I thought it best to call later. I started to call Heidi. She would be crying and unable to talk. Finally, I put on my jacket and went to the Dreamland. As I opened the door, someone laughed. The men were standing at the bar, their feet twisted to the rail. They talked barroom talk. They laughed the deep, rich laughter of black men drinking beer. They smiled and nodded when some woman glanced into the cafe. They played the pinball machine as if nothing had happened today. I watched them for a moment, turned, and went back home.

Monday afternoon was set aside for the friends of Six to view his body. I left school and walked slowly through the snow to the place where the casket lay.

There is a funeral parlor on Chicago Avenue and Thirty-Seventh Street. The wooden colonial columns are white and the bricks are red. In summertime a row of carefully kept flowers surrounds it. In fall, the big maple trees shower the lawn with leaves, and in the evenings the fresh smoke of maple leaf bonfires drifts across the opening. But in winter it is a tomb. When the snow falls gently upon the city, there is a blanket of white on the tile roofs and on the stone sills. Inside, the sweet smell of burning incense mingled with the tallow from the candles. Inside, there was a blue casket, and therein lay the body of my friend. Last summer we stood on the corner, wondering where to go. In winter we knew where to go. With faltering steps and heads bowed, we approached the building. We paused before the big oaken doors and, as they opened, the first conscious pain of loss filled the heart and I walked down the aisle to the empty seat reserved for me between Heidi and the ruddy-faced mother of the boy who pledged to be my brother.

A minister stood before the casket and looked solemnly over the sober young faces. He spoke of the youth of the world, of suffering the young to come unto Him, of facing life without those who were called from us. Heidi held my hand and sobbed. The minister bowed his head in prayer, then quietly left the room.

The attendant raised the lid of the coffin, straightened the tie, and motioned us to come and view the body. We rose, Heidi clinging tightly to my hand as we formed a line to take our final, respectful look at the still, sallow face of our friend.

They will put him in the ground and I'll never see him again.

We're not going on the road this summer. It would have been fun. I felt the splash of a tear on my hand. Ashamed, I brushed it off. Dry, hard sobs racked Heidi. One of the guys from the YMCA touched the sleeve of my coat. "You know how to pray. Will you?"

"Please, Nels," said Heidi.

I paused, afraid of what babble might come out if I opened my mouth. A Bible was placed in my hand. Something I knew from memory, something I could read through the tears: "The Lord is my shepherd . . . "

They all knew the verse. A few of the more religious ones joined me in the twenty-third psalm: "I shall not want . . . He maketh me to lie down in green pastures. He leadeth me beside the still waters, He restoreth my soul. He leadeth me in the path of righteousness for his name's sake. Yea, though I walk through the valley of the shadow of—of—"

Heidi broke down. She placed her hand tenderly against the still, lifeless face. I slowly pulled her hand away. Maybe there is something. Maybe you just don't die.

" . . . of death, I shall fear no evil."

I finished the psalm. We filed past the casket and went back to our seats. The attendant with solemn finality closed the lid. The memorial was over.

We filed quietly out of the building. It was snowing again—big, soft flakes. No one said good-bye. Our friend was gone and we were sad. Heidi held my hand as we stood with Mrs. Peterson until she caught a cab. A quick "God bless you," and we were alone.

"We'd better go."

"All right, Nels." If I had said let's commit suicide, that would have been the answer.

We walked down Chicago Avenue toward the bus line. An advertisement for beer flashed off and on, splashing the snow in neon red. A man came out of the beer hall, looking over his shoulder at us. I glared back. He shrugged and kept walking. Halfway down the block, Heidi turned, grabbed the lapels of my coat, pressed her face against my chest, and cried. It was different from her earlier suppressed sobbing. The floodgates opened, then nearly closed to gentle, childlike crying to ease the way to the pain. I wanted to comfort her. There was nothing to say. I held her for what seemed hours before the tears stopped and she released my lapels. Our thoughts shut out the rest of the world and we walked on toward her house. Six was gone and everything between us had changed. She seemed so hurt, so afraid, and so alone.

I could feel her spirit close to me, listening, waiting for me to speak to her. It clung to me and I turned to it and thought, "I'll look after you. I love you, you know that. But we don't talk about that. We never dare look into each other's eyes. We never speak of, or cross the bar that they placed between us. You know how I feel and I know you understand, but I can never tell you.

"He's dead and we're still alive and have to face tomorrow. The sun will still rise and the moon will still shine and I'll love you and can never tell you. We'll grow up and you'll marry some man with blond hair and blue eyes. Maybe he'll be something like Six was—but it won't be the same, and sometimes you'll remember how we were. I'll be gone, because all I want is to run away from everything. I know why hoboes hobo—ramble this country— searching for peace within themselves, no worry and no regrets. It can be found only in what these savages call the jungle.

"There I can be myself and you'll forget the Negro guy you liked. You'll never know these things, and I can never tell you."

"What are you thinking, Nels?"

"I don't know. Nothing, I guess. Maybe about all that's happened in the past few years. Pretty soon, maybe I'll never see you again. You'll live through this, and someday you'll forget tonight. I know I never will."

We walked a little farther before she spoke.

"No. I won't forget. Never. It sounds funny, but you're all I have now. Mom and Dad—they don't know me. Six did and you do—I think. I feel funny about it all. I never—not in the last few years—loved Six the way people thought I did. Gee, we had been going steady for the past six years, ever since the sixth grade. I was his girl. Nobody else even dared to ask for a date."

We kept walking. There was no place to go.

"Funny, the way we were. He was more than a big brother, but he wasn't really a boyfriend. Do you understand?"

"I think so."

"Do you think I'm a bitch for talking like this and he isn't even buried?"

"No, long as you're telling the truth."

"I guess if it hadn't happened, we'd have gotten married in the next few years. I'd been happy with him."

She pushed her hand into my coat pocket and held my hand tightly.

"Maybe, I shouldn't tell you this, but last summer we decided to do it. We tried, but he was too big. He used to tease me and tell me we couldn't get married. We never tried it again."

I was silent.

"Now that he's gone, will we still be friends? Will you still like me?"

"Sure, kid. We'll still be friends."

We approached her house. The warm lamplight shone through the big front window. It looked neat and clean inside.

"Well, I guess we say good night here."

"I wish I could invite you in. I feel like a liar, saying that we're friends and then not inviting you inside. He would never come in here after what my parents said about you."

"It's all right. Not your fault. Things are changing, you know. All over they're changing. We'll see it different some day."

She looked up at me. The gray eyes were soft and greenish in the light that filtered through the snow. She impulsively pressed her cheek against mine and whispered, "Good night. You're a good person."

I watched her walk into the house, turned, and walked toward our part of town.

That's the way it began.

★

Mort wasn't much of a talker. When others talked, he listened and thought. Sometimes, a day or so later, he would comment on what had been said. When he did talk, we knew he had thought over what he was going to say. He was looking serious as he approached me in the hallway at school.

"What'cha say, Mort?"

"Not much. I saw you was alone. I want to talk about something."

"OK. What's up?"

Mort looked at me, embarrassed by what he was thinking.

"Ain't really my business, but it sort of is—"

"Hey, man. You can say whatever's on your mind. You know that."

"It's about you and this chick."

"What chick?"

"You know, man. The Ofay."

"You mean Heidi?"

"Yeah. I been hearing some talk—some of it is 'he said that she said' sort of shit, but I hear that some of those YMCA people we're trying to work with are talking about you and her."

"Goddamn, Mort. I've known her since eighth grade. Besides, I hardly talk to her."

"Well, you know how those people are. They see one of us colored guys talking to a white chick, first thing they say is we're trying to fuck her."

"Well, that ain't what's happening. We've been friends for a long time—that's all."

"You know me, man. If you're in love with her—fuck them people, you got to live your life. But if you're just tryin' to hose the chick, it's going to hurt what we're trying to do."

I didn't think anyone had noticed. I had tried to be so casual about it all.

"There's nothing happening, Mort. I'm not trying to make something happen. I know what you're telling me, and I appreciate you putting me hep to the shit. I bull jive with a lot of these chicks at school. But I'll be more cool."

Mort's usually jovial black face was unsmiling. His eyes were always bloodshot and yellow, as if he worked in the bright sun too long. They weren't smiling either. I knew what he was thinking. Just last week, Senator Bilbo had made a speech in the Senate on the resolution of the "Negra problem."

"Bring them all to Mississippi," he roared to an amused Senate. "We will give them each a fifth of whiskey and a switchblade knife. At midnight we'll parachute one white woman into the middle of them. By morning the Negra question will be permanently solved."

"That stinkin' son of a bitch," I thought. "But he's just saying what they all think. So my Christian friends think all this is just to get next to a white girl! They think Bilbo is right. I don't want anything to do with those people. They can keep their lily-white Christian association. They're not going to let us get a foot in the door. If it's not one excuse, they find another. I'm not going to kiss their ass for what's rightfully mine."

After all the frustrated thinking was done, I knew I couldn't walk away from this fight. I had pulled the gang into it and I'd have to stick it out. The choice was clear. I couldn't let this thing with Heidi develop any further.

I could not avoid her. We were constantly meeting in the hallways or on the steps of the school. I knew she wanted me to know that the smile and "hello" were special and just for me. I would give her as casual a "Hi" as possible, followed by an awkward moment of silence when a conversation should have begun. Hurt by my silence, she would leave.

Sometimes, we would find each other in the school yard or the drugstore across the street. During the few moments we talked I would wonder if anyone was watching and, embarrassed, would cut the conversation short.

I hurt her by distancing myself from her. I was hurt because I was betraying something important. More than that, the longing to touch and hold her was almost unbearable when she was near.

Winter thawed and began to melt away. Spring came to the North Star country. Our Y club, The Cavaliers, won the city championships in basketball and most of the indoor track meets. Our names were in the papers and older people congratulated us, but we knew that we were playing a losing game. We didn't talk about it, but we had failed to do what we intended. It was already 1941 and the YMCA had still failed to integrate. We made a lot of white friends, and our acceptance at school was better. That was not our goal. Our little separate-but-equal organization had legitimated the segregation. Not only was that a failure but I had lost my chance with Heidi to boot. I began looking for a way out.

I hadn't spoken to her for over a month. She was avoiding me with an if-that's-the-way-you-want-it recognition of my avoiding her. Suddenly, she was directly in front of me, waiting at the side door I always used at the end of the school day. Her arms were crossed, clasping her books to her breast. The pleated skirt and bare legs still a bit pigeon-toed in her bobby socks and brown-and-white saddle shoes all showed her rapid maturity to womanhood. The brown hair was still held together with the cow ear clip she had worn since the eight grade. At seventeen, the uneasy, childlike half smile made her even more radiant. A deep breath and my heart began to beat again. Happy to see her, I didn't care who was watching.

"Hi, Heidi. God, I'm glad to see you."

"Really? If you are, I'm glad. I thought you were avoiding me."

"Heck no. I guess we've both been busy—"

"I haven't been busy. I thought you might call."

This was the fork in the road, the last chance. If I messed up now—"I should have called. I always intended to. It's just that I've been trying to do something, and nothing worked out."

"I talked to Ernestine. I asked her why you were avoiding me."

"What did she tell you?"

"She said you were trying to break up the discrimination at the YMCA and you didn't think it would look good if you were going with a white girl."

Suddenly the blood was pounding in my throat and temples. It sounded ugly, and more than ugly, it was true.

"That's not the way it was—there's more to it than that."
She turned and pushed the door open. The glint of tears was in her eyes.

"Then it is true." She turned her back to the door, pushing it open. A few students were still sauntering in the hallway. Behind her, the April sky was brilliant blue and the grass springtime green, alive against the patches of winter dun. Her gray eyes were accusing—hurt and defiant.

"All the years we've been close friends—more than friends—I thought you were beginning to like me, like me for myself, not just because I came along with Six—the way I was beginning to like you." She closed her eyes for a moment. When she opened them they had softened, the harshness of accusation fading to the softness of pity. "Did you throw it all away to please people who hate you?"

"I—I didn't know. I didn't believe that you—"

She began walking slowly toward the street. I fell in step with her, knowing she wouldn't have said all that if she wanted to end it and walk away. I touched her arm. She shifted the books to free her hand and slid it into mine.

"Honest, Heidi. I didn't think you'd feel like I do. I thought you were just being friendly."

"Gee, you're dumb. How can you be so smart and so dumb?"

"How am I being dumb? I can't make something happen just because I want it to happen."

"You're not just dumb about me. It's everything—like the YMCA. Don't you know you can't join their world? They won't let you. You wouldn't even like it. Why do you care about them?"

"That's why I didn't get in touch, Heidi. Even you think I want to join their world. I don't want to. I just want my rights. They can be prejudiced all they want. I ain't going to take their discrimination and segregation."

"What do you mean, that's why you didn't get in touch?"

We were sliding into an argument. The fork in the road was reappearing. I wanted to put a stop to it while it was still possible.

"I mean, I can't join their world, and I can't be with you without joining it." I knew that she knew I was lying. There were too many interracial couples in Minneapolis.

"Let's not fight, huh, Nels?"

"I don't want to fight. We just got things straightened out. If you got time—let me buy you a Coke."

We sat side by side in the booth sharing a coke, confessing how terrible the past few months had been without even talking together. When she finally left for home, I knew we had crossed the line and there would be no turning back for either of us.

11

WE WERE STUCK in our segregated little community. If some way out opened to us, we never had the money to take advantage of it. Poverty checked and held us there, held us together with chains stronger than the segregation imposed by law and custom. We didn't want to scatter out and join with the white guys in their YMCA clubs, and we could no longer justify accepting a segregated club.

When we let the YMCA know our intentions, they sent Chuck Cline out to talk to us. We all liked and respected him. Trying to understand our contradictory thinking, he could only shake his head at the damned-if-you-do/damned-if-you-don't position we put him in. Disregarding his pleading to keep up the fight, we disbanded our segregated little club. There was no sense of loss. We were seventeen, and spring was calling us.

★

The parks were important to us. More than a baseball diamond, more than a swimming pool, the park was the place to tell a high school sweetheart all the things that seemed inappropriate anywhere else. It was a place for laughter and conspiracy, a place to lie back, watch the sky, and feel at peace. We enjoyed these things only so long as the white ethnic gang that controlled the park allowed it.

In the beginning, the park gangs were hardly more than baseball or football teams. As their members grew older, they laid claim to the park in their neighborhood to guarantee that a field or diamond would be open for them. By their late teens the park had become their fiefdom.

Our neighborhood lay between two parks. A mainly Irish gang dominated Nicolet to the west. We had friends among them, and in many ways we were closer to the poor Irish than to any other whites. A group of Negro-hating Irish thugs took over the park at night. To be in Nicolet park after dark guaranteed a fight with the Paddys. Chicago Field was closer and controlled by a mainly Italian gang. They went to our school and some lived at the edge of our neighborhood. We knew most of them and were good friends with some. They were vulnerable, because we knew where they lived and met them individually on the streets.

The Fascist movement in the city, spurred on by Gov. Harold Stassen's crude, anti-Semitic political campaign, was big and growing. The Polish Blue Shirts, the German American Bund, and the Fascisti all had youth divisions. Their thinking spilled over onto the youth around them. The brutal conquest of Ethiopia made us hostile to anything Italian. We believed the Italian guys thought they could do the same with us. Some in the Chicago gang were deeply influenced by fascism. Others, whose parents fled Mussolini's fascism, took every opportunity to let us know they wanted to be friends.

The tension between our little gang and the Chicago gang increased as the weather warmed up and we went to the park more often. In one week, there were two fistfights between some of our members and theirs. We knew that sooner or later we would have to settle with them, or they would drive us from the park.

Our fighting with the Chicago gang was not very serious.

From their point of view, the growing threat of invasion by the Nicolet gang overshadowed our sporadic fistfights.

The rumors at school about a coming fight between Nicolet and Chicago increased every day. One night someone splashed a Chicago gang member's car with yellow paint. The fight was on. Arrangements were made to meet that Thursday afternoon in Chicago Park and fight it out. Our little gang, split between the two gangs geographically and to some extent by friendships, was implicitly involved.

Finally, Chuck, Mort, and I talked it over. "Look, Chuck," I said. "If things go the way they're going, four of us will end up fighting with Chicago and three with Nicolet. What say we get together and fight on one side or the other, in exchange for protection in the park from now on?"

Both these gangs were bigger than our little group. We had the reputation of being good fighters. Whichever gang we sided with was going to win, and everybody at school knew it. We agreed on our plan and set about mobilizing all the Negro guys in the area. We sensed our strength and knew that for once, we were going to come out on top.

All day Thursday, the halls and study rooms buzzed with the air of the coming battle. The girls were excited. The guys wore high-topped boots and dungarees for the scuffle. Rubber hoses and miniature baseball bats or silk stockings stuffed with sand crammed the lockers.

Chuck and I worked to keep our little band of eleven warriors together as we marched from school to the park.

"There's gonna be blood spilt today," someone in our gang said.

"Yeah. But we can't stop it now," another answered.

"Shi—it, man. I don't want to stop it. Let her roll."

The two sides gathered at opposite ends of the field. Few of the guys knew what the fight was all about, nor did they care. Springtime gripped them, turning their fancy to war.

Our little gang stopped in front of the field house and watched.

The leader of the Nicolet gang approached Mac, who lived at the edge of his neighborhood. "What's the matter with you guys? You turned yellow?"

"Nope," Mac said. "What's in it for us?"

"What'cha mean, man? You're on our side, ain't ya?"

"Maybe. What's in it for us?"

Chuck and I stepped in and told him the terms. We get protection in the park. We get any diamond and the pool when we want it. That was OK with him because they seldom played here. He went to talk it over with his gang.

Two of the Chicago gang came over and asked why we weren't with them. We told them the terms and they refused. Halfway across the field one of them turned and shouted, "You Goddamned backbiting black bastards!"

Chuck started to run after him. We held him back, waiting for the decision of the Nicolet gang.

The guy came back and agreed to the terms. His gang would protect us in Chicago, and in return, we would always help them against the Chicago gang.

We walked across the field and joined the Nicolet gang. The two groups moved slowly toward each other. As we closed together, we could hear the battle cry of the Chicago gang: "Get the niggers!"

Chuck darted back and forth in front of us, his asthmatic breathing louder than ever. "Stay together—stay together for protection. If they separate you, they'll kill ya!"

Only a few yards remained between us. We closed with them, sparring and shoving until angry enough to begin the fight. Somewhere, serious fighting started. It spread quickly, and suddenly it was mortal combat. After the first swing, I lost my club and fought with my fists. Rolling on the ground, we slugged it out. Yells and dust filled the air. Chuck refused to fight any single person. Instead, he darted through the crowd, doubling up with any one of us who might be in trouble. We caught on and used the same tactic. The biggest guys in the Chicago gang kept charging into us. We would meet them two or three on one, a fistful of black knuckles fixing their mouths so they couldn't say "nigger" so easily tomorrow. For us, this was a fight to the finish, and we were winning.

The scream of sirens overrode the yelling and cursing. I turned to Chuck. "Cops!" We knew what they'd do to us.

"Thud!" The sky was full of red flashes, stars, and whirligigs. I fell to the ground. I knew I had been hit with something—a pipe or club. The blood ran into my eye, burning and blinding it. Mac helped me to my feet. Chuck and Mort wrenched the club from the guy who had hit me. Chuck clutched the white guy's face, digging his fingernails into the eyes. Mort grunted with the effort of long, loping, overhand blows to the face and uppercuts to the guts. They dropped the guy. He lay still, hurt a lot worse than I was.

The cops were running across the field, followed by a group of firemen with a hose.

"Let's cut out!" Chuck yelled.

Held up by Mort and Mac, I followed the gang across the field, through a group of screaming white girls who had come to watch the battle, up the embankment to the safety of the street. The white guys joined forces now, trying to battle the cops. The cops beat the leaders with billy clubs and dragged them off to jail. The firemen turned the hose on the rest, scattering them like leaves. We went back to the corner. I didn't stop. Doc Brown was at home and drew together the gash in my forehead with two stitches.

★

The next day I went to school with an eye swollen shut and a bandaged forehead. At lunch period, Heidi winced. "Nels, what happened? Were you in that gang fight?"

I smiled.

"God, they'll kill you someday. Don't fight, you just can't win."

"We did win. We can go to Chicago park now, and nobody's going to bother us."

She looked at me as if I needed protection. "Honey, you can't fight the whole world."

I liked the tenderness. I wasn't used to it. As we walked down the hall she kept her hand on my arm, finally slipping it into my hand. I started to pull away but stopped. Everybody knew we were more than friends.

The excitement of being in love filled the days that followed.

Friday afternoons were always special because I would walk partway home with her. Sometimes we would plan some clandestine meeting for the weekend, but mostly it was our special time together, our time to sit in the park and talk. She never missed a chance to read me her new "favorite" poem and tell me what she thought it meant.

The *World's Best Poetry* was a thick collection of verse through the ages. After we sat down, she opened the book to the marker and read Keats's "La Belle Dame Sans Merci."

There were no explanatory notes. She closed the book. "What do you think it means?"

"I don't know. Guess I'll have to think about it."

"I like it. I read it before. You know what I think?"

"Huh?"

"I think this guy went through life. This woman without mercy is life. Life's like that, isn't it?"

"I don't know. Sure, it's tough. But it doesn't have to be that way, and I don't think it will always be that way."

She drew her knees up under her chin, clasped her arms around her legs, and laid her head on her knees so that the fine brown hair fell over one side of her face. "I don't think it will ever change. Just war and people fighting and dying over nothing. I wish I believed in God—believed in something. I wish I had something to believe in."

"There's a lot of things outside of God to believe in. I believe in you. I believe we're going to get pulled into this war and I believe when it's over there'll be a better world."

"It won't get better." She added wistfully, "They tell you it'll be better to make you fight."

"Maybe we're going to have to fight here. But one way or another, war is coming. The people who own everything aren't going to let it change without a war. Look what happened in Spain. Down South they're driving us back into slavery. We're going to have to fight."

She gazed blankly ahead in forlorn silence, as if the world no longer mattered. I put my arm around her, and she leaned against me. "Tell me something pretty."

I told her a story about my secret moccasin flower in Wabasha. She smiled, unclasped her legs, and, taking my hand, turned her mouth toward mine for our first, fumbling, real kiss.

It was not the place, it was not the time. Breathing deeply, she pulled away from me. "I'd better go home. Mom will worry about me."

It was dusk dark, as the black hoboes would say. We walked slowly, hand in hand, to the bus line. The bus approached. She turned to me, eyes glowing with passion. "I love you."

The bus pulled away. Clasping and unclasping her hand in a babylike wave, she smiled good-bye.

As I walked toward the drugstore, I counted out thirty-five cents in nickels and dimes. I had to be ready. I'd never bought a "raincoat" before, but the older guys always said Trojans were the best. Any other kind, they said, made it like washing your feet with your socks on.

12

As spring blossomed into summer, the dogs of war crept closer. The gut knowledge that we were being drawn into another world war chilled the warmth of May 1941.

For once I saw Ernestine walking home alone. I held the door open for her. A pert thank-you smile brightened her brown face.

"How've you been, stranger?" she asked.

"Stranger? You're the one running steady," I said.

"Got to keep moving. Talked to your girlfriend last week. She's good people."

"Yeah, I know you did."

"Hey?" She rolled her big brown eyes. "I didn't say anything wrong, did I?"

"No, she just told me you all had talked. What do you think about it—our going together?"

"I don't know—I don't think about it." She kicked into the weeds along the curb. "Men are lucky, Nels. You can do what you want—when you want. Heidi is a good girl. At least you two are honest. There are so many white boys who make passes at me—some of them ask to go out with me—but it's always that back alley stuff. When a Negro fellow and white girl go out, they do it in the open, but a white man wants to do things under cover. They're ashamed of what they themselves want."

I squeezed Ernestine's hand. She was my friend. "I wanted to talk to your dad. When do you think I could come by?"

"He said he wanted to talk to you sometime. You going to talk to him about the Communist Party?"

"I wanted to find out what it was all about. I've made up my mind about one thing; I've got to do something. I've got to join something. They're the only ones doing anything."

"He's home now. Come on by. Mom isn't home. You know they're always fighting about dad's being with the Communists."

Mr. Thomas was sitting in the living room, a copy of the *Daily Worker* on his lap. His finger moved slowly beneath the line of print as he read the latest developments in the Scottsboro trials.

"Hi, Dad. I brought Nelson home to talk to you."

"Well, come on in. Sit down, sit down. Yes, I thought I'd talk to you. You seem to be—be involved in activity. The party people here, you know Vicky and Doug, you know Evangeline—"

"I know them when I see them. Sometimes they're passing out leaflets on the corner, but I don't know them."

"Well, anyway, they know you. They asked me to talk to you—perhaps you'd like to come to a meeting."

"I don't know very much about them. I don't believe what I hear on the radio about the Communists, but I wanted you to tell me."

Mr. Thomas had come north from Beaumont, Texas. Barely literate, a deep thinker and a heavy drinker, he was a sweeper in one of the major plants in the area. "I don't quite know what you want me to tell you."

I sensed he was uncomfortable with my quizzing him about the party. "I just wanted to know what the Communists are trying to do—what they stand for."

Mr. Thomas pursed his lips. "You got way more education than I have. You got to read up on these things. Communism comes from common—common people, things owned in common, the common good. I'm not good at explaining things, but I know they're the only people fighting for those kids down in Alabama. Even the NAACP won't help them. I was about to starve to death when the Communists got me this job. They're good people. They do good things. They help our people. They practice what they preach. That's all I can tell you."

I knew I shouldn't pursue it. I would find out later that most of the blacks recruited into the Communist Party came in because the Communists were "good people" or had helped them get jobs in plants where they controlled the union. I thought they were more than "good people," but I'd have to find that out elsewhere. Mr. Thomas handed me the leaflet. I thanked him and left.

I put the leaflet in my pocket and walked the few blocks to the meeting.

★

We all knew Vicky. At one time or another she had been to every house in the neighborhood selling *Daily Worker*s. She never moved as our little black community crept outward. The family of the intense, friendly redhead was Communist. So was her boyfriend, Doug, a soft-spoken labor organizer. Sometimes, they would come to the corner and hand the older guys leaflets announcing meetings on the Scottsboro case or the Spanish Civil War. They had friends on the corner. We treated them differently than other whites in the area. Some of the guys would go to their meetings and come back, saying there was no discrimination in the Soviet Union and the Communists would put an end to it here. They were on our side, even if we didn't know how or why.

★

A light rap and Vicky opened the door, welcoming me with a smile. I knew a few seated among the ten or twelve people present. Evangeline and Carl, seniors at school, were known as Young Communist League members. Vicky introduced me around. Sam Davis stood up and took my hand in a firm, handshake. I said he had spoken at our church during his campaign for governor. He smiled, nodding that he remembered. Chain-smoking, holding the cigarette in the middle of his mouth, he constantly blinked and turned his head to keep the smoke from getting in his eyes. I immediately liked that man but wondered why he didn't hold the cigarette in the corner of his mouth, as everyone else did.

Martin Mackie shook my hand. The tall, rawboned Finn from the Iron Range spent a year in the trenches of Spain. He would say a few words about the war. Doug would report on the Scottsboro case. Three Negroes were present. I didn't know the middle-aged man and his wife. I knew Frank, the studious, close-mouthed man from Duluth who always had a friendly word for our gang. Unlike the rest of the guys in the neighborhood, he never hung around the corner or the tavern.

Vicky opened the meeting, welcoming Frank and me as friends of the party. She spoke of how the Fascists in France, England, and America were using the *sitzkrieg* to prepare for a united war against the Soviet Union. She concluded that we had to fight for peace to thwart their plans. There was plenty of news about the phony war, but I never heard it analyzed so clearly. The facts at her fingertips and her sincerity impressed me.

Martin spoke of how the Fascists in Spain now had a free hand and were carrying out a massacre of Communists and anti-Fascists. Speaking deliberately and softly, not wasting any words, he explained how the democratically elected Republican government of Spain lost the civil war. He spoke bitterly of Roosevelt's policy of neutrality, adding, "There can be no neutrality with the Fascists."

During the discussion I finally got the courage to ask, "Who are the Fascists here?"

"They are in every section of business and politics. People like Bilbo, Rankin, and Father Coughlin are Fascist, but they are only mouthpieces for the industrialists and bankers who want the Fascist system."

Martin had hit the nail on the head. The chips began to fall into place. Those were the people I hated. If the Spanish people had been fighting the likes of these men, then I was sorry the war was over. I would have gone to fight.

By the time we said good night, the world looked completely different. Scottsboro, Spain, the fight for the unions—the fight against Jim Crow and segregation—all were one fight against the Fascists. The Soviet Union was the only country that had defended Spain, the only country that had protected the people against Hitler and the Fascists. How clear and simple it was.

When Martin spoke about guys my age being the heroes of the war, I understood that one of the reasons Spain lost was that the people didn't know how to fight. It suddenly became clear that we Negroes always lost because we, too, didn't know how to fight. I made up my mind to learn.

I didn't say anything about the meeting at home. Pop, who at one time supported the Soviet Union, was becoming more and more vocally anti-Communist. Part of the reason was his government job; but mostly he intended to be on the winning side.

13

SCHOOL WAS IN its final week when I noticed the poster on the bulletin board. The army had established a new program to train officers for the army reserves. The Civilian Military Training Camp would pay thirty-five dollars plus traveling expenses for a month in the army. It was what I was looking for—a chance to learn to fight. I believed in the military. It was the highest level of organization and force. That was the route to freedom.

I went directly to the principal. Glad I was interested, he wrote a long recommendation and told me he would send it in with my application. I had a feeling he thought it was a good way to get rid of me.

Heidi and I decided to celebrate my birthday on June 21, the day before my birthday. That way we'd have time, and we both knew the time had come.

With a little pleading, I got Pop to give me the keys to the car. I called Heidi and arranged our date. I was at the park fifteen minutes ahead of time, watching as she walked toward me. A picture of ripe womanhood, she held the purse closely with one arm and swung the other to the slight, twisting motion of her hips. Her mouth, painted a startling scarlet, set her face aglow with the warmth of her smile. A quick embrace. We entered the car and headed for the Negro community on Franklin Avenue and the best barbecued ribs in town.

Stuffed with pork, coleslaw, and hot sauce, she sat there licking her fingertips. Watching her innocent sensuality, I conjured fantasies of tonight.

"Want to play the nickelodeon?" she asked.

"Sure. What do you want to hear?"

"I don't think I know anything there. You pick out something I like."

Three records for a quarter. I punched out three of my favorites and sat opposite her in the booth. Jelly Roll Morton began tickling the piano with "Mamie's Blues." Heidi had never heard blues before. Erskine Hawkins's new album, "After Hours," was next, already so popular we called it the "Negro National Anthem." Jay McShanns's "Confessin' the Blues" said all I wanted to say to her. Heidi leaned toward the music, hands in her lap, eyes closed, captivated, swaying in rhythm.

"God, I really like that. Too bad we can't dance here—that music makes me want to dance."

I smiled at her.

"I always heard that the places colored people go to are more fun than white places. I guess it's true." She chattered on, "It's so relaxed here. You can be yourself. Are you going to take me out to a dance someday?"

This wasn't a tavern or dance hall, but I began wishing I hadn't brought her here. So many young white women get caught up in the easy life and first thing they know they're in the sporting life. Perhaps for whites, it's hard to tell where one ends and the other begins.

The clock above the cash register showed eight.

"We'd better go. It's already eight."

She nodded in agreement. I started the car and turned toward Lake Nikomis and its lovers' lane.

★

"What are you going to do this summer?" I tried to make conversation.

We passed the White Castle hamburger joint. I was reminded of why I had to learn war.

"I don't know. Not very much. Have you made any plans?"

Jesus! This is the summer Six and I were going to hit the road. I pushed it out of my mind lest it spoil everything.

"Yeah, I did have a plan for a month. Did you see the application for the Civilian Military Training Camp at school?"

Her eyes widened when she heard "Military." "You're not going to join the army or something, are you?"

"No, heck no." I forced a laugh. Jesus Christ! This is going to ruin our date. I would have to tell her now. "It's a month-long training thing like the ROTC in college."

"And then you'll have to go into the army?"

"No, it's just training. After three years, you become a reserve officer."

I could feel, more than see, her glancing at me, looking for a sign of the truth. We consciously talked about small things until I swung the Oldsmobile into a darkened area overlooking the lake.

Comfortable in the backseat, we listened to the radio playing soft dance music. I sat in the corner of the car, she half stretched out, cuddling against me. Her breast pressed tightly against my chest; her face nuzzled against my throat. The radio was playing the love theme from *Romeo and Juliet*, "Our Love." She was half humming, half singing along in whispers, her lips against my throat, "I speak your name in every prayer . . . "

The three buttons at the top of her dress were easily undone.

"I see your face in stars above . . . "

How the hell do they undo these things? I can't unsnap it. She partially sat up, unsnapped the brassiere, and lay back in my arms. Another few moments of petting and kissing. The brassiere, pushed up and out of the way, revealed a full, sweet hemispheric breast. A dark shadow in the moonlight, my hand covered it.

"Our love, I see it everywhere . . ."

Little whimpers of passion punctuated the hushed deep breathing, as I nervously slid my hand inside her dress, beneath the elastic to the warmth.

"Heaven can wait. This is Paradise/just being here with you . . ."

She smiled between kisses. "How did they know?"

"The whole world knows. It's the most important thing happening tonight."

I had carefully put it in my shirt pocket. I fumbled for it, tearing at the tinfoil cover. With one hand I unbelted and unzipped, then tried to get the rolled, powdered sheath on. Heidi half sat up.

"Let me do it."

Her fingers encircled and teased as she unrolled the Trojan over it. Leaning back, fighting for control, I realized the music had stopped. Gabriel Heater's oily, hateful voice was droning, " . . . three complete armies . . . smashing through Communist defenses . . . Red Air Force destroyed . . . led by German Panzer divisions . . . through the Red Army like a hot knife through butter."

"Oh, Jesus Christ!" The adrenalin bolted through me.

Lips parted, wide eyes frightened, she stared at me. "What's the matter? What's the matter with you?" She released the limp, half-sheathed thing. I pulled up my pants.

"Didn't you hear? The fuckin' Nazis invaded Russia!"

"God! You frightened me. You always said they would. You always said they'd go to war." She looked up to me, her eyes matching the pleading in her voice.

"There's nothing you can do about it. Don't spoil tonight."

She doesn't understand. She doesn't understand! She has to understand!

"I have to do something about it. Heidi, Russia is all we got. If Russia is defeated, there is nothing to defend us. They'd have already hanged the Scottsboro boys if it wasn't for Russia telling the whole world about it. They'll drive us back to slavery—or worse."

" . . . and all the ships at sea! Come in, Berlin!" Walter Winchell.

We sat quietly while I listened to the detailed account from Berlin on the developments of the war. Then I realized she was crying, sobbing, and smearing the wet mascara into her eyes. I tried to put my arms around her, to comfort her. Cold and stiff, she wiggled away from me.

The dashboard clock showed ten. We had to leave then to get her home on time. It was over for tonight.

"I'm sorry."

The silence was stony and cold.

I reached over and opened the door on her side. She slid out and got in the front seat. I pulled the Trojan off and threw it into the bushes.

Panzers and Red Army and I fucked it up royally tonight, I thought as we drove home.

I parked in front of her house, not caring if her father liked it or not. She turned to me in cold resignation.

"Happy birthday."

"I couldn't help it. I'm sorry—I really am. Call me?"

She slid out of the car, gently closing the door, and walked to the porch without turning around.

★

With ten birthdays a year in the family, we couldn't afford a celebration. We did have a special dinner, and when it was over, Mom brought in the cake with its eighteen burning candles. I blew them out. My brothers shouted "Happy Birthday" and reached for their slice. Eighteen punches on the arm from six brothers can make a person sore. We laughed and scuffled around the room as we always did, but the chilling news from the eastern front dampened our laughter. Spain, Austria, Poland, Czechoslovakia, Denmark, Norway, Holland, Belgium, France—now the Soviet Union. With the gates opened by the Fifth Column, fascism seemed invincible. Would it come here and place the Klan and Rankin and Bilbo in power? The Fifth Column was here and mobilizing with the slogan of "keeping the niggers in their place." The guys on the corner seldom spoke about it, but it was on their mind.

Vicky and Doug came to the corner with a leaflet calling on the people to defend the Soviet Union. There was nothing we could do, but we sympathized with them, and some of the guys told them so. Vicky explained to me that the United Front was more important than ever, and she still believed that the front should be based on the struggle of the Negro people for freedom. I liked that idea. I didn't know much about the revolution, but I did know we were leading the fight here, because our fight for equality was against the Fascists. I was learning many new words and grappling to understand new ideas.

The next day, I received a notice and a check for a first-class train ticket from the army. They ordered me to report for duty to the post commander at Fort Riley, Kansas, on the first of July. I had already made up my mind to hobo my way and give the money to Mom. To take the freights, I would have to leave within the next day or two. There was much to be done.

I called Heidi. The lingering anger melted away when I told her I had to leave the next day.

"You're going to see me before you go, aren't you?"

"Sure, honey. That's what I'm calling about."

The soft, warm, late June night began to settle in the park when she came to our rendezvous bench. Saddle shoes, knee-length pleated skirt, fluffy sweater—Central High on vacation.

The kiss, soft and questioning at first, turned firm with parted lips that said everything was all right. We sat down and talked about the things we would do after I returned from camp. She was a dreamer and wanted some promise to build her dream on. This time it was dancing and fun. I couldn't dance, and I no longer knew what fun was. I let her talk and didn't answer. Finally, tired of small talk, she leaned against me, sending the blood hammering at my temples.

"I want you so much," I whispered.

"You have me."

I touched her. She wasn't wearing panties.

"Honey, I don't have any protection with me."

God! I hadn't even thought of it!

A moment's silence. There was no turning back this time.

"It's OK. I'm going to get the curse in a few days. It's safe." Sighing deeply, she closed her eyes, tilting her mouth to mine, lips parted.

She calls it French kiss—we call it soul kiss. . . . From the soul—to the soul. . . . Stay on the bench—she'll stain her dress on the grass. . . . Just relax, sweetheart, relax, it won't hurt. . . . Jesus Christ, I love you so much. . . . There, there, now—now . . . God, you're so sweet. . . . Yes, more than that, more than you love me. . . . Yes, I know you love me. . . . Yes, sweetheart, I'll come back—then we'll never part again.

★

In front of her house—one last desperate kiss, one more pledge of love, and the last good-bye.

I walked home, content and happy. She was in love with me and in a few weeks I'd know how to shoot a machine gun and fire a mortar. I would learn strategy and tactics. When the war came here, if the bell should toll, it would not toll for me. The next morning, I kissed Mom good-bye and walked to the freight yards.

Part Two

THE LONESOME HOWL OF
A FREIGHT TRAIN

14

AFTER THE HOT shower and the vaccinations, we teenage volunteers passed through the supply building and received our allotment of used clothing, mess kit, canteen, World War I tin hat, bandolier belt, and an old Ensfield rifle. Then we billeted in a tent encampment set up in the old Ninth Cavalry parade grounds.

We began hard ten-hour-a-day, seven-days-a-week doses of becoming a soldier. The first thing I learned was that it never rained in the army, only on the army. Sometimes we drilled ankle-deep in mud while the Kansas wind blew dust in our faces. I qualified as expert with the rifle, and learned elementary tactics and strategy and to make and read maps. We spent days marching behind the captain on his white horse, running for miles carrying mortar barrels and heavy machine guns, crawling through tear gas, and swallowing the sweat that collected in the gas mask. We learned to live in cadence and by the numbers.

There were some other basic things I learned. First, I was not simply a soldier. I was a black soldier. The officers seldom court-martialed the black soldiers of the Ninth Cavalry. The sergeant simply took the offender out to the stables and beat hell out of him. If the sergeant lost the fight the victor got the stripes.

The post was rigidly segregated. As with all segregation, the worst of everything belonged to us. In the post theater, we sat only on the sides, while the white soldiers occupied the center. The white commanders ruled that blacks didn't like to swim, so the pool was for whites only. In any argument between white and black troopers, the MPs always ruled that white was right and God help any black trooper who struck a white one—no matter what the provocation. Our appeals for justice were made against white men to white men. Such appeals generally meant hours of extra duty or even a stretch in the guardhouse. My first and only trip to Junction City taught me that the power of the police, which backed up the more subtle, pervasive power of whites in general, relied ultimately on the unlimited might of the military. We soon learned to find our recreation strictly among ourselves. Then we learned to nod our heads in agreement when some white man, secure in his perceptual knowledge, stated that blacks preferred to be to themselves.

It wasn't all bad. Soldiering was a respected profession among the blacks. The employment was secure; a soldier could save a few dollars a month. Housing for a black soldier's family was way above that afforded by the average black civilian. The segregated schools provided better education than those in civilian life. After thirty years he retired with a respectable pension, medical care, and burial guaranteed. Segregation and worse was everywhere, not simply in the army.

I'd had a bellyful of the United States Army and laid aside any notion of making it a career. It was so different from what I had imagined. The violence of and in the army is almost indescribable. The coarseness of a life mainly among men, away from women, clashed with everything I was striving for. At Fort Riley, I began to learn that a respectful love and close association with women is the first step toward the civilizing and softening of a man.

A part of our military training appealed to me. In our field exercises or in maneuvers, it was exciting to move the theoretical infantry and artillery and have the umpire wave his flag in my direction, showing that I had outflanked and crushed the enemy. I liked bayonet practice, running, cursing, and stabbing through the row of straw dummies.

Long thrust to the throat, grunt with the effort, "Hah! You Ku Klux son of a bitch." Withdraw. Butt stroke to the nuts, "Ya! Fuckin' peck!" Butt stroke to the face, short thrust to the guts, "Huh! Nazi bastard." Withdraw. That's the way to make them pay attention to you! It was thrilling to learn the meaning and use of force in history and conjecture what it could mean when black America understood how to use it.

The orientation bull sessions were the best of times. Led by an officer, we spent hours in political discussion. The knowledge I had gained from my limited association with the Communists gave me a political clarity beyond that of the other troops. I often found myself in a dialogue with the officers. We all agreed that we would soon be at war. I never discussed it, but I deeply believed war would give us a chance to be free. If war should come, they would need us more than we needed them. The blacks should make themselves indispensable both as soldiers and as workers and then force the government to bargain.

★

Heidi wrote warm, cheerful letters full of the dreams reserved for those in their teens and in love. The last day of camp, the mail orderly entered my tent. "Sugar from Minnesota." He threw the letter to me. Opening it, I leaned back to read it slowly. After a few lines I sat up straight and then leaned forward, scanning and res-canning the lines:

Darling,
. . . I don't know how to tell you. . . . already two weeks late.

I got very little sleep that night. After bed check I crept outside and chain-smoked, grappling with the biggest problem of my life.

We would get married. God! No job. No prospect of getting one. Not in Minnesota. I'll head west. California, Oregon. I hear there's work out West. Tomorrow, they pay us off and turn us loose. I'll send the pay to her and grab a fistful of the first freight train heading west. Satisfied that I was doing the manly thing, I went back to the cot and slept.

Training camp ended. I wrote a short note telling her I was going west to get work and would send for her. I wrapped the note around the postal money order and sent it off.

15

MOST OF THE GUYS took the freights home to save money. A huge group of us walked down to the yards and grabbed trains going in various directions.

I didn't have a conscious plan. The hoboes in the jungle told stories about a couple of railroad dicks using rifles to shoot the 'boes off the train as it made the hairpin curve crossing the Sabine into Texas. They warned me not to try getting to California through Texas.

"They's 'specially hard on you boys," a skinny white youth from Arkansas said.

I decided to head due north to Fargo, and then cut west to Seattle. Maybe then I could get safely down to California.

The next morning I caught a slow local freight, the only thing heading north.

I felt good sitting in the open doorway, legs hanging down, watching the vast expanse of America unfold before me. I felt a little seasick watching the oceans of wheat bend and sway under the gentle breeze and the hot Kansas sun.

All that day we rumbled through a gigantic area that could feed half the world. The great army of the unemployed was beginning to disintegrate as Roosevelt's "Arsenal of Democracy" plan began pulling men into war production. There were fewer men on the trains. The whites got the jobs and a greater proportion of the hoboes were black than a year ago. It made hoboing that much tougher. The vast rear guard of that army was still on the road—searching, wandering, begging. I was always with them in spirit; now it was reality for me.

This was the way to know America. The rivers and bluffs, the vast fields, the miles of vacant land seemed to call us. "Rest easy, my sons. There is much wheat in our house and much corn. I am your mother, your beginning and your end. You who wander alone and despised, come rest in my house, come close and love me."

There was no resting. The farmers hired guards to protect their vegetables and corn. The land was theirs. If we approached it, the dirty little jail cells packed with roaches and bedbugs awaited us. An edge of fear and apprehension is part of any hobo's life. That, added to being black, kept us together on the train. We would get off to splash water on our faces or run and hide in the weeds when the train stopped and the railroad dicks came to inspect the empty boxcars.

We moved into the Great Plains of South Dakota. Although still in America, we were glad to leave Kansas and Nebraska with their vigilantes, unpainted shacks, and rich wheat lands.

The nights turned cold in Fargo. I went into the huge jungle and shared in a pot of mulligan stew some good brother had carefully left behind. There was a sign nailed to the tree: "Dear gentlemen of the road, help keep our home clean." I realized that I had seldom seen a dirty jungle.

The young hoboes had to team up and protect one another. The wolves, those womanless men who had become aggressive homosexuals, might grab and gang-rape any young man caught by himself. It was one of the facts of the road. In Kansas I teamed up with Jerry, a black guy my age. A thickset, muscular youth from the cotton fields of Alabama, he entertained the hoboes, mimicking the sounds of the freight train with his cheap harmonica.

We cleaned up and went into downtown Fargo to forage for food. The small shops cleaned up early in the morning. I waited at a small meat market and when the owner opened, I approached him. "Mister, I wonder if I could clean up your place for some bacon butts or baloney ends." He hesitated. I quickly added, "Mister, I'm hungry. I'm willing to work—I don't want to plain beg for something to eat."

That got him. I carried out a few boxes and swept the sidewalk and left with a sack full of odds and ends of meat that would have been thrown away.

Back in the jungle, Jerry was waiting for me. He had a few potatoes, a sack of coffee, six eggs, and an old overcoat. He tossed me the coat.

"If you're goin' over the hump, you better keep this here. It most likely colder than hell already."

After our feast, which we shared with several other 'boes, Jerry and I shook hands and said good-bye. He was going east looking for work. I was going west looking for work.

At Bismarck, I jumped off the train and went into the jungle. A woman was sitting on one of the logs, talking with a few of the white men. A piece of twine held her hair back, and her dress was hiked halfway up, exposing her thin thighs. The dried skin tight across her cheekbones emphasized how beaten and down this poor woman was.

★

"Hell, baby," one of the hoboes said, "If I had fifteen cents, I'd give it to you. I ain't got nothing."

One of the men handed her a tin plate full of stew. She half smiled and, without looking up, gulped down the food.

"Ya know," she said. "A bum is the only decent guy left in the world."

One of the guys mumbled something.

"Hell," she laughed. "I'd give you some, but it'd get around that I went for free."

I wanted to look at her but the white men would say something. I turned my back and heard the guy who had given her the stew say, "I ain't turned down nothin' free since I voted for Hoover." They walked away toward a string of empty boxcars.

She was from the South. I thought of the Scottsboro boys and moved farther away from them all.

The train assembled. The coupled big engines would pull the mile-long freight through the Rockies and over the Divide. The sixteen driving wheels ground and spun, letting out blasts of steam, and finally the engineer gave a frightful whistle for the right of way.

I threw the gunnysack across my back and ran for the freight as it pulled out into the main line.

The next day, I jumped off the train at Butte, washed up at the roundhouse, and walked into town looking for food. A group of men from the train stood in front of a beer hall listening to a tough-looking, heavyset man.

"Now, if you want ta work, we'll give ya five bucks a day and take out for your food, an' ya gotta stay on company property."

Five bucks a day was an unheard-of wage. The men quickly agreed to work. I wanted to raise my hand. Surely, they wouldn't allow a Negro kid to earn that kind of money. The men grouped together and the fat man started to walk away.

"I'd like to work, Mister."

He glanced at me, narrowing his eyes. "Naw, we can't use no . . . " He turned to a man beside him. "He's small—we can use him in the old vein. We're still short-handed."

He turned back to me and said, "Come on boy, but do what you're told."

I fell in with the rest of the men. My head was in a swirl. God! A job. Five bucks a day! This is it! Things are going to work out.

We trudged up the steep street behind the two bosses. Ahead stood a series of corrugated iron buildings supporting a big sign: ANACONDA COPPER COMPANY.

A group of forty or fifty men carrying signs stood in front of the main gate. STAY AWAY! ON STRIKE! LIVING WAGE! UNION RECOGNITION!

The fat man walked over to one of the pickets. "Might as well get the hell out of the way, Jim. We're comin' through."

"Don't scab!" one of the strikers yelled. "You guys are workers, too. We're hungry just like you are!"

The little group of hoboes began mumbling. One said, "I knew Goddamn well it was a trick. I might be a bum but I ain't no fuckin' scab." He started to walk away, turned, and yelled to us, "Come on! Anybody who'd take a job in there is taking food outta some kid's mouth. Go through that gate and you're a low-down son of a bitchin' scabbin' rat.'"

I figured I didn't need a job that bad. One by one we started back toward town. A middle-aged man in a dirty suit fell in beside me. "It's true. The workers should stick together. The Lord made plenty for everybody."

"Yeah?"

"Of course. We have to learn to be Christians. I'm a preacher. I never wrong my fellow man."

The guy actually was a preacher. His satchel was full of religious tracts and small Bibles with tiny print. We walked slowly down the hill toward the tracks, stopping now and then to look at the finely wrought copper horses and other souvenirs of Butte. Hot inside his suit, the preacher kept wiping his forehead with the sleeve of his coat. We got back to the tavern.

"Do you drink beer, brother?"

"Sure."

The pudgy bartender shifted the stump of his cigar to the other side of his mouth and said, "What'll ya have, mister?"

"We'll have two beers."

The bartender jerked his thumb toward a series of signs tacked above the bar. One of the signs said, "We do not solicit colored trade." The other was more explicit. A caricature of a black guy sitting on a fence, grinning and eating a big piece of watermelon, the sign said "We serve 'em—" and ended with a drawing of a pig raising its tail.

I got up and walked out of the tavern. The preacher followed me.

"It's not right. The Lord . . . "

I wasn't for religion then. I wanted to fight. How was I going to fight in Butte? They lynch white people in this town. I was so terribly alone. This was a Ku Klux town, and I wanted to get out before something happened to me. We sat beside the tracks waiting for the train to assemble. I wouldn't talk to the preacher about God. I believed he was trying to convert me because I was black. He was a good guy though, and I didn't want to insult him.

The sun dropped behind the foothills. The preacher unrolled a long loaf of bread, cheese, and bologna. I got a bottle of water and we sat together munching until the freight made up and pulled out. We sat together in the opening of our side-door Pullman, watching the country slipping away beneath us, listening to the two big engines groaning with their load, pulling us through the wild, desolate land of the Rockies.

Paradise is a misleading name. The small town just inside the Idaho border, hidden in the Rocky Mountains, was isolated from the rest of the world. A major freight junction, the town was overrun with hungry, sick hoboes. My preacher friend left me there. He heard there was a need for the Lord in Boise. I walked down the tracks looking for the jungle. In the weeds a rattler buzzed and drew back his ugly diamond-shaped head. I turned and went in the other direction. A girl saw me and ran toward the station. That was a bad sign. A white guy about my age whistled and beckoned to me. "They roundin' up the bums. We better get out of here."

We ran across the tracks and slid down the embankment across from the station and down the gully, out of sight of the town.

"I know this country good. There's a big curve ahead. The train got to slow down. I think we can catch her on the run there." We crouched in the underbrush, waiting for the train laboring through the gorge to the east.

For the first time in days I thought of Heidi. How was she? Had her parents found out? What was she doing? The ceaseless search for food and rest had pushed all other thoughts from my mind. The road was beginning to wear me down and get the better of me. The dirt and grime and sweat scratched my body. My hair was full of cinders. I was hungry and bone tired with the kind of weariness only a hobo can know. Was I going to spend the rest of my life like this? Never resting. Never clean. Never gaining. Was I always going to be the constant prey for the cops and the railroad dicks and the hunger? Christ, the only emotion a hobo knows is fear.

The train stopped and filled the boilers, and after a shrill whistle the doubleheader jerked the freight onto the main line. Its driving wheels spinning, belching cinders, the train picked up speed and, making fifteen miles an hour, lurched into the sharp curve. My new buddy and I ran for an open car, caught the side of the door, and swung inside. Two young people crouched at the far end of the car. My buddy walked over to them.

"For the love of Christ! Two girls."

The young women—still teenagers—remained seated but moved closer together. They had probably closed the opposite side of the boxcar to make sure no man would get in. That was the side facing the Paradise station. The Scottsboro case flashed into my mind.

"I'm getting off."

"How come? We're safe here."

"Don't want to ride with no women."

The train was gathering speed. I slung the sack across my back and lowered myself within a few inches of the ground. Pacing the train for a moment, I let go, plunging headlong into the brush and stones. When I got back to my feet, I looked ahead to the three young faces leaning out of the boxcar. They waved. I waved good luck and turned back toward Paradise.

The second train pulled out. I climbed into an empty car, closed the door, curled up in my overcoat, and slept.

Who does not know the beauty of Oregon? I sat in the doorway of the boxcar, watching its splendor unfold before me. There on the western slopes of the Rockies is a land I love. We crossed the Great Divide and rumbled down the mountains toward the sea. The jumbled rocks of the highlands began to disappear; the scrub growth gave way to tall, green, stately Oregon pines. They seemed to march confidently up the slope of the mountain, saying to me, "Eighteen? You're only eighteen? God, you're so young. If you're going to grow old like me, you have to do as I have done. Sink your roots into the earth. Then you will grow as tall and sweet-smelling as I am."

And I said back to them, "You're a pine tree and the earth is your home. I'm a black boy and I ain't got a home. I'd rather be a tall pine tree than a black boy. I'd look down from the mountain upon the freight train and the hungry hoboes. I'd stand there for a thousand years and shake my head at the crazy people who fight over crumbs when there is so much. God was good to you."

We moved past the tumbling streams, the logging camps, the long wooden shoots where the logs skid down faster than any freight train, crashing into the river and making rainbows that hung for hours in the brilliant sunshine.

Whoo—Whaaa. The big engines sniffed the mountain air and with one big eye saw the countryside and bellowed to the land that they were happy too. We roared through the gorges and tunnels, along the side of the mountain where Chinese slaves had gouged at the earth, quarried a ledge, and laid the tracks so a black boy with little beauty in his life could see Oregon. Twilight settled over the mountain. The engines, Phaëthon's fiery steeds, jerked my chariot onward, chasing the setting sun, racing down the mountainside, through the valleys, westward toward the distant, sparkling lights of Portland.

The next morning, in the roundhouse, an older man with steel-rimmed glasses and clean coveralls was going over an engine with a huge oilcan. Steam was rising from the big brick holding tanks where the boilers emptied.

"Mister?"

The oil man turned around. There was pity in his eyes. I must have looked terrible. I'd been two weeks on the road without a bath or washing my clothes.

"Well, son, I guess you want to bathe. You need it."

"Yeah. I know I do. I got to get cleaned up so I can find a job."

"How old are you?"

"Eighteen."

He shook his head slowly and the look of pity deepened.

"I got a kid your age. It's a damned shame what's happened to this country. Go ahead, but hurry up before the next crew comes in."

I pulled off the army boots, the filthy socks and underwear and slid into the hot water. The Fels Naptha soap felt good cutting the grime and soot. After soaping, rubbing, and rinsing the clothes, I soaked in the hot water until the oil man gave me a nod. I put on the wet, clean clothes and made for the jungle, where I could hang them out to dry and use my overcoat to cover my nakedness. Afterward, I went into town to see who and what lived there.

Poverty lived in the streets near the railroad tracks. It stalked everywhere; it clutched the broken sidewalks and the withered trees. The crowded slums of Portland mirrored every slum in the West. Japanese men and women sat quietly on the steps of the storefronts, their faces masks of hunger. Their little black-haired girls laughingly flashed their white teeth as they played hopscotch on the sidewalk. White men in sailor caps and dungarees walked aimlessly, pausing to spit or pick up a cigarette butt. Everywhere, Negroes milled about. Their black faces merged into the dirty streets and the white faces and the storefronts. The children, in their ignorance, were happy.

Darkness settled over Portland. It engulfed the streets. It came silently, rising in the alleys, hiding the man who was slowly and deliberately sorting garbage, putting the less-rotten pieces in a dirty paper sack. It put fire into the cruel, beady eyes of the rat darting along the walls searching for a way to the baby crying inside the dirty building. Night covered the green tubercular spittle, the broken wine bottle, the hopscotch game and all the shame of the day. It brought out the whores—black, Japanese, Filipino. Fat dirty slim pretty painted drunk hungry defeated unloved unloving uncaring uncared for unwanted women—who had no faces no names no yesterdays no tomorrows, who only knew and hated tonight. It brought out the men: the pimp who stood in the doorway watching his women, urging them to work harder. It brought out the black staggering down the street trying to walk so the loose sole of his shoe would not trip him. It brought the rich white boys to skid row in search of a fast, cheap lay so they could take their girlfriends home safe in their virginity. It turned the skid row into a fantastic and dangerous human jungle where everyone was at once hunter and hunted. The whores looked for men to fleece. The pimp followed the whores, afraid they might keep a dime. The muggers stalked the pimps. They needed money to get to the whores. In front of and behind this jungle were the eyes of women. Mothers eyes watching their sons and daughters sold on the block for cash or broken on the rack of gotta get a job.

With my last thirty cents I ate a bowl of stew and bought a sack of tobacco, then went back across the railroad tracks to the warm laughter and tall tales that made hoboes love their jungle.

The next morning I started looking for work. I tramped up and down the streets asking, looking, begging. The answer was always the same: "Can't use you, boy." "Sorry." "Don't need you." Toward evening I felt like an animal to be used or not used, instead of a human being. I didn't like the feeling. Absolutely destitute, I turned back toward the jungle. I had not eaten that day. As I neared the tracks a truck full of young Japanese men and women and a few blacks pulled up alongside me. The driver stuck his head out of the window. "Hey, boy, you wanna work?"

My heart leaped. I'd work for food, let alone money. I disregarded the "boy." "Sure, mister. You got a job?"

"Ever work on a farm?"

"Sure."

"Hop in."

I climbed into the truck. The Japanese young women giggled and moved away from me. I hated to think how I must have looked and smelled.

"What kind of work is it?" I asked one of the black guys.

"Pickin' peas. Ever done it?"

"No, but I reckon I can get by all right."

"Tough work. We sure ain't makin' nothin'. But I gotta eat."

"No lie."

The truck left Portland and headed into the rich countryside.

"What do they pay an hour?"

"Fifty cents a bushel; it ain't too bad."

I figured I could pick a bushel an hour. Four bucks a day! I'd be on easy street.

We arrived at the farm after dark. The driver said to us, "We'll start at daybreak tomorrow. You fellows sleep in the shack over here, the girls over there."

Inside there was nothing save cobwebs and the rough wooden floor. The guys began to grumble. I didn't mind sleeping on the floor or the ground. The rest of the crew had blankets; I had hidden my sack in the jungle and had only the clothes on my back. One of the Japanese fellows offered to share his blanket. I thanked him and declined.

The next morning we were given baskets and led to the open fields. Endless rows of pea vines stretched from one end of the valley to the other.

"Now listen," the boss was saying, "I'm gonna accept only good stuff and the baskets have to be level with the top. If you got any rotten stuff, we ain't gonna count it."

I took a row between two young Japanese women and prepared to make my four dollars for the day. I had never picked peas before and my hands were clumsy on the vine. I watched the women and tried to copy how their fingers flew over the vines, each seeming to work independently of the other. At ten o'clock, soaked with sweat, I had barely made a basketful. I took the basket to the truck. The driver emptied it on the canvas, putting only the fresh full peas back into the basket. There was only a half basket now. I worked three hours for twenty-five cents! By noon I had a basket of carefully culled peas. I earned seventy-five cents in six hours. Twenty-five cents bought a half loaf of bread and a chunk of salami. I knew I was going to have to work like hell to earn enough for supper. I had two more baskets of culled peas by night-

fall. Supper cost fifty cents, twenty-five cents went to pay for sleeping on the floor. I worked fourteen hours and had seventy-five
cents to show for it, and no way to get away from this place.

The next afternoon I straightened my back and looked down
the rows we had gleaned. With nearly a quarter of the field
picked, I was about as hungry and broke as the moment I arrived.
The peas were in the warehouse, and what money I earned went
right back into the boss's pocket for food and the shack.

One of the young women said to me, "Don't feel bad, none of
us are making very much."

"This ain't nothin' but slavery." I thought of the pickets in
Butte.

"We're saps to be working for this guy by the bushel. We
ought to walk out for an hourly wage."

The young woman smiled at me and then looked to the
ground. "I know we should. I've been doing this work for ten
years, since I was eight. Some people tried it. You just can't do it.
They'll call you an agitator."

The day drew to a close. Another seventy-five cents. I sat
down that evening trying to figure how to get out of this place.
The two women I worked with came over to me carrying a basket
of peas between them.

"We made an extra bushel today and saved it out. You can
have it if you want. Then you'll be able to leave."

I had never felt so grateful to anyone in my life. I took the
bushel to the boss and told him I was quitting. He shoved me fifty
cents. On the way out I saw one of the women.

"Thanks."

She smiled, her teeth white and even in the gathering darkness. The bangs and straight black hair framed her pretty face.
Looking at her beautiful eyes and lean, strong body, I wanted to
embrace and kiss her.

"Thanks very much."

"That's all right. Good luck."

Back in the jungle at Portland, I wrote a long letter to Heidi,
telling her I was moving on. There might be work in Seattle.

The next morning the train pulled into a siding at the out-
skirts of the city. The brakeman walked the length of the train,
warning the men that the dicks were rounding up the hoboes in
Seattle and we should get off here. I slung my sack and started
walking through the light drizzle toward the city. As the drizzle

intensified I took shelter under a bridge and, looking out into the rain, tried to think of a way out.

I had to get out of the jungle and the skid row, away from the filth and hunger and hobo eyes. I couldn't go home. I had to find work and prepare for the baby. There wasn't any work. The system was set up so we barely existed. Hand to mouth, never saving a penny. I wrapped my coat tightly around me. Almost crying, I formed a vivid resolve. I'm not going to live like this. I'm not going to beg and I'm not going to take low. They fight me—I'm going to fight them. For a long time I huddled under the bridge, looking out into the rain.

The tracks led to the warehouses of the Canadian and Northern Pacific Railroads. In the gully off to the side, three Negro men stood beside a fifty-five-gallon steel drum. The youngest of the three was softly strumming a guitar and singing. The other two were in their middle or late fifties; the gray stubble of their beards stood out against their black faces. I stopped a few yards from them and sat back on my heels.

> *Cruel fireman, lowdown engineer*
> *Cruel fireman, lowdown engineer,*
> *I'm tryin' to hobo my way,*
> *An' they leaves me standing here.*

The men glanced in my direction.

"Heard the music. Thought I'd come over and listen."

"Ace, damn if'n these babies ain't all over the country."

Ace spit a heavy slug of tobacco and, half smiling, said, "Don't pay no 'tention to that son a bitch. He thinks he owns the railroads."

I smiled. I didn't want to be drawn into any argument.

"Where you comin' from?" Ace asked.

"Just got in from Portland. You'll starve to death there."

"You hongry?"

"I ate yesterday."

He nodded to the big steel drum sitting on a makeshift fireplace of stone. Halfway down the barrel was the most food I had ever seen—potatoes, carrots, cabbage, lamb chops, beef, okra, peas—all cooked together and covered by a thin coat of grease. I turned to the friendly old guy.

"I reckon you all will want to eat pretty soon. I'll get some firewood."

No one answered. I gathered an armload of wood from the boxcars and went back. A fourth man was there. Instinctively, I didn't like him. He was dirty, with heavy jowls and closely set pig eyes. He looked at me for a moment and said, "Another boy, eh?"

"What say, man?" I acknowledged his remark and started the fire. Before long, the stew was steaming and the smell of good food filled the air. Ace turned to his friend and said, "West Coast, this here boy seems OK. We can take one more in. Want him?"

West Coast looked at me. I hadn't the slightest idea what they were talking about.

"We got a good setup here. You act like you ain't scared of work. We get food from the commissary for cleaning it up. If you wanta, you can come in. That means you works one day a week. Me an' Ace here, we's the boss, an' you gotta do what I say. I ain't concerned with what you do outta this end of the jungle."

I nodded my agreement. I'd agree with anything that meant food—food three times a day. The fellow with the guitar began to finger the chords. Tin plates came out of gunnysacks and bags. Using a big tin cup, they dipped into the barrel, filling their plates.

After the second helping I began to pick up the names of the men. Ace and West Coast were the two old-timers. Ace got the name by bragging that he was the best hobo in the country, with the longest time on the road. He claimed over thirty years. West Coast always started his tales with, "I knows this West Coast like the palm of my hand." The guitar player was Car Boy. He washed and simonized cars for what money he earned. Big John was the guy with the pig eyes. He was big, well over six feet, and seemed disliked by all, especially by Ace.

During the afternoon, a few more men drifted into the jungle—Little Joe, Big Daddy, Sweet Man, and Sam. They had been farmers, factory workers, and janitors. One of the fellows had been a college student. The Great Depression brought us together in Seattle, in the jungle, in search of food.

After dinner, two of the men went to the commissary to clean it up. I sat next to Ace and West Coast, listening to them swap lies and warmed by the deep-throated, free laughter. I finally pieced the setup together.

Several months before, Ace and West Coast had gotten to

know the man in charge of the commissary and freight warehouse. They came to an agreement to keep the commissary clean
in return for all the meat, fruits, and vegetables that were too ripe
to ship. This allowed the warehouse man to pocket the janitor's
wages and assured the hoboes of food. There was so much food
that Ace and West Coast took other men into the combine. This
lightened the workload and there was still more than enough to
go around. With me there was a total of fourteen men. They
were all black except for one white man. Fred didn't hang around
with us, but he showed up for work and food. We all liked him
and never felt embarrassed cussing out the white folks in front of
him. He agreed. The week's work amounted to about six hours.
If a person didn't do his work well, Ace would run him away and
get someone else.

What a setup! All kinds of food. It may not have been much to
those who ate three times a day. To those who ate once every three
days, this was nothing short of heaven.

Near the gully the men were building a Hooverville. Their little shacks of cardboard, corrugated iron, scraps of wood—whatever they could find—nestled among the scrub. I asked Ace if I
should build a shack over there, too.

He looked at me. "Boy, I don't give a damn if you builds or
not. You can sleep in the boxcars if ya wants to—course, the bulls
is gonna whip yore ass if ya do—or ya can build next to mine—
over there. Now, don't ask me no more damn fool questions."
The scowl beneath the graying stubble didn't match the twinkle
in his eyes.

Big John came over and said, "Look, boy. Ah'm aimin' to
build too—what say we go in together, OK?"

Ace looked hard at me. Everything in his lined black face was
a warning.

"No, thanks. I reckon I'll build alone."

Big John shot a cold stare at Ace.

"OK, boy. I just wanted to be yore friend. I got a kid 'bout
yore age. Hope somebody's tryin' to look out for him."

I felt a little sorry for Big John. Maybe he was OK, but I
wasn't going to go against anything Ace said.

During the next few days I built my little shack from crating
wood and tar paper. In the evenings after the big fire under the
barrel had gone out, I would sit with Ace and West Coast, listening to the tall tales that ended the day's routine.

Ace had been a bit of everything: farmer, miner, sailor, and hobo. He kept his sparse frame covered with three or four layers of clothing. His dark brown complexion highlighted the gray stubble no matter how often he shaved. He laughed easily, showing the tobacco-browned stumps of teeth. His short hair receded far back from his forehead, and a hearty laugh would wrinkle the shiny skin over his dome.

West Coast was one of the blackest men I had ever seen. He was nearly sixty, robust, and strong. He defended his big belly as all muscle. The harsh hobo life kept him hard and the sun had burned the whites of his eyes to a yellowish red. He enjoyed bugging those sunburnt eyes into a murderous glare and then bursting out with belly-shaking laughter. His favorite stories were of outsmarting Ace.

On the road since before World War I, they had a deep, manly love for each other. West Coast was full of bluster and threats but I wouldn't want to cross Ace.

After I had completed my new home, Ace called over to me. "Looky here, boy—"

"Great Gawd!" West Coast broke in. "Look out. Every time that old bastard opens his mouth, a lie flies out."

"Shut up your mouth, I ain't funnin'. I'm tryin' to straighten the boy out."

Ace was serious.

"Most and generally, I don't mess in nobody's business. You can take it for what it's worth. You understand that?"

"Sure, Ace; I'm listening."

"Now, I'm tellin' you that pig-eyed bastard ain't no good. Stay away from him. First time he crosses me I'm gonna lay his guts out on the ground where he can see 'em."

A moment of silence while Ace rolled a cigarette.

"West Coast, remember that time we stole a pig in Louisiana an' put a hat on him and the dick thought he was a bum?"

With an almost fatherly look, West Coast said to me, "He ain't tellin' you wrong, boy. That bastard is shootin' at you."

He turned back to Ace. "Lawd, Ace, you oughtta stop that shit. One of these days your food won't go down, all them lies comin' up."

Car Boy tuned his guitar and started to sing.

Twilight settled in the jungle. Hearing the singing, the rest of the men came out of the shacks and boxcars to join in. Before long each person found a place for harmonizing. The singing turned to our sorrowful past. First the country blues and then the spirituals. The rich, deep bass and the tenors made the jungle a warm and friendly place.

Someone took up a collection for a gallon of applejack. Mellowed by the cider, they sang long after the moon started to fall toward the Sierra Nevada.

★

The good life was beginning to tell on me. I gained twenty pounds, stopped reading, and hadn't written a letter in three weeks. I needed clothes and was desperate for money. I decided to talk to Car Boy. He found some kind of work almost every day and put his money into Postal Savings.

"I'd like to put a day in with you, Car Boy."

"Sure, two people can do three times the work of one. But I don't let no grass grow under my feet. You work with me, you got to jump steady."

Simonizing cars is hard work. We finished one in about three hours. Car Boy knew how to hustle. He took the five dollars we earned and bought beer with it. We took the beer to the docks and traded beer for tuna. The we ran the tuna to the farmer's market and ended the day with over fifteen dollars. That was big money. We went halves on a gallon of wine and took it to the jungle to share with the men. It was getting dark when Car Boy held up the wine. The men left the crap and tonk games and came over for a swig. Then the evening discussion got started. There were only three real subjects. We called them the three "Ws"—women, white folk, and war.

"Sure there's gonna be a war. How you think work is opening up again?"

"Damn if I'll fight. A Negro is supposed to go hungry for twenty years and then jump in and fight for the bastards that been keepin' him hungry."

"I hate this fuckin' country. I wouldn't fight if Hitler was in Spokane."

"America, my ass. Let them that owns it fight for it."

"I'll tell you all something," Ace said. "Now, you all say you hate this country. I was a farmer. Any farmer knows you can't hate the land." He picked up a handful of brown Washington earth. "I hates some of the people in it, but you can't hate the country." He let the dirt fall. "You can't hate this. Hell, I loves the land. Makes me mad when you all talk like that. I ain't got shit, ain't never had shit, but I ain't gonna say I hates the country. Sure, hate the white folks for what they done. They ain't had nothin' to do with the land. They took it from the Indians—and took it from me too."

"You sure right, Ace."

"Damn if he ain't."

I had never thought in those terms. It made sense. I didn't hate the Wabasha valley. I couldn't.

The talk continued.

"I tell you, the whole Goddamn system gotta be changed."

Everywhere there was the talk against the "system." This vague thing was like the night. It covered everything. How could you fight the night—or the system? It was everywhere and nowhere. It was a good and easy thing to hate, but what can you do about it?

The talk died down. Soon the wine was gone and a few of the men stumbled out into the darkness to sleep.

Big John and a woman came down to the jungle. She sat near the fire. "Any of you all want to turn a trick?"

I looked at her. She was a youngish, good-looking brown-skinned woman. She caught my eye.

"You want to trick, baby?"

I didn't answer. Ace looked up from rolling a cigarette.

"You liable to pull an alligator from outta there for all I know."

The men laughed, but one of them jerked his head sideways and the woman followed him into a boxcar.

"So now that red-eyed son of a bitch is tryin' to pimp."

Big John looked at Ace for a moment, opened his mouth, closed it, and walked away from the fire.

"You'd better be careful, Ace," I said.

Ace slowly reached into his belt and pulled out an eight-inch hunting knife.

"He'd do better tryin' to get some tame pussy off a wild bear." He slipped the knife back into his belt. He wasn't smiling. His lined black face was immobile and there was no twinkle in his eyes. I knew that Ace would kill if anyone pushed him too far.

★

Sunday afternoon I put on my new sweatshirt and clean pants, intending to see one of the dime movies. Big John met me at the edge of the yards.

"Hey, boy, you want to pick up some fast money?"

"I'm goin' to a movie."

"Wait a minute. We can pick up five or ten bucks in an hour if you wants to."

"How?"

"You don't have to do nothin'. We'll go into the white neighborhood and catch all them church folks. You can make out like you're my son. I'll do the talking. We'll pick up plenty."

I never begged outright, and I didn't want to become involved with Big John in any way. Ace had said to stay away from him—and I really intended to.

"Naw, I don't want to take no chances like that."

Big John offered a cigarette. A tailor-made—his woman must have picked up quite a bit of change last night.

"Look, I don't know what Ace been telling you, but I been treatin' you right, ain't I?"

"Yeah, you been straight."

"All right, then. I ain't askin' you for nothin'. I'm interested in making some money for both of us."

I had been on the road long enough to know that the lure of free money is the opening to every sucker game. But this seemed foolproof to me.

"OK, Big John, let's go."

We went to the residential section of Seattle. Big John's pleading worked magic. He would approach a woman, take off his hat, and say, "Ma'am, I hates to bother you, but my boy here is hongry. We jest got into town and I ain't found no work. I ain't askin' for me, but could you let me have a little something so's he could eat?"

No one refused the contrite father.

After working the street for two hours, he suggested we knock off. We had over twelve dollars. He split it fair. Back at the skid row, the hamburger steak dinner was a welcome change from the stew. Big John went into the liquor store and got a quart of apple-jack and a pint of whiskey.

"Come on, boy. Let's drink. It's all on me."

It was dark back at the yards. I opened both doors of the box-car. If he tried to rob me, I could get out.

For half an hour we sat at the end of the car drinking. A slug of whiskey, a drink of applejack. I began to feel the liquor. I got to my feet. I was dizzy.

"Got to go, Big John. Thanks for the drink."

"Sure, boy, might's well have one more before you go."

"OK, one more."

I took the bottle and tipped it back. There was fire in my mouth and in my stomach. I sat down, afraid I would fall.

Big John's voice droned on, "Stay here if you want to . . . sure is pretty out . . . ever get down to California?"

Fighting against falling asleep, I tried to muster the strength to get up. Finally I gave up and stretched out on the boxcar floor.

Big John shook me.

"Hey, boy . . . Hey . . . "

I felt him reach for my belt. I tried to get up; the whirring of the boxcar was too much. I tried to turn over.

"Go on, man."

I couldn't even talk straight. He cut through my belt and pants with a straightedge razor. Panic gripped me then. My head began to clear. "I've got to get up. This son of a bitch is going to mess me all up." He laid the razor down. My mind was function-ing; my body would not obey. Big John was drunk too. He could hardly keep his balance. Gathering all my strength, I stood up. He bumped against my shoulder and fell. As he did so, I grabbed the razor to cut his throat. I couldn't get it open. Staggering to his feet in the darkness, he looked seven feet tall. I had to get out of there. The ground seemed miles below. Big John stumbled toward me.

"What's the matter, kid? Hell, I ain't gonna hurt ya."

I sat down and jumped. He tried to sit down and fell. I was too dizzy to run. As he tried to get to his feet, I kicked hard into his face. The animal growl was frightening. Another kick to the side of the head. He rolled over. My close combat training at Fort Riley had saved me. I knew I had to kill him. Sickness enforced the dizziness. I started to vomit. The retching left me sweating and weak. There was only one coherent thought left—get out of there.

Ace and West Coast were sitting by the fire. Ace looked up at me.

"What the hell got ahold of you?"

"Big John tried to fuck me."

"Where's that motherfucker?" His hand slid to his knife.

"Down in the yards. I knocked him out—kicked him. He's gonna try to kill me sure. Let me use your knife, Ace. He comes to, he'll kill me."

"We can't have no killin' here. That's all the cops want. We just have to run him off."

I stumbled to my shack, got the razor open, and fell asleep.

The next morning, Big John came into the jungle, the side of his face one big bloody abrasion. His parted swollen lips showed blood on his teeth.

"What you sayin'?" he greeted Ace.

"Get." Ace pulled his knife. "I don't want no rotten son of a bitch like you in this part. Now get."

John reached to his belt where he kept the razor. West Coast moved toward him. Ace shoved his knife to Big John's belly.

"Don't get no crazy ideas, ya low-down bastard. I'm countin' to three. If you ain't gone—you gonna stay."

West Coast moved closer.

"We don't want no wolves here, you rotten motherfucker. I knowed what you was up to all the time."

Big John was trembling. He narrowed his eyes at me. I knew that if we met again, one of us would die. I cursed myself for not having bought a knife. Big John turned and walked toward the yard. For a moment Ace watched him leave, then turned to me.

"I oughta slap your ass clean back to Minnesota."

"Thanks, Ace."

"Thank the Lord."

"Anybody can act a damn fool once," West Coast said. "You got to pay for your learnin'. You done paid. From now on don't never drink with no one person. If anybody tries to be so God-damn sweet to you—take care."

I had to have a weapon. I looked over all the knives at the hardware store and bought an oversized linoleum knife. It handled easier than a dagger and could slash better.

The following week, Ace called the group together. We assembled around the food barrel. Ace stood up, concern and anxiety etched in his face.

"There's something you mens ought to know. I was talking to the boss up at the commissary. He told me that a dick by the name of Red Anderson been transferred from the Southern Pacific up to here to clean the place up. Me and West Coast, we know this fuckin' guy from way back. He used to sit on the coal tender with a .30-06. When the train makes the hairpin curve crossin' the Sabine into Texas, he could look into and between every car. He'd shoot the bums off the train, or force 'em to jump into the gorge. Don't know how many he kilt."

"What must we do, Ace?"

"I don't rightly know. I suspect we just keep doin' what we doin' until somethin' happens."

"Jesus Christ," I mumbled, "this must be the dick I heard about in Kansas. Hear about him all over the country. He must be a killer."

It happened two days later. Four city cops with rifles, a fire engine with six firemen, and the new dick came to the jungle. The cops rounded us up and read the vagrancy law to us. Each of us had the necessary ten dollars. They couldn't arrest us. The firemen told us our shacks were a menace to public health. They gave us ten minutes to get out. I stuffed my belongings into the gunnysack. It was fuller now than ever. The firemen doused the shacks with kerosene and set them on fire. I glanced over at the new dick. He was a redneck if ever I saw one. The broad-rimmed, sweat-soaked felt hat shaded the perpetual scowl on his ruddy face. The warts on his neck stood out. Heavyset, with huge, thick hands, all he needed was a whip to become a picture of the driver man.

The shacks burned quickly. As we turned toward the skid row, Big Red walked over to Ace. "Listen, old niggah—I want you to stay outa here. I know all about your racket at the commissary. You lazy niggers try to live off the fat of the land. If I catch you on Great Northern territory, I'll kill you. You understand that?"

Ace glared back into the white man's eyes. "Fuck you, white man. I'm on city property—you ain't gonna kill nobody."

The jaw muscles trembled in Ace's black face. West Coast had tears of rage in his eyes. A feeling of rapport and unity swept through the hoboes. Red felt it too. He didn't reach for his gun.

"I ain't warnin' you no more." He turned and walked toward the commissary. We watched until he was out of earshot.

"That white son of a bitch."

"Somebody ought to kill that bastard."

"I gets a chance, somebody will."

"What the hell we gonna do now, Ace?"

"I ain't sure. Looks like we better get. You can kill Red, but you can't kill Big G. They'd get somebody else."

We began to drift by ones and twos toward the end of the yard. We had to leave the city. Red wasn't playing and I knew he was a killer.

I heard there was work in San Francisco. It was the middle of September. If I couldn't find a job soon, I would have to decide to head back east or stay on this side of the Divide until spring. Until darkness would hide me, I waited for the evening freight in a dime-dinger, the ten-cent skid row movie.

The freight for Stockton was pulling out at 10:30. By walking slowly I could make the yards just in time and wouldn't take a chance on meeting Big Red.

The train hadn't made up. I climbed into a boxcar to wait. Both doors were open. As I began to close them, I saw Ace and West Coast four or five cars down from me. I saw someone else too. Red climbed between two cars. I started to yell a warning. Ace saw him too. West Coast turned to run between the cars. Ace stood there, refusing to run, giving West Coast a chance to get away.

It was a chilly, windy, cloudy night. The clouds raced beneath the moon and intermittently the scene was in darkness and then in the light of the bright September moon. West Coast stood hiding between two cars. He wasn't going to leave Ace. Red saw Ace, and his cold rasping white man's voice broke the night. "Halt! Heh—caught ya, huh?"

Ace didn't answer. Big Red's voice cut the night. "Put up your hands, nigger." Red pressed the gun against his chest.

"Bustin' into boxcars, huh?"

Ace raised his hands slowly. Red drew back his fist and, grunting with the effort, hit him in the face. Ace stumbled back against the tracks and fell.

"Get up, you old black bastard."

Holding his jaw, he got to his feet and raised his hands again. Big Red moved toward Ace, the blackjack dangling from his hand. West Coast swung from between the cars, the bowie knife dull in the moonlight. With the sixth sense of a cop, Red crouched and began to turn toward the danger. By crouching, the blow intended for his heart caught Red in the base of the skull. The blade crashed through and protruded from his mouth. Even in death, Red struggled for balance and then lunged headlong across the tracks. West Coast turned to steady Ace. I jumped from the car, wanting to run away. I couldn't leave Ace.

"Come on, Ace."

West Coast shoved me back.

"Get gone, boy. Hurry."

I glanced down at Big Red. I had never seen a man killed before. I had never seen a dead person except in a casket. The point of the knife jutted from the open mouth. The mean, brutal brains oozed from the other end. West Coast shoved me again.

"Go ahead, boy. Hurry."

The scene sank into my consciousness. A white man was dead. I saw it happen. I turned and ran in one direction; Ace and West Coast went the other way. The bright light of an engine shone down the eight-track right-of-way. In the dark it was impossible to tell which track the train was on. I crouched until the engine passed me. It was a fast rattler, an all-steel refrigerated train that ran the fruits and vegetables to Walla Walla. The topside catwalk was a part of the car and impossible to hold on to. The rear and side ladders were indented steps and impossible to hold. Between the cars was enough room for a man to stand on the coupling and hold on to two iron bars. The train, gathering speed, jerked me off the ground. The noise was deafening. The engine highballed its good-bye to Seattle.

The next night, I jumped off the train, gulped down a bowl of stew, got a paper, and grabbed the first freight going south to California. Two days later, I jumped off in Eureka, thinking there might be work in the timber.

The hoboes stood in a small group listening to a man standing on a wooden crate. I walked over. It had to be a preacher or a Communist. He was explaining how the capitalists were responsible for the Depression. Now, they were dragging us into a war so they could continue to make profits and come out of the Depression.

"If we get into the war, it has to be on the side of the people—with the Soviet Union and the Chinese people. We workers got to get something out of this war and not let the capitalists make millions off our blood again."

The man went on to explain that he was a Communist and the party had to alert the working class to the danger of being dragged into war on the wrong side.

"I learned a song during the first war, when I was a Wobblie. You need to learn it too, 'cause sometimes a song says more than a book." Without a trace of self-consciousness, he threw back his head and sang.

In a boss's war, a worker gets
In a boss's war, a worker gets
In a boss's war, a worker gets
A bellyful of bayonets,
Boys, let's turn the guns around.

In a worker's war, the worker gets
In a worker's war, the worker gets
In a worker's war, the worker gets
A government of Soviets.
Boys, let's turn the guns around.

I listened for a while and walked toward town to get a bowl of stew. I agreed with the man. The system had to be overthrown. There had to be a revolution. If the Red Andersons ever came to power, it'd be worse than Germany.

I soon found out there was no work for me in the timber. I pushed on to Stockton.

The picking season in the north had just ended and the workers were heading south to get in on the harvest. The jungle was full. Scores of white hoboes came in, some with families. No one set up a Mason-Dixon line but blacks were on one side of the jungle, whites and Mexicans on the other. In the area where the two groups merged, they all socialized.

A skinny white youth sat on an upturned bucket, strumming a guitar. His clothes were in tatters, his face a picture of exhaustion from the road. I moved closer to hear him.

I been way down in jail on my knees, darlin' baby.
Been way down in jail on my knees.
Way down in jail on my knees, God knows
I'm goin' back to my long lonesome home.

Everywhere there was talk of the killing. A black hobo told me the cops had picked up and beaten every Negro hobo in the Seattle-Tacoma-Portland area. I walked from group to group listening to the news, hoping someone would tell me where they needed men. The black hoboes said they needed men for the lettuce harvest but the Okies wouldn't let the blacks in. It was white man's work. That went for the peaches, too. These white hoboes from Arkansas and Oklahoma were friendly enough individually, but I knew as a group they were dangerous.

Over at the roundhouse I washed up and went to the skid row to spend another precious fifteen cents on a bowl of stew. I passed an old black 'bo huddled in a doorway. I gave the "hello brother" nod and looked again. It was Ace. I helped him to his feet and we went to a little dingy cafe on one of the side streets.

"They got West Coast," he said wearily. "Me and him separated, but they caught him. Fella told me they took him in the elevator and beat him 'til his head looked like a clod of dirt." Ace ran the back of his hand beneath his nose and looked dully down into the steaming coffee mug.

There was nothing to say. All the compassion seemed drained from me. I was so tired. Tired of the road. Tired of the unending violence and the threat of it, the segregation, the constant fear of the cops and dicks, and the whites. I was sick of having to take the work and food that no one else wanted. Tired of keeping my hand on my knife whenever someone approached. The road was beating the spirit out of me. I was becoming a bum. I was not going to let that happen.

I forced myself to think of old West Coast. What did they do to you, old friend? I know how they did it. Handcuffed you to the rail and used their clubs and blackjacks. I could almost hear those jackals laughing as they kicked your testicles and gouged your eyes with their clubs. You said "fuck you" when they asked where your friend was. They called you a Goddamned nigger and rammed the club into your mouth and laughed as you coughed out the teeth and blood. They knew how to torture—break the legs and arms, grind the penis beneath the heel. They always went for the sex parts of a black man. When the moaning stopped they beat the corpse some more, angry that you dared die and stop their fun.

God, I hated them. I was ready to trade my life for one of theirs.

★

Old West Coast. I can see the black face and hear the rich laughter. I'll not forget you. Neither will I forget the Great Northern Railroad. The Big G—with their Nazi cops who hunted us down and killed us because we were black and defenseless. I won't forget how they stopped their train in the eight-mile tunnel and fired up the boilers to smother the hoboes. Fourteen men and a woman!

Big G said that would teach the hoboes a lesson. Someday, when we have the revolution, I'm going to find out who the Big G is. Who's the brains and the executive board. I'm going to indict them and testify against them. I'm going to ask to be in the firing squad. I'll press my cheek tight against the stock so the barrel is steady, breathe deeply, and squeeze off. If the revolution don't do nothin' but let me get even, I'm for it. Rest well, West Coast. You'll never again clutch the blinds, cold and hungry. The big mountain-jumpin' engines highballed for the last time. From now on, you've got the right-of-way.

"Boy."

"Yes, Ace."

"Boy, I like you. You respected what I said, an' you treated me right."

"Sure, Ace."

"Go home, boy. Get off the road. It ain't no life for a human. It ain't no life for a dog. You hangs around the freights and the jungles and after 'while you gets cinders in your blood. Then you can't quit. It's worse than dope."

I sat beside him in silence.

"Ah'm tellin' you 'cause I likes you like you was my own son. Go home. Promise."

"OK, Ace. I'll go back."

"Don't get back on the road, boy. Me and West Coast done bummed every line in the West. Thirty-five years. West Coast dead. Me—I'm almost gone, too. If yore heels itch, wash 'em, boy. There ain't no future here. You young. Our people needs young men who know the score. You done learned it. Go home an' don't forget."

We sat for a moment in silence.

"OK, Ace."

I paid for the coffee and shoved a dollar bill into his hand. "I'm goin' home, Ace."

"Good-bye, boy."

We didn't shake hands. We looked at each other for a moment and I left.

I bought a sack of food and a couple of cans of Sterno. In the twilight I found an empty mail car hooked to a passenger train that was heading for Chicago. Back through the Rockies, Helena, Butte. Back across the Little Big Horn and the Big Horn. Across the badlands. Across the high bridge at Valley City and into Minnesota. Four days from homeless to home. Four days from adrift to family. Four days from all alone to sweetheart.

Heidi was thinner than I had remembered. The gray-green eyes seemed saddened and veiled. I didn't ask her about the abortion. The slight sagging of her youthful breast told the story. We kissed and pledged our love and did all the things reunited lovers do. She was slipping away I knew she felt I had deserted her in a moment of need. I felt she would never know me.

There were changes in me, too. All the little things and all the big things I had seen and done remolded me. I couldn't shake off the feeling of being outside even our little black community. I chafed at all the rules and regulations, all the things other people said I should and shouldn't do. Disgusted with their fawning on the authorities, I no longer fit in. I was restless and longed for the freedom of the open road. I had crossed a Rubicon. My heels itched and there were cinders in my blood.

16

I HATED TO go back to school. Eighteen, older than most of the other students, I was no longer part of their half-adult, half-child world. It was my senior year and I had to have that diploma. I had already missed more than a month and my grades last semester had been terrible. The principal did not want to let me come back. I had been in military training, and war was drawing near. That made his position—as he expressed it—"uncomfortable." The schools adopted a policy of immediately graduating any senior who enlisted. He suggested I might think about that.

The guys in our little gang and the young women around us were changing. Being away for even a short while made it so clear. They were already giving up. The school routed the women to the home economics classes and trained them for nothing but maid service. The guys were routed to the shop classes and trained for factory work. Only grades of consistently B or above and the most vigorous protests by parents would move a black student into college preparatory classes.

Making out my program, I asked for the class in creative writing as an elective. The principal slowly looked over my very poor English grades and shook his head.

Determined to take the course, I decided to see the teacher in charge of the class. When the school day ended, I went down to her office and peered through the glass-paneled door. Sitting at her desk, wearing glasses, reading through a pile of manuscripts, the teacher appeared stern—almost frightening. With her iron-gray hair knotted at the back of her head, her sharp, middle-aged features looked almost hawklike. I decided not to try it, but she glanced at the door, smiled, and beckoned me in.

At her desk, I forgot the speech I was going to make.

"Ah, I—"

"My name is Miss O'Leary, Abigail O'Leary. What's yours?"

"Nelson. Nelson Peery."

"Well, sit down, Nelson. I'm glad you came in. I've got all this stuff to read. My God, don't you kids do anything interesting anymore?"

She pushed the pile of manuscripts aside and swung her chair around to face me, nodding to a chair beside the desk. I took it. She went on talking, interrupting herself with laughs that crinkled her face, making her look kind and pleasant. Finally, she stopped chattering about her class and asked, "What is it you want, Nelson?"

Her talk put me at ease and now I wanted to talk about all the things I had to tell the people. How they are used against one another, how the Fascists planned to take over the country, tell them. . . . "Well, Miss O'Leary, I want to write. I want to get in your class, but I got some bad marks in English and the principal said no."

She smiled again. "You also use some bad English, but that's not important."

I completed the form she handed me and gave it back to her.

"Peery—Peery. Have you always lived in Minneapolis?"

"I lived in Wabasha before here."

"I thought I knew that name. Did you know Abigail Quigley?"

"Sure," I laughed. "Once I beat up her kid brother and she grabbed a shoe and chased me into a briar patch. She spent an hour crying for me and picking the needles out of my foot. Then she gave me candy to boot."

Miss O'Leary laughed. "She's my niece. She told me about that."

We talked and laughed about Wabasha until the sun set and

darkness gathered outside. Saying good night, we shook hands warmly, my hand between the two of hers. I knew I had found a friend.

The next day I met Heidi in the hall and told her I was going to learn to write. She grabbed my hands and leaned close to me.

"I'm so glad, hon."

Her eyes were deep and damp. The students walked by, some looked; no one said anything. I fought down an urge to kiss her.

"See you tonight, huh?"

"Sure. Write true, won't you? Not like you hate everything . . . "

"I do hate everything."

She pressed against me for a second and hurried to her class. Chuck walked up behind me.

"One of these days, you're gonna lose sight of the world."

Before Miss O'Leary's class, Chuck and I went out for a smoke and I ran in just as the bell rang. The chairs were arranged in a semicircle, and there were a few extra ones in the back. I walked toward them, not anxious to sit near anyone.

"Nelson, your seat is right there." Miss O'Leary pointed to an empty seat between two white girls.

I hesitated. She smiled.

"Hurry now, we only have an hour."

I slid into the seat. I slightly knew the brown-haired, plump young woman to my right. To my left sat an aristocratic, very blond young woman. She smiled and said, "My name's Katherine."

I was startled. Her voice was thick with the South. I glanced at Miss O'Leary, thinking, "What the hell kind of trick is this?"

"What's your name?" the Southerner was asking.

"Ah . . . Nels. Nels Peery."

I swung my legs away from her. I didn't want to give anyone any excuse to say anything about me. I was uncomfortable between the two women, but no one else seemed to notice.

Class started. Miss O'Leary had a terrible, explosive temper, and the students were afraid of her. After being angry, she would smile and act as if nothing had happened. I shrugged it off, thinking it was just her Irish temper. It was just Miss O'Leary.

The class was the last period of the day. No one seemed anxious to leave. Everyone continued the discussion, genuinely interested in one another's work.

Miss O'Leary motioned to me.

"You have a lot of catching up to do. As soon as you can, I

want you to hand in a piece on what happened to you during the summer."

Katherine came over. A bit embarrassed, she tried to start a conversation. "I thought you took a dislike to me because I'm from the South. I wouldn't blame you, but I do want to be friends."

Miss O'Leary smiled. I knew she had placed me next to Katherine on purpose. I stopped being angry with her.

"Sure . . . I'm sorry. I didn't mean for you to think I didn't want to be friends. I . . . "

"I know," she said. "But none of my family ever believed in segregation or discrimination. That's why we left Shreveport."

Jolted to the bottom of my race consciousness, I smiled at her. These refugees from Jim Crow were white. I went out of my way to be friends with Katherine.

I loved our writing class. Miss O'Leary pulled material out of every student. She would start the day threatening, cajoling, praising, and coaxing the work out of us. She would lead us toward thinking we might be budding geniuses, then knock us down for thinking it.

I wrote from fear of not writing and from an overpowering urge to express myself. If I handed in something trite or trivial, she raised pure hell.

"My God! Don't you know any real people? Don't hand this sort of trite writing to me again. Here, read this—if you can understand it. You're lazy and writing is the hardest work in the world. If you want to work, all right. If you want to play, get out of this class."

As did the rest, I would leave swearing never to come back. I always did.

I handed in a short sketch of Ace and West Coast. Overjoyed, she said, "It's about time, you simpleton. Everybody lives and has so much to say. You have to *learn* to write. Keep writing about real people."

As the school year wore on, Miss O'Leary guided me toward social and political maturity. I realized in later years that she personified the last of a great and noble part of American intellectual development. The Christian socialists of her caliber are gone. They tried so desperately to turn the tide of war and social oppression by living Christianity and struggling to plant the seeds of social morality in everyone they touched. She was my first real teacher.

As soon as I finished one book, she handed me another. From Hawthorne's *The Scarlet Letter* through Du Bois's *Souls of Black Folk* to Sandberg's *The People, Yes!* and scores of books in between was an unending, exciting awakening.

A teacher commented that one of her students was becoming too friendly with a black athlete. Flushing to an angry red, Miss O'Leary told her to kindly stay out of her classroom, and not to bother speaking to her again. She learned that Negroes were not welcome even to visit the Park Avenue apartments where she lived. She invited me to tea that very evening, making sure the manager was aware of my presence. After tea, she showed me her old-fashioned apartment. I couldn't see any value in old flatirons and tea pots but listened respectfully as she explained the period and history of each. Then she showed me her real hobby. Opening a trunk full of manuscripts, she said, "These are my children. I've written sketches on nearly every student I've had since 1912."

Under her forceful hand, the class published a quarterly literary magazine, *Quest*. The envy of every high school in the country, *Quest* had won at least one National Scholastic first prize every year for the past eighteen years. Few knew what went into making that magazine. She wrung it out of those students: fussing, belittling, humiliating them until the young women cried and the guys would almost quit. They came back for more. *Quest* won the prizes and she would throw an ice cream and cake party.

As time came to start organizing for publication, Miss O'Leary made recommendations for the various posts of the magazine. The class discussed the recommendations and approved them. Hank Franklin, a brilliant, shy, nominal member of our gang, was chosen editor. J. C. Wiggins, another member of the gang, was chosen business manager. I was chosen literary co-editor; Chuck was coopted from the art class to work with the art editor. Four young white women filled the remaining posts. After school, on the corner, we realized that we had a staff of black guys and white women. The class did not notice it. They elected according to talent and ability. Aware of it from the very beginning, we set out to make this the best magazine published in the country.

When the work, the crying, and the frustrations were over,

National Scholastic published its awards. Hank took first prize in poetry. Chuck took first prize in art. I took first prize in autobiographical sketch, short story, and essay. J. C. took second prize in essay. No high school magazine had ever taken such a sweep of prizes. Plus it was a huge financial success. Miss O'Leary was ecstatic. Ring Lardner, Jr., and Dalton Trumbo wrote encouraging letters to me.

Miss O'Leary called me into her office. "Nelson, you've got to start taking lessons from someone else. There is a teacher here who I think is the best there is in structure." She bit the end of her pencil. "I've hesitated sending you to her. She's a Communist and I'm afraid you're at that point where they can influence you."

"Nobody can influence me against my will."

"That's just it. I'm afraid it might be your will. Oh! I'd turn over in my grave if you wrote for the Communists—but I'm going to send you to her if you promise me one thing."

"All right. What's that?"

"Promise that as soon as the class ends, you'll leave."

"Sure, why shouldn't I?"

She smiled her special Irish smile. "I imagine they might have coffee afterwards for the inner sanctum."

I wasn't sure what she meant. I promised and she handed me the address.

"Now understand. When the class is over, you go home. If you don't, Miss Le Sueur will tell me about it."

I laughed again.

"I'm not afraid of the Communists."

"Oh, Nelson! I'm not afraid of them either. People are always calling me a Communist. It's just that I don't want the responsibility . . . "

I laughed at her contradictory statements and she knew why. If they called her a Communist, that proved they were good people. She handed me a book and I left.

After dinner I found a chair in the least noisy part of the house and opened *Native Son*. I could not put it down and finished it at five the next morning. I sat back thinking. Wright presented Bigger Thomas, the depiction of the Negro people, as ground down beyond redemption so the white folks would publish the book. Wright is one of us, and a Communist, too. He knows, as we know, that a slave is more moral than the master. All that stuff about Bigger Thomas had to be written so Wright could get the

main point across. Here are the Communists. Here's what they
stand for and what they do. How the hell can anybody, especially
any Negro, be against the Communists? I had to talk to Vickie
and Doug again.

Tuesday night. I walked over to Miss Le Sueur's house on
Twenty-fifth and Harriet. She opened the door for me.

"Come in, Nelson. I'm Meridel Le Sueur. We were expect-
ing you."

I recognized her right away. She was the woman who came to
our house with the *Daily Worker* when we first moved to Minneapolis.

"Hi. I remember you."

I stepped inside. All the seats were taken by an assortment of
people. Some looked to be university students; some looked rich;
some were workers. All were intensely interested in the discussion.
Sitting on the steps, I hardly heard it. There must be more to
communism than I had thought. They must be after more than
feeding the hungry and equality for the Negroes. What makes a
white person a Communist? What makes a writer a Communist?
I tried to imagine a time when I could ask her. The class ended
and Miss Le Sueur laughingly told me of her promise to Miss
O'Leary. I left determined to get into that coffee-drinking inner
sanctum.

17

THE THREAT OF war increased almost daily during the fall of
1941. Factories began limited hiring. As the white workers went
into the factories, the lowest level of employment became available to us.

I shall forever love the Walgreen's drugstore. They gave me a
job washing dishes. I had to work only fifty-four hours a week for
the wonderful sum of $16.74, paid in cash every Saturday night. I
felt like a millionaire. Between school and work there was no time
for fun. That was OK. I bought some clothes, paid Mom room
and board, and had money left over for Saturday nights with
Heidi. Bustin' suds was hard, hot work. The women at the
counter were great. They would send me milk shakes and sandwiches along with the pans of dirty dishes.

My little contribution to the house helped, but there was never enough of anything. My parents proudly told our neighbor, who was a railway waiter, that I had a job at Walgreen's.

"Thirty-one cents an hour ain't bad money—but it ain't good either."

"No, Mr. Beck. But it sure beats a goose egg."

"That's true, son. Where is your derby hat?"

"You know I never wear a hat. I don't own one."

"Boy," he chuckled, "Don't you know why darkies wear derby hats?"

"No, I never thought about it."

"When you have a poorly paying job, you got to wear a derby hat. You can put a pound of butter under a derby. Most anything fits."

We both laughed uproariously. I had never thought of anything like that. I bought a derby and we ate butter instead of the lard-looking margarine. I had nice silverware and a few thick coffee mugs, too. I loved Walgreen's.

★

The thunder of war to the east and west threw the seniors together with a special sense of urgency. The rules of conduct relaxed and no longer forbade holding hands in the hallways. No one interrupted the long, intimate talks beneath the stairwells or in darkened corners. The growing threat of parting brought the young men and women together with desperate passion.

Winter clamped Minnesota in its frigid grip. The snow bent the boughs and the thirty-degree-below weather burst the limbs, which sounded like rifle shots as they cracked in the night.

Heidi and I loved the cold outdoors. We spent hours walking through it, holding hands and talking about our tomorrow. So many paths and doors open to young lovers were closed to us. We did not want to live in the twilight world of interracial couples. Slowly, hardly aware of it, we made our plans to leave this country.

Heidi wanted to go to a nightclub. In Minneapolis, if you wanted to take your date to a nice dinner, you went to the airport because federal regulations protected you against segregation. It wasn't any fun. If you wanted a fun night, you went to the Negro Elks Club up on the north side.

The Elks Club didn't admit anyone under twenty-one. I knew

the doorman well. He held the door open, saying politely, "Good evening, Mr. Peery."

After a wonderful dinner of fried chicken, candied yams, and collard greens, we sat in the darkened corner watching the people dancing to the plaintive, sensuous blues.

"Well, what say, Nels? Long time no see. How are you, Miss . . . ?"

Brown, handsome, immaculately dressed, pimp chain hanging almost to the cuff of his draped pants, two sparkling rings on each hand, Reggie was the picture of the up-and-coming pimp. I remembered back before his eyes were bloodshot and full of that I-know-it-all expression. What a nice guy he had been. Polite, intelligent, inquisitive. We elected him president of our Salvation Army Camp group because we knew he wouldn't steal our dues. That was before his knack for persuasion turned into conning. That was before he gave up the struggle of the Negro youth. That was before his constantly stated "We should be all for one and one for all" became "I'm for me and fuck you!"

I didn't like pimps and I didn't like Reggie.

Before I could protest, he said to Heidi, "You'll join me for a drink?"

She smiled acceptance. He slid into the booth beside me, looking into her eyes, openly calculating which approach would pay off the best. The waitress came to the booth. Reggie turned to us and asked what we wanted.

"Gin and tonic for her, bourbon over for him, and scotch and milk for me."

Heidi smiled knowingly at him.

"Bogart's drink, huh?"

Reggie smiled at her. "Maybe he got it from me."

Bogart my ass. Every nickel-slick pimp and two-bit whore on the north side drinks scotch and milk. Fucking sissy-ass drink, anyway.

After what seemed an agonizing hour, she finished her gin and tonic.

"Can I ask her for this dance?" Smiling.

"We really got to go, man." Cold.

"Night's just beginning, Nels. Don't rush off." Accommodating.

"It's so nice here. Can we stay and dance?" Ignorant.

"We have to go. I have to go to work in the morning." I held her coat; she smiled in thanks to Reggie as we left.

As we got into the jitney for the ride back to the south side, I said, "Look, Heidi, stay away from that guy. He's no damned good."

"He seemed awfully nice. I thought he was your friend."

"He's not my friend. He's a fuckin' pimp."

"I wish we could have stayed and danced. It was an awfully nice place."

★

November faded into December. That Sunday dawned bright and clear. By nine o'clock the salted slush began to melt. It was my turn to go to the drugstore for the paper.

Some of the gang were already there. Chuck, Mac, Carl—same dumb jokes that ended up playing the dozens and probably in a fight. Mr. Spiegel was guarding his merchandise out of the corner of his eye. The radio was playing dance music.

"We interrupt this program . . . Pearl Harbor . . . Manila . . . The Japanese Imperial Army . . . "

The drugstore was silent. Mr. Spiegel's eyes were sadder than ever. Chuck's laughing lips were open, his asthmatic breathing loud and rattling. The announcer finished. We were at war.

The older fellows started drifting into the Dreamland and the drugstore to hear the comments of the rest.

"Fuck it. I ain't goin'. For what?"

"The hell you ain't. This is going to be a big one! The whole fucking world! Every living ass is going to go."

I left the drugstore. Pop was moving the dial from station to station for the latest news, declaring that he was ready to go again. Mom shot him a mean glance, mumbling something about "old fool" and looked over her ripe brood. Three ready for the slaughter now. At least one more if it lasts very long. She silently cried a little and rose to fix dinner.

During the following weeks our white friends at school began to disappear as their Guard divisions activated. The hallways buzzed with talk of enlisting. This was the real thing. A radio announcement had changed all our lives.

Winter blew itself out in the fury of March winds. The Fascist armies poured across Asia and Africa. I got the library's copy of *Mein Kampf* and spent a week digesting it. If I had any doubts about what Hitler stood for and meant to do, his book erased them.

So the Negroes are first cousins to apes and you will exterminate them? You will destroy the Soviet Union? This isn't a race thing. We're going to have to stop this crazy bastard. I remembered Ace picking up the handful of American soil and saying, "Man, you can't hate this."

Almost without realizing it I slipped closer to the Young Communist League. Although I never formally joined up, I attended meetings when I had time and was close enough to be called and to call them the endearing term "comrade." They taught me new concepts, new ideas, and new ideals with lectures and songs.

> *I'll give you ten-o,*
> *Red fly the banners-o.*
> *What is your ten-o?*

Ten for the days that shook the world. (I got and read the book.)
Nine for the days of the general strike. (I never knew that English workers had fought their capitalists.)
Eight for the Eighth Route Army. (How I loved Mao Tse-tung and the Chinese People's Liberation Army!)
Seven for the Seventh World Congress. (I read Demitrov's report calling for the united front against fascism.)
Six for the Haymarket martyrs. (Albert Parsons became my model revolutionary.)
Five for the years of the five-year plan. (Which proved the superiority of socialism!)
Four for the four great teachers. (Marx, Engels, Lenin, and Stalin.)
Three, three, the Comintern. (The Third Communist International, created by Lenin.)
Two, two, the opposites, interpenetrating-o. (That was my introduction to dialectics, to the thesis and antithesis.)
One is worker's unity that ever more shall be! (Someday, it will be possible.)

★

I knew I was going to enlist. I hadn't been called up because no openings existed in the segregated Negro infantry organizations. I didn't want to be called up. I wanted it to be my own decision to go fight along with the people of the world. I told Mom. She cried a bit. I knew that she had prepared herself for this moment.

"I knew you'd go." She sighed. "I can't stop you. I guess men have to fight to prove something to themselves. It's just that I hate to think that I raised seven sons to become cannon fodder."

I had to tell Miss O'Leary. She looked surprised and then hurt.

"My God, Nelson, don't be a fool. I watched the young men go to the last war. For what? To make United States Steel richer. They made the war. Let them fight it."

"I have to go, Miss O'Leary," I said quietly. "Part of it is so I can say, this is my country. I fought for it and you can't deny me."

After dabbing her eyes with her lace handkerchief, she smiled. "I know how you feel—you're so young. It seems such a waste to educate for peace and then see you all go to war."

It was hardest of all to tell Heidi. The muscles in her face twitched and then very calmly she asked me, "Why, Nels? Tell me why?"

"Honey, you know I have to go. This Hitler will have us back in chains—or worse. We can't have a life while he is alive. Feeling the way I do about Russia, I think I should fight to save her. If I'm going to get the world we want, I got to fight for it."

She cried then—hot, bitter tears that brought tears to my eyes. "What has this country ever done for us? Even a dog has more rights. Please don't join."

When she saw I wouldn't change my mind, she threw herself against me with a protective, helpless passion, clinging to me and crying over and over, "They'll kill you—they'll kill you. You won't come back. Please, Nels, please."

A few weeks before graduation I received my notice from the army reserve. Keeping my promise to myself, I went down and enlisted. The adjutant understood what I was doing and smilingly congratulated me on not allowing the army to tell me what to do. He gladly wrote out a two-week delay in route so I could graduate.

★

On June 12, 1942, the principal called my name and I stepped forward to receive my diploma. The assembly noticed my brown shoes and the cuffs of my khaki pants beneath the purple robe. At first a few—and then the entire audience—stood and applauded as I left the stage. After the warm and sometimes tearful embraces and farewells to my many friends at Central High, I walked home, kissed my family good-bye, and left for Fort Snelling.

The next morning a jeep took me to the train station with orders to report to Fort Huachuca, Arizona.

The train backed into the station. I stood for a moment looking over Minneapolis and down the skid row toward Seven Corners.

I'm only eighteen, but I know you, America. You whore mother of democracy, you who strangle the dreams you've birthed. I know your wheat fields and copper mines and hobo jungles. I've left sweat on your prairies and, as an eagle, perched on the pinnacle of your Rocky Mountains, I've seen your splendid beauty from Kansas to Oregon. Grant me one wish. Be more good than beautiful. Show me yams and cotton and steel and coal unstained by corruption and tears. You would be a gentle thing without your thugs and lynch mobs. Someday I'll tear out your claws, come close, and love you.

The engine highballed—a sound I loved.

"All 'boo—aard!" The conductor swung on behind me.

Part Three

"WITH RESPECT, OR ON THEIR SHIELDS": THE MEN OF THE 93RD

18

FORT HUACHUCA IS in the high desert of Arizona. The valley and its surrounding chain of mountains form a lovely jewel in the beauty of the Southwest. In the evening, the sun bathes the ragged mountains in a reddish afterglow. The sage takes a soft purple hue. The winds rise to moan through Montezuma Pass and spread their melancholy across the desert floor. A word of the Apache Indian, Huachuca means "Mountains of the Wind."

★

The military never dreamed of using the black soldiers as anything but hewers of wood and drawers of water. They sent them into the Quartermaster, Port, Water Supply, Graves Registration, Laundry, and Engineer Battalions. These combat support groups freed up white men to fight a white man's war in defense of a white man's country.

The black press matured as a fighting organ within the Abolitionist movement. It led the fight to force the government to accept the slaves and black freemen as combat soldiers. Its tactic was to buy first-class citizenship with the blood of the Negro soldier. The black press thought that institutionalizing the black soldier as a laborer—a second-class soldier—would strengthen second-class status after the war. The tactic of sacrifice failed in the Revolutionary War, in the War of 1812 and in the Civil War, in the wars against the Indian, in the war against Spain, and in the war against Germany. The consistent failure of this tactic was no deterrent.

The black masses were of a different opinion. Poll takers in Harlem found that most blacks believed they would be treated better by the Japanese than by the whites. They believed they should force concessions rather than make the sacrifice. Mrs. Roosevelt tacitly supported them, saying, "The U.S. cannot expect the loyalty of the Negroes under present conditions."

A movement is led by a press. Without its own press, the militant movement of the blacks fell under the influence of those who had a press. That press, controlled by the ambitious black upper class, was little more than a safety valve for the militancy of the masses.

As they regained control of the movement, the bourgeois owners of the black press began a national clamor for an integrated army. The generals wouldn't even consider it. They disregarded the fact that blacks, whites, Chinese, and Filipinos were fighting side by side, shoulder to shoulder, in an integrated army on Bataan.

During World War I, the white population had angrily asked why black men were not dying at the rate of whites. Now they were questioning why blacks weren't being drafted at the rate of whites.

★

The generals had nothing to draft them into. Whites were drafted by number and blacks were drafted by quota. Although they were 10 percent of the population, their quota was 6 percent of the army. All the black organizations were up to strength. They could not create any more service units without creating more combat units. The answer, over the bitter complaints of the black press, was to form two segregated infantry divisions. This would allow them to draft blacks in proportion to whites. Giving in to both sides in a seemingly democratic gesture, they ordered the reconstitution of the old Ninety-third Infantry Division (Provisional).

Black regular army units—the 9th and 10th Cavalry, the 24th and 25th Infantry, and an assortment of army reserve troops—provided the cadre sent to Fort Huachuca. Half the regular army 25th Infantry, caught in Bataan by the Japanese invasion, was fighting there. With the remainder of the 25th as its core, forming a new 369th, and federalizing the 8th Illinois National Guard as the 368th, they called the 93rd Division to the colors. Gen. C. P. Hall took command.

★

There was no end to the troop trains that pulled into Fort Huachuca in the spring of 1942. Throughout the blistering heat of the days and the soft cool of the nights the trains puffed and wallowed into the sidings, disgorging the men and their baggage. Engines turned around and headed back for more.

They came from the plantations of the Black Belt, from the mines of the Virginias and Alabama and Pennsylvania, from the slums of New York and Chicago, from the hill towns of Kentucky and Tennessee. They came from the sea islands off the Carolinas

and Georgia and from the assembly lines and relief lines of
Detroit and from the blast furnaces of Cleveland and the open
hearths of Gary and the open plains of Texas.

Some came with scars of shackles on their legs and the indel-
ible mark of Parchman's Farm stamped into their eyes. They
came with college degrees and parole papers. They came with
pockets full of loaded dice and fingers supple from shuffling the
deck. Some with jet-black skin and untamed eyes had tense
mouths quick to state that they had no white blood in their veins
and were descended pure from the Original Man.

Drafted, they came grumbling and cursing, dragged from
wife and home. Some came as volunteers. They came damning
America, her Jim Crow and her lynch law. They came cursing
Hitler and the Fascists and eager to do battle for human rights.

Brothers separated for years met in the barracks, hugged and
kissed and cried. One man, seeing a picture of his wife in another
soldier's wallet, calmly picked up an ax handle and hit him in the
face. Bitter enemies from rival policy houses met as long lost
friends. Men from the peonage of Georgia and Alabama and
South Carolina took bunks near one another and talked far into
the night about coon hunting and fishing and the meanness of the
white man.

Some turned their faces and took sips from little bottles. As
night settled a few would slip away to The Hook, the whore town
of tents and tin shacks outside the gate, and lie with one of
the three-hundred women who serviced Fort Huachuca's thirty-
thousand lonesome, isolated soldiers.

19

I LEFT MY barracks bag outside and entered the Orderly
Room of Headquarters Company, 1st Battalion, 369th Infantry.
Knocking politely at the door, I waited until the officer sitting
behind the desk looked up. Snapping to attention, I gave my best
salute.

"Private Peery reporting for duty, sir."

He halfway returned the salute and waddled out of the chair.
The sign on the desk said Major Betha. Soft and paunchy, he
didn't belong in an infantry outfit.

"Glad to see you. We're just forming the regiment. I'm the only officer here and there's only a few other enlisted men in the company. The clerk will show you around. Where is your home, soldier?" The lazily slurred voice was Black Belt South.

"I came from Minnesota, sir. Minneapolis."

"Hummh. I didn't know they had colored people up there. Just wondered. Your voice sounded strange."

I stepped back to get out of there before the cracker said something worse. I thanked him, saluted, and, turning to leave, bumped full body into another officer.

"Beg your pardon, sir, I . . . "

This man was a soldier. Lean and athletic, about twenty-five, his overseas cap with the silver first lieutenant bar sat exactly at the proper angle. His uniform, pressed and clean, clung close and unwrinkled to his body. Hazel eyes studied me carefully.

"Who taught you to take a step back when you salute?"

"I was in the Civilian Military Training Corps, sir."

"My name is Lieutenant Harper. I got mine in the Citadel. What's your name, soldier?"

"Private Nelson Peery, sir."

"Next time, look first." There was the faintest outline of a smile. Harper was also from the South—but what a difference from Betha. I held the door for him; Harper thanked me and went in to report for duty.

Corporal Moore, the company clerk, took me to the barracks. As we were climbing the steps, a twenty-year-old, tall, slender soldier was coming out, his big, wide mouth in an almost perpetual grin.

"Well, hello, White Rabbit."

"Hello, Welby. My name is Mr. Moore. This is Mr. Peery." Welby and I shook hands.

"Back in Memphis, everybody calls me Bunky—Bunk McGee."

The name seemed to fit. I soon found out that he had earned his nickname by telling a series of ridiculous stories of his sexual exploits. Halfway through, someone was bound to say, "That's a lot of bunk!" His easy and complete smile parted his full lips to show a mouthful of big white teeth. The nostrils of his wide, flat nose seemed to extend when he smiled, which was often. His hair was slicked straight back with heavy, sweet-smelling grease. I turned to look at Moore. He did look a bit like a rabbit, with his pointy ears and closely set eyes. His light tan skin completed the picture. The nickname White Rabbit would stick to him for the duration. From Baltimore, with a year of college, Moore married shortly before being drafted. His only goal in the army was to get out soon and in one piece. He accepted the safe and easy job of company clerk as the regiment formed, and kept it until the end of the war.

For a few moments we talked together with the ease of young people pulled away from the warmth and security of family and forced to create the camaraderie of the infantry. Bunk pulled out a picture of himself standing beside a smiling, pretty, dark-skinned young woman who barely came up to his shoulder.

"I call her Little Bit." The smile widened, showing the big white even teeth. He waited for me to comment on the sexual implication. Afraid of saying something offensive, I quoted from a popular song,

> *She calls you her lover*
> *And says you her beggar, too.*

Bunk's smile broke into laughter. "I heard you was from way up North. Where you learn that shit, man?"

"Even Eskimos ask for a little bit."

Moore's grin broke into laughter. I followed him up the stairs. He pointed out my bunk; we shook hands and he left.

★

While I was making my bunk two noncoms came in—one, a first sergeant, the other a corporal. Noticing that I was a new man, they sauntered over to the bunk.

"You must be Peery."

"Yes. Just got in."

"This is Corporal Jackson, acting platoon leader. I'm Sergeant Thompson."

"Glad to know you, Top. Pleased to meet you, Corporal Jackson."

The Top Kick at forty-seven had been in the army thirty-two years. He was an old cavalry soldier from the Ninth at Fort Riley, Kansas. A brown-skinned, handsome five foot ten, Top was hard as a desert stone. He trained recruits the regular army way—beat them down until they either came up fighting or crapped out. He eased up on me when he found out that I soldiered with his old outfit at Fort Riley, Kansas.

Pete Jackson was the type of guy the army prays for—an intelligent, arrogant, beautifully built, physically coordinated, ambitious man. He loved the security of army life and gloried in the petty privileges of a noncom close to the Top Sergeant.

At first, it was almost fun being in the army. I was eighteen and a large number of the incoming recruits were under twenty-five. We younger men became friends quickly and tended to group together in the rough-and-tumble of basic training. We didn't purposely stay away from those "over thirty." We lived a different life. They were too quick to fight and too involved in serious gambling.

The daily convoy from the rail depot to the fort pulled in. I watched from the window as one of the trucks stopped at the Company Headquarters and another group of men unloaded. Assigned to different platoons, they made for the corresponding barracks. The first guy up the stairs was about thirty-six but looked older. His long, puffy brown face was frozen in a hangdog expression. Huge bulging eyes, reddened by years of whiskey, looked scornfully around the barracks.

Jeff, from Chicago, who had gotten in that morning, looked up from his bunk and started laughing.

"Goddamn, if it ain't Juicy Jones."

"So they got you, too."

"Yeah. How the hell you pass the medical exam?"

"One a'them fuckin' doctors put a flashlight in my ear and this other motherfucker looked in the other ear and said he didn't see no light—so here I am."

When the laughter died down, I asked Jeff, "Where'd he get that name?"

"Well, he was one of the biggest bootleggers in Chicago till he drank hisself out of business."

Juicy mumbled something about "kiss my ass" and stretched out on the bunk.

I glanced over at him. He must have been a handsome young man—tall and straight. His oval face still expressed something gentle, and behind the redness of his eyes there still shone an intelligence and quickness of mind. Juicy was an indictment of America. Like so many bright black men, he could express his sharp mind only in the underworld. An intelligence the country wouldn't use was slowly being destroyed by whiskey.

Juicy let everyone from the company commander on down

know that he hated the army, hated America, and didn't like anyone who disagreed with him. We were always friends, but when he found out that I volunteered he looked at me with amazed disgust.

"You stupid little sonofabitch . . . " And that was his title for me from then on.

Lee came in with a group of recruits from South Carolina. Overseas cap sitting crossways on his head, he carried one bag and dragged the other up the stairs. Nineteen and drafted from one of the Sea Islands, Lee was short, thin, and very dark-skinned. His round head seemed too big for his body. If ever the term "Geechie" fit a person, it was Lee. He walked down the aisle looking for an empty bunk. Finding none, he turned to the men, straightened his shoulders, and said in his best Sea Island English, "One of you Southern boys get up and let the General have a bunk."

He looked like a playful pup with twinkling eyes and a devilish grin. Few would ever take Lee seriously. He would provoke howls of laughter saying things that would get anyone else knocked down.

We became immediate and fast friends. He knew that behind the silly grin and the banal vulgarity, I saw the sharp and inquisitive mind.

A new recruit, short, stocky, dark-skinned, his hair plastered down with Murrays and a half smile lurking at the corners of his full mouth, entered the barracks. He carried a trumpet case in addition to his army gear. Harold, a natural and talented entertainer, played with a band in Houston. He looked like a good-timing East Texan. He could make up songs at the drop of a hat and tap-dance in combat boots. Equally at home with the trumpet, guitar, or piano, Harold quickly became a favorite of everyone.

Hewitt came quietly into the barracks. He looked at and spoke to no one. The self-sufficient haughtiness marked him a West Indian. Small, black-skinned, with piercing eyes, Hewitt spoke with a calm, modulated British accent, carefully enunciating every syllable. He had a talent for starting arguments. He never lost his temper. Arguing in an angry, icy voice, he made everyone else lose theirs. Hewitt was a brilliant part-time student at Columbia. A militant Pan-Africanist, he quickly became the abrasive intellectual leader of our group of young soldiers.

Joe took the bunk across the aisle from me. Joe was twenty-four and from Memphis. A husky five foot eight, he seldom raised his voice and never swore. His father was a minister and Joe a devout Christian. After a few days of exchanging friendly greetings and small talk, Joe called me aside.

"I noticed the book and the dictionary on your shelf. Were you a teacher?"

"Heck no, Joe. I just got out of high school last month."

"When I was in basic training I started a class with some of the men who wanted to learn to read and write. Two or three men in the company want to start another class. Will you help me?"

Of course, I would help. I sent a letter off to Central High asking for the necessary books. They were sent immediately. The after-hours class was one of the most rewarding experiences of my life. Early on, Joe and I were given the affectionate respect of the men in the company. Soon the whole battalion knew and had a special "Hey, man" greeting for the two teachers trying to uplift their race.

★

They say a healthy army gripes. We griped about the chow, the heat, the dust, the water, and the things that made the army the army. Most of all, we griped about the white supremacist attitude of most of the white officers.

The War Department, dominated by the Southern elite and Northern reactionaries, followed the old discredited line that the segregated Negro outfits functioned best if staffed by Southern officers, because "they understood the Negro." Most of these officers were reservists. Many were Klansmen. Some of them tried to treat the regiment as if it were their antebellum plantation. They expressed their belief in white supremacy with body language and tone of voice. The worst expression was their slave term, "boy."

Sometimes, the officer would catch himself and change the "boy" to "soldier." Most of the time when the braver of the soldiers would carefully say, "Sir, my name is Private Johnson," the officer would glare at the insolence, realize he was wrong, turn on his heel, and walk away.

Everyone could see trouble coming. After a few minor incidents, I talked to our little group individually. We held a small meeting to see what could be done. We decided to talk to Chaplain Watkins. I didn't like the idea because it exposed us too much. The majority was for it. Hewitt was to be the spokesman.

Chaplain Watkins said he would be happy to talk to us. After the introductions, Hewitt carefully explained why we had come. The chaplain sat looking at his hands. I knew that he had heard the story a hundred times that month. Finally, Hewitt summed it all up: "Sir, what are we fighting for if we can't get elementary human dignity here?"

Chaplain Watkins looked at us individually and breathed deeply. "Of course, I'll keep everything you've said in confidence. You ask me what we are fighting for? I guess it's that chicken and rice. God knows, you have very little else."

There was nothing more to say. When the chaplain got demoralized it was time for some action. We looked at one another, thanked him, and left.

"I guess we'll have to take matters in our own hands," Hewitt said.

"I can't take matters in my hand," Lee said, extending an outstretched palm, "but I can take a rifle."

"Naw," I said. "We can't do that. Not yet, anyway. We have to wait until something happens, something to make all the men mad. Then we can do something."

"We'd better have our shit together, some sort of plan," Bunk said.

"Let's talk about it tomorrow," Joe said. "But be quiet in the barracks. I hear they already got some squealers in the company."

We all agreed and split up as we neared the company area. The next day we assembled to exchange our World War I rifles for the new semiautomatic Garand M1. We formed a loose semicircle in front of Major Betha to learn the nomenclature and care of the rifle. The men sat with their pith helmets back from their foreheads, chins in their cupped hands, staring into the dirt before them, half hearing the lecture.

"Now, this here little doodad is called the seer." Betha was clearly irritated by the lack of attention. Holding the seer up, he said, "Now, what is this called?" He glanced over the group and pointed to one of the men. "You. You, black boy . . . "

Electricity shot through the group. Heads flew up. Betha mumbled something but was unable to cover it up. Jeff got to his feet in a boxer's stance. His eyes narrowed.

"Major, sir. You know Goddamned well there ain't no boys in the army . . . "

Everyone was shouting at once and then began to chant: "Apologize! Apologize!"

Betha tried to call the company to attention and then turned to the First Sergeant. Top rose to his feet, saluted, and about-faced with a spin on one heel: "Ten—hut!"

We quieted down; some of the men began to form ranks.

"Sergeant, dismiss the company."

"Com—pany, dismissed."

We headed for our barracks. We knew this was it.

"If this peckerwood gets away with this, there ain't no tellin' where it gonna stop," Jeff said.

"Shit," somebody mumbled. "Let's write Mrs. Roosevelt."

"That ain't gonna help anything today." I looked around at the agitated soldiers. "Let's strike."

"Yes, Goddamnit," Bunk said. "Let's strike!"

"How the hell you gonna strike against the army?" asked Corporal Jackson. "We'll all get court-martialed."

"Let 'em do it," Lee said. "We's in prison now—ya just cain't see the fence."

"We can do it if we stick," I said.

"OK, gentlemens, here the lick," Jeff said, making the decision. "Nobody answers any formation until that peck apologizes. They ain't got no legal case. What's more, they can't stand this kind of publicity. There ain't nothin' gonna happen if we stick together."

There was much talking as we entered our respective barracks, each man trying to put forth his idea or opinion. Moore stood on one of the bunks and shouted for the men to shut up.

"Now listen, men, we got to get some kind of plan if we gonna do anything. Let's elect somebody from each floor of each barrack to see that not a living ass falls out for dinner or for any formation after dinner."

"Jeff and Nels take Headquarters."

"Harold and Juicy take Pioneer."

"Hewitt and Lee take Anti-Tank."

"Joe and Bunk take Service and Supply."

There was a tremendous enthusiasm as each team left for their platoon barracks. The men flopped on their bunks waiting for battle.

Harold blew mess call. Even under tension he put a beautiful quality into the bugle sound. Jeff and I stood beside the steps. The men were eyeing one another to see who would be the first crab to pull away. No one moved from his cot.

Within a few minutes Lieutenant Harper entered the barracks.

"Ten—shun," Moore shouted. We knew we must not break military discipline. We stood at an exaggerated, rigid attention. Lieutenant Harper walked the length of the barrack, his hazel eyes glancing over each individual, summing up his temperament.

"At ease, men," he said in a deliberately quiet attempt to calm and disarm us. Hands were clasped behind backs and feet were separated in a formal at ease.

"I know that most of you men have been in the army only a few months, some of you a few weeks. What you are doing is mutiny, and in time of war it is punishable by death. I'm not talking to you as an officer to enlisted men, but as man to man. I don't think Major Betha realized or meant what he said. He is willing to apologize to Private Gaston. The rest of you men must fall out for mess and for all other formations."

Turning smartly on his heel, he walked the length of the barrack. There was absolute silence save for the clack of his boots on the wooden floor and the heavy breathing of the men.

"Lieutenant, sir." Hewitt stepped from beside his cot. "Sir, I'm sure the Lieutenant realizes that Major Betha's remark insulted the entire company. I believe that the entire company deserves an apology."

Lieutenant Harper glared at Hewitt, his eyes cold, emotionless steel. Hewitt returned the glare without anger, but without fear. There could be no backing down now.

Harper shifted his eyes from Hewitt to glance around the barrack.

"Rest. As you were." He returned Moore's salute and left the barrack.

Hands reached out to congratulate Hewitt, to slap his back and shake his hand.

"Good goin', fella!"

"Goddamn. Get him, Hew." Lee was giggling, "You all see that? Toe to Goddamn toe, eyeball to fuckin' eyeball. Do it, Hew!"

"Aap, Goddamnit, come 'ere." Sergeant Thompson entered the barrack. "Goddamnit, gentlemens, I'm all for this thing, but Goddamn it, you all done put me on the spot. The major told me to order you all out to the company area. There's gonna be some talkin' done down there. Now fall out. That's a direct order."

We trusted the Top Kick. He was all army, but he never forgot what he was.

"Look, men," Moore said. "We'd better make this formation. They've already give in a little. If they don't come across with the straight shit, we come back in."

The tiny concession had strengthened determination. Sensing the possibility of victory, the men became more militant, and worse, more sullen.

The men fell into squads. Squads became platoons. Platoons became the company.

"Dress right. Dress!"

"In a little, Bunk. Out a bit, Joe. Steady, Front!"

Eyes focused on Lieutenant Harper. Top about-faced, saluted, and awaited orders.

"Have the company report."

"Report!"

"First Platoon present. Second Platoon present or accounted for. Third Platoon present."

"The company is present or accounted for, sir."

"Give the men at ease."

"Company!" We clicked to parade rest. "At ease."

Hands behind backs, feet separated, we tensely stood at ease.

"Men," Lieutenant Harper spoke with the clipped sharp words befitting a fifth generation of professional soldiers. "I called this formation to extend to the company the apologies of Major Betha. I also want to warn you that the commanding officer will not tolerate this strike to go on any longer. Sergeant Thompson, call the company to attention."

"Compan—ay, Ten—hut!"

Salutes exchanged, Lieutenant Harper walked away toward the Orderly Room.

"At ease, men," Top said softly. "I've been in the army thirty-two years and I've never seen this done before. Let this be the end of it—there ain't no hard feeling on either side. Now get your mess kits and fall out for chow."

We knew we had won a terrific victory as incomplete as it was. A bunch of Goddamned recruits defied the Jim Crow army and won.

20

No LONGER A conglomeration of men, we were soldiers in a military organization. Our uneasy truce with the Southern white officers held together through strict adherence to the Articles of War. We sensed the growth of our consciousness, unity, and strength. We wouldn't give an inch toward their cherished illusion of the "good old darky of the South." They made us pay. We used army regulations as protection. They used the regulations against us. We walked at 104 paces per minute in prescribed and complete uniforms. Clothing was immaculate, shoes shined, rifles and equipment shone like new money. That was all for the good. It was easier to believe that we were fighting men, worthy of respect, when we looked and acted like it.

Major Betha transferred out. Harper, promoted to captain, took command of the company. Lt. Arnett Hartsfield, commissioned from the ROTC at UCLA, was the first Negro officer to join the company. (In 1940 Col. Benjamin O. Davis and his son, Lt. Benjamin O. Davis, Jr., were the only black officers in the army except for three black chaplains.) The only black ROTC man at the university, Hartsfield had expected but did not get any credit for that. Son of a comfortably well-off family in Los Angeles, he had been a law student. The thin, sensitive face of this slender, athletic young man reflected a cultured, intellectual background. He came into the company with a complete gung ho attitude. The aloofness of the white officers soon crushed that. We enlisted men understood. We soldiered for him, making him look good in front of the commanding officers.

As we went into a rigid relationship with the officers, we settled into an easy but structured relationship with one another. The society of the company began to form. The gambling men grouped together. They made and enforced rules for debt payment and conduct of the games. The drinking men began to hang out together. Our little group, based on an elementary social consciousness, had a small but definite intellectual striving. Most of us, recently out of high school, read and passed around books. We wrote letters for the illiterates and taught our school.

We were a company. There was interaction among all. Juicy and Lee were the polarities. Juicy would drink quietly, reserving for himself the right to be miserable without disturbing the rest of

the men. Lee would take one drink, and under the guise of being
drunk, completely upset the evening's routine in the barrack.

When Juicy did talk, he would hold court on how Jim Crow
America had thwarted his every honest effort. There was enough
truth in it for him to excuse his alcoholism. He saw the frustrations of the Negro people as simply an enlargement of his own.
He knew better, and it forced him to drink more.

Lee would mimic and, jesterlike, end up poking fun at him.

Juicy's grumbling and Lee's harassment began with the
morning first call. After reveille, Jackson snapped on the lights.
In various stages of awakening, the men swung their legs out
from the covers, lit up the smokes, and tried to rub the sleep from
their eyes.

Juicy followed his own routine. Sitting up in bed, taking a swig
from his bottle, he started a morning soliloquy:

> *A chicken ain't nothin' but a bird,*
> *A hunkie ain't nothin' but a turd,*
> *And us niggers ain't shit.*

The next pull at the bottle woke him a little more. His huge,
menacing, protruding eyes glared around the barrack in search of
disagreement. Seeing none and reflecting on his statement, he'd
mumble, "Shit."

Lee walked over to his bunk. "What you mean we ain't shit?
Joe Lewis is heavyweight champion of the world, John Henry
Lewis is light heavyweight champ, Henry Armstrong got all the
other titles, and Father Divine's God." Lee turned toward the
men. "Tell him what I said."

Laughter drowned out his reply. Juicy gave up and stretched
out on the bunk mumbling, "I wish your mammy hada' crossed
her legs and bust your Goddamn neck on the way out."

★

A few more men joined the platoon. As soon as Parker walked
into the barrack, we knew this was a guy you didn't fool with. His
jaw protruding with a wad of chewing tobacco, he gave off an air
of belligerence. His eyes seemed to constantly glare behind the
steel-rimmed glasses fitting tightly against his face. His first act
was to open the barrack's window and spit out the cud of tobacco.
He looked around with a you-want-to-make-something-out-of-it

glare. A husky five foot ten, from rural Alabama, Parker was what the Southern whites called a "crazy nigger." He let them all know that he didn't mind dying and would take some of them to hell with him. He finally stood up and said, "My name's Parker." After the introductions had been made and the talking began, we realized that Parker was an OK guy. He just didn't joke around with anyone and didn't want to be joked with.

Joe Harrison joined us from Company C. Six foot two, he became regimental boxing champ. He wasn't a boxer. He was just big and strong. The first day in the barrack he had us howling with laughter with his exhibition of how to knock down a mule. We knew he had done it. Joe, from rural Georgia, was a gentle and thoroughly likable person. An easy smile accompanied his greeting, "Everything is lovely." We gave him the name "Big Joe" to distinguish him from our other Joe.

Lonnie Vaughn came in to be a driver for the message center. Smiling almost constantly, quiet and religious, he melted into the company. He never got into an argument and seldom swore or drank. Sometimes we called him "Snake Eyes" because his green eyes contrasted with his brown skin. He was one of those soldiers whose calm and efficient work made the army function.

The company completed its complement with two black officers and one white officer. Lieutenant Christmas, formerly the dean of men at the segregated Alcorn College of Mississippi, was a soft-spoken, nervous, brilliant administrator. He could flawlessly type as fast as a person could speak.

Lt. Joel A. Powell had just graduated from the Officer's Training School at Fort Benning. Those of us who knew him as a line sergeant in the Twenty-fifth used to called him "Jap." If no one else was near, he'd still call us "motherfucker" and grin.

The white officer, a graduate of the Citadel, was from Jackson, Mississippi. He entered the orderly room with his shirttail almost out, pulling up and adjusting his pants around a body without sufficient curves to hold them in place. This disheveled officer spoke the worst English I have ever heard.

Corporal Moore and I stood up as he entered.

"Corporal Moore, company clerk, sir," Moore reported.

"Company commander here?" Half returning the salute, he set his bag on the floor. I glanced at the stenciled "Lt. Jack Akeley." As I raised my eyes I knew he was looking at me.

"Wanta know how to pronounce it?"

"Well. Ah—yes, sir."

"It's Akeley—Ah-killy."

I suppressed the grin.

"Glad to know you, sir."

Moore and I glanced at each other in surprise as he stuck out his hand. The embarrassment of the handshake over, Moore informed him that Captain Harper was gone.

"Well, never you mind. You all see to it that my bag get over to the officers' quarters." He turned and left the room.

Moore just shook his head. Strange cat. Mississippi cracker. Shake hands with you like an equal and then tell you to take care of his clothing. Oh, well . . .

Despite his being from Mississippi, we liked Akeley better than the other white officers. He had the same easygoing smile for the black enlisted men as he had for his fellow Southern whites. He butchered the King's English and didn't care. He never said "ate." The word was "et" for present, past, and future. In the security of the barrack we called him "Lt. Mush Mouth."

Akeley became the operations officer of the battalion. A regimental order promoted me to staff sergeant, and because of my CMTC training, Akeley assigned me as his assistant.

Akeley managed to call me "boy" every day. He said it in such a way that I could never tell if he meant part of the team or immature servant. His morning greeting was, "Well, now. Good morning, Sergeant. How's the boy?" I made a point of pretending that I didn't hear him speaking. Repeating himself, he would always drop the "boy."

We received one more soldier into our company.

Barrack bag over his shoulder, personal possessions under his arm, this last newcomer walked into the barrack after we stood retreat. Half smiling, nodding to whoever looked his way, he stopped at the empty bunk across the aisle from me. His bag, stamped with his serial number, showed he was from Co B, 369th Inf.

"From a rife company, huh?"

"Yeah, it's a damned good place to be from and stay from."

"My name is Nels. This is Juicy, Lee, Jeff . . . "

Speaking and nodding to all, he grinned and said, "My name's Bradley."

Brad was twenty-four and from Marshall, Texas. He had

eighteen brothers and one sister. He showed it by being completely at ease in the constant shuffling, talking, and gambling of
the barracks.

Their farm could barely provide for them. Brad left home and
worked in the fields until drafted. A husky five foot ten, he had a
sharp face that showed an Indian ancestor. The brown skin
stretched tight over his high cheekbones, giving a severity and
seriousness to his face. Not so with his large, soft, fawnlike eyes.
The whites were clear and the hazel pupils contrasted with the
coloring of his skin. I found separate sides of his personality
reflected in his face and eyes. Speaking softly with a Texas twang
instead of the more familiar Southern drawl, he quickly integrated himself into our group. An easy guy to like, he built a
friendly relationship with everyone.

Our basic training ended. So did many of the romances and a
few of the marriages. I had felt so secure, but I was soon drawn
into the common set of circumstances. The daily, loving little one-
page notes from Heidi became twice-a-week letters and then one
a week. Almost imperceptibly the tone of her letters changed from
passionate, to warm, then friendly, and finally cool. When I
received the final letter, I didn't have to open it to know it was the
end. There were no good-byes or recriminations. The stiffness
and formality said it was over. For the first time I began to notice
what so many of the men were going through. Some never mentioned it when the letters stopped. I watched them withdraw to
the bottle and the solitary comfort of staring at the floor after
lights out. Some, like Juicy, covered their hurt with jokes. He took
the floor, bloodshot eyes protruding more than ever, waving his
Dear John letter like a trophy.

"Would you listen to what this here motherfucker done told
me? She done put me down! Listen to this—'Those little things
you been sending to me are no longer necessary. I can't use you no
more. I still wish you good luck and God bless you.'"

"What else she say?"

"That's all she wrote."

Bradley got his letter from Ruth. He read it over and over, and
as the message finally sunk in he smiled and said, "I hope she fall
through her ass and breaks her Goddamn neck."

He never mentioned her again.

Joe got his letter. He kept to himself for several days and then made detailed excuses for her breaking it off. Each night as he knelt beside his bunk he included her in his prayers as he always had.

Hewitt broke off with his girlfriend. "She is simply too light-skinned."

Bunk was frank and honest. He handed me his letter, saying, "When I read this letter, my heart took sorrow and the tears come fallin' down."

We were all just a bit envious of Lee, who every night put the picture of his fat little wife on the clipboard and scribbled out a love letter from Huachuca, "Mountains of the Wind."

The breakups were affecting morale throughout the army. Finally, Congress passed a law making it illegal to divorce a soldier.

The vast majority of the men had close-knit, stable relationships. Those of us who didn't had no other arms to run to. Hurt and bitter, we had absolutely nothing we could do about it. We were in the all-powerful army. Army gave a damn about a broken heart. Army said, "Goddamnit, soldier, straighten up. Get on the ball. You got to soldier for the man. Snap to."

With the rest of them, I wallowed in my misery, missing her lips and the yielding firmness of her body. In the loneliness of Huachuca, I'd daydream of her, giving her qualities she never had, qualities I'd always wanted in a sweetheart. Then I would hate her for taking them from me. Unthinking, I began to slip into the "whore this" and "bitch that" talk of some of the men.

One evening just after taps I made some particularly vulgar remark. Jeff waited until I was pulling off my shoes to say, "You one of the better-educated men in the company."

"Yeah, I guess so, Jeff . . . "

"You supposed to be pullin' the rest of the men up, not lettin' them pull you down."

I knew what was coming.

"I see you write your mama every week. You love your ma?"

"Sure. What's that got to do . . . ?"

"Just remember she's a woman." Jeff turned away and pulled the covers over himself. I had known better. Playing tough guy looked foolish. It was the last time I ever made such remarks.

★

As ties to home and lovers weakened and broke, the soldiers turned to one another. The intense attachment of buddies, especially in the infantry, was an emotion they would never again experience. It would remain throughout their lives testimony to their capacity to love selflessly. Never again would they so completely bare the heights of their idealism or the depths of their despair. They would never find another person with whom to be so honest and so selfless. They would never again feel that those deepest and most damning secrets are secure in another's hands. The buddy becomes father, brother, drinking companion, banker, untiring confidant to all the hurts and hopes and fears. Buddy gets the last nickel. Buddy gets the last cigarette. Buddy becomes wise by giving quiet advice, brave by hiding his cowardice, and more of a man by confidently giving that dignified special kind of love that exists between men of combat. They were unable to understand the love they felt for another man, and the most endearing term that passed between them was "you son of a bitch."

★

After settling into the platoon, Brad and I spent a lot of time talking about our backgrounds and hopes and dreams. We were drawn together by a hatred for and a desire to do something about our second-class citizenship. We agreed that Hitler was the main enemy and had to be fought. We also agreed that we weren't going to knuckle down. We would fight fascism where we found it and we knew it was closer than Germany or Japan. Barely having finished a segregated Texas high school, Brad was political. He quickly grasped my shallow idea of a socialist America, run by and for the workers, without competition for jobs. As did most Negroes, we saw that competition as the basis of discrimination. We had a common experience on the open road and in our work as migrant laborers. He had been what we hoboes called a "rubber bum." We felt a bit superior to them. With their cars chained around their necks, they had little left over for themselves. We 'boes rode the side-door Pullmans, secure in the knowledge that we would get where we were going and save the fare to boot.

The friendship that developed between us grew and deepened throughout the war. Brad was my buddy.

★

The total segregation of the all-black fort shielded us from the violence that the black soldier faced everywhere, especially in the South. Enveloped by the "Mountains of the Wind," isolated in the vast wilderness of the high desert, we soldiers of Huachuca lived beyond the reach of sheriffs and night riders. Our relative safety only increased our anger and frustration as we received news of mistreatment of the black troops and civilians.

The black newspapers, in a minimal way, kept us informed. We infantrymen did not trust them. We knew that their strategy to gain equality for the black people (and leadership for themselves) was having the black soldier make greater sacrifices and show more patriotism than the whites. Before we were through basic training, they set up a howl to commit us to combat. We hated the black newspapers for their constant appeals to the government to send us into action.

The spontaneous transfer of information by the soldiers themselves was much more dramatic and reliable. Eighteen thousand threads of information daily entered the fort as letters from friends and relatives, from servicemen and local papers. The commanders, fully aware of the inevitable outcome, were incapable of stopping them. The rumor mill ground on day and night. The rumors were seldom as bad as the realities. America was telling us that just because we were going to have to fight and perhaps die for the country, we better remember our place—in uniform or out.

★

As the weeks ground on, we found more and more to fight against, less and less to fight for. The "B Squad" movement rose spontaneously in the rifle companies. When two men from the 369th met, one would shout, "What's your outfit, soldier?" and the other would answer, "B Squad: Be here when they go over, and be here if they get back."

21

THE MORE THE government spoke of democratic war aims, the greater became the Fascist terror against the blacks. The cops in Alexandria, Louisiana, shot down twelve black soldiers. The sadistic lynching of Cleo Wright in Sikeston, Missouri, was a carnival of horror. After the torture and burning was over, scores of cars filled with white men, women, and children dragged the broken body of the black youth through his neighborhood. They stopped a few times to challenge the blacks to fight. With their men bottled up in Fort Huachuca, there was no response from the women and children.

The sullen demoralization of the soldiers ripened toward violence. Army G-2—military intelligence, something akin to a military FBI—fearing the explosion, warned the black newspapers that they would draft their personnel if they became inflammatory. If necessary they would (and on occasion they did) confiscate their papers. When the small local press, the *Southwest Georgian,* exposed a lynching in Newton, Georgia, in 1943, the editor was immediately drafted and his paper folded. Half the staff of the militant *California Eagle* was drafted. Finally, the G-2 warned that although the seizure of individual issues of papers was permissible, banning the black press would "only serve to supply ammunition for agitation to colored papers." The issue of freedom of the press wasn't even involved. The black press's response was to militantly declare its patriotism.

Shaken by the low morale of the Negro people for the war, *Time* magazine ran a special edition exposing the wretched, segregated conditions of the Negro soldier. Its aim was to force the government to do something about it. The Negro press attacked *Time,* stating that such information would make slackers out of the Negro soldier.

Most of us understood that Hitler was worse than Senator Bilbo or Rankin or Talmadge or Thurmond. We understood that his concentration camps were worse than the chain gangs and prison farms. The historical base of our consciousness was firmer than this understanding. The chain gang and lynch mob preceded Hitler and would be here after he was gone. There was no room for illusions. Somewhere along the line we would have to fight it out here.

The battle began at Gurdon, Arkansas. The black Ninety-forth Engineer Battalion from Fort Custer, Michigan, was on maneuvers. A few isolated fights between the troops and the police and MPs escalated to an attack by police and the town's mob against the unarmed soldiers. Northern white officers were beaten and called "nigger lovers" while the MPs stood by. The unarmed black troops scattered into the woods. Some of them caught freight trains back to Michigan, where the Army court-martialed them for desertion. We began to secure and hide ammunition.

When the United States entered World War I, the economy was almost at full employment for white workers. The rapid expansion of war production created an immediate and severe labor shortage. The employers sent agents into the black labor reserve of the South. They pulled millions of sharecroppers and service workers into well-paying jobs in the factories at the very beginning of the war. That war had something in it for everyone.

World War II began during the Depression. Millions of unemployed white workers had preference in hiring. In the spring of 1942, blacks constituted fewer than 3 percent of the war workers. The labor shortage began late in the year. Then the doors opened a crack to the black workers. The head of the Brotherhood of Sleeping Car Porters, A. Philip Randolph, organized the march on Washington to force a fair employment policy in the war against fascism. The government had no intention of giving in until Secretary of War Stimson, an open white supremacist, convinced Roosevelt that Randolph's real aim was to prevent the Communists from taking over the civil rights movement. Mark Eldridge, appointed chair of the Fair Employment Practices Committee (FEPC), immediately went on a speaking tour that spring to assure whites they had nothing to fear from the FEPC. He received a standing ovation from a Southern white audience when he stated, " . . . not even all the mechanized armies of the earth, Allied and Axis . . . could force the Southern white people to abandonment of the principle of social segregation."

By February 1942 the war was in full swing. The whites of Detroit rioted and attacked blacks moving into a federal housing project at the edge of "their" community. Thirty-five thousand white workers laid down their tools and walked out of the huge Douglas Aircraft plant when one black was hired. In the summer of 1942, poll takers in Harlem found that only 11 percent of the blacks believed they would be better off after the war.

The Marine Corps had never admitted blacks. The navy stopped accepting them between 1919 and 1930. In 1930 they accepted a few mess men. After World War I, the army had practically stopped recruiting blacks. Congress, under political pressure, developed a quota system and put a lid on the size of the army. The Negro-hating generals got around congressional intent. While keeping the names "infantry," "cavalry," and "artillery," most of the black combat outfits became labor and service organizations. On paper, each black combat soldier became two soldiers, one combat (on paper) and one labor (actually). The trick cut the black slots in half and assigned the other half to the recruitment of whites. The generals were then able to form a lily-white Tank and Air Corps.

Self-appointed black leaders, and those appointed by the white political structure, appeared as if by magic. They began maneuvering to take control of the simmering movement of the working-class black. Forced to fight Hitler, the working-class black deeply believed the fight should start here and now. The army held the greatest concentration of blacks, and the Ninety-third was the pawn to be fought over.

★

The Ninety-third Division plus the post complement numbered close to twenty-five thousand men at Fort Huachuca. The commanders realized the danger of keeping that number of men bottled up in the desert without decent recreation and almost completely cut off from social contact with women. The United Service Organization (USO) never stopped at Huachuca. The commanding generals trembled at the thought of white women dancing and singing before black troops. The USO directors didn't want it to happen, and we didn't expect it.

In June 1942 our pay went from twenty-one to fifty dollars a month. Suddenly we had money to spend and nothing to spend it on. The tension increased.

Fry, the tent and tar paper town near the gate to the fort, became the scene of unending fights as the soldiers turned more and more to the whores and the bootleg whiskey. A few rough bars with names like Yazoo City and Selma Beer Garden sprang up. They made matters worse.

We nicknamed Fry "The Hook." Anyone who went there was going to get caught by something—the clap, a knife blade, or, if he was lucky, a tough black fist. The army built a huge recreation center we called the Green Top. With its hundred-yard-long bar, it was to be an alternative to The Hook. The latest easy-riding blues jelly-rolled from the jukeboxes. Neat young black barmaids imported from Texas and Louisiana served five-cent beer. Everyone flirted with them, and though they were not allowed to dance with the soldiers, for three dollars they would slip away or make an after-hours date.

There was no directive against going to Tucson, Bisbee, or

Nogales. Phoenix was off-limits. The black 364th Infantry regiment, ordered to Phoenix from Hawaii, resisted the segregation and police brutality. A hundred of them took up arms and fought it out with the MPs and cops. They killed one officer, one white enlisted man, and a white civilian before being overwhelmed.

Getting out of the fort was almost impossible. As the tension neared the flash point, the decision was made to provide army trucks for transportation.

Trouble began the first weekend. A convoy from the 368th went to Bisbee. A restaurant owner told a soldier, "We don't serve niggers." The soldier knocked him out and his pals trashed the place. In the ensuing melee a black soldier was shot by the cops. The soldiers tried to set the town on fire and retreated toward their trucks. The city cops and military police from the Eighth Air Force surrounded them. The soldiers were savagely beaten and some received long prison sentences. The generals declared Bisbee off-limits. The merchants lost a million dollars in trade and the soldiers lost a place to relax. The convoys were still going to Tucson and Nogales. Our little group in the platoon decided it was better to go to Mexico, even though it was farther away.

★

The convoy bounced over the dusty secondary roads for three hours before it reached the border. Without stopping at any of the bars in the newer section of town, the convoy drove straight to "Ranchita," the old walled city. Ranchita had always been the hangout for black soldiers. White soldiers from the Eighth Air Force went to the newer section of town. No one challenged the segregation and it became entrenched.

Ranchita was wall-to-wall prostitution, gambling, and games. Brad, Bunk, Lee, and I went from bar to bar drinking Modelo and Dos Equis. We played soccer with the kids, who were all over the place. Wearing huge mariachis, we had our pictures taken sitting on painted burros. As the afternoon darkened into evening we grew weary of Ranchita and decided to see the rest of the town.

Inside Ranchita, black MPs patrolled with the Mexican Policía. Outside the walls the Policía patrolled with white MPs. We stepped outside the walled area and started walking up one of the main streets. Before we had gone two blocks a patrol approached us. The white MP pulled his club from its holster,

Brad slid his right hand into his pocket, Bunk moved to the left, Lee to the right so the MP couldn't cover us all at once.

"Where you all boys goin'?"

We ignored the "boys" stuff

"Lookin' around," Brad said, glaring at the MP.

"You all ought to stay in your own part and there won't be no trouble." The MP knew that he was the one in trouble.

I translated a sentence in my head, hating that I hadn't learned Spanish in school.

"Señor, quieremos ir allí. OK?" I said, waving my arm to the south and east.

El policía grinned and said, "All this is Mexico. You go where you want as long as you obey Mexican law. No fighting and no bothering the girls."

"Thank you. We just want to look around."

He glanced at the MP and back to me. "I'm glad to see you are learning Spanish."

"I have Mexican friends. They tried to teach me." I knew that went over.

★

Buying trinkets and exchanging glares with the Eighth Air Force men, we wandered for an hour through the town. Tired and broke, we returned to Ranchita and the first convoy back to Huachuca. A group of soldiers were milling about near the convoy. The four of us went over to see what was happening.

Two soldiers from the 368th were standing in the middle of the crowd talking excitedly. They had been in a hell of a fight. Both were bloody. One of the soldiers had a nasty gash above his eye. He gazed at the crowd with a who-is-with-me? look in his eyes.

"We might have to take it in Mississippi, but we ain't got to take it in Mexico. I'm getting me a equalizer an goin' back there." He looked slowly over the crowd and said in a low, deliberate voice, each word standing separately, "I'm ready to die like a man before I'll live like their fuckin' dog. Who's goin' with me?"

I turned to one of the soldiers.

"What the hell happened?"

"Looks like they went into town and went to a bar to get a drink and a gang of white soldiers jumped 'em. The Mexican police got 'em out and brung 'em here so the white MPs don't get 'em."

The soldier with the gash above his eye continued to look over the crowd, pausing to stare into each set of eyes until there was a nod of agreement or the mumbled "I'm in."

Thirty soldiers were ready to fight.

"Where we gonna get the iron?" a soldier asked.

"Ah'm ready to get it on. What's the plan?" another asked.

There was a moment of awkward silence. There were no guns, no plan, no leader, only a mission. Brad glanced at Lee and Bunk and then at me, securing our agreement that he should speak on our behalf.

"Look, men. You all been in this fight long enough to know that we got to have a plan. We got to get organized. Them crackers are waiting for you. They figure you're coming back. They got their MPs ready and right now it's about twenty of them for each one of us. We ain't gonna get but one crack at it. What say we do it right?"

"He's right, men," the bloodied soldier said.

"How we gonna do it?" another asked.

"First thing, we got to break up this crowd before the MPs come or some handkerchief head gets wind of what we're doin'. Me an' my buddies here are from the 369th. A couple of guys from the 368th and the 25th meet us over at the gate. We're infantry. There's eighteen thousand of us. We can take care of them sissy-ass air force crackers."

At the gate we agreed to think things over and meet up at the Long Bar on Monday after supper. There we could organize and work out some plan of action. We started back to the fort, full of exhilarating whispers and youthful bragging about how we were going to whip some ass next time. The laughter subsided and some of the men drifted off to sleep.

It was time for introspection. I knew that I was being drawn further down the road to rebellion, a road from which there is no turning aside and no return. If we were going to fight, it had to be offensive, not defensive. If these white soldiers got the slightest hint that we were afraid—. I thought back to the roots of those ideas.

★

The night of New Year's Eve, 1934, was unusually warm for Wabasha. A light, powdery snow began to fall about eight o'clock when the party began. By ten, the light powder had covered the packed snow and ice already on the ground. It made walking slippery and slow going.

Pop's New Year's party was in full swing. Mr. and Mrs. Mason, the Riesters, the Stroots, and the Barens family were all there. I turned eleven that year. The grown-ups were spiking punch with illegal whiskey and telling jokes. I showed off my birthday gift to their kids. Pop's railway mail clerk job was steady and we were better off than most of our neighbors. I had gotten an elegant gift. My new .22-caliber rifle was the finest gift any country boy could receive. Mom gave me a stern look. She didn't like guns and she didn't like whiskey. I could tell she was upset now that both of them were present. I put my gun away.

"Say, Laddie Buck." Pop always called me that when he was drinking. "Take this fifteen cents, go to the store, and tell Mamie to give you a pack of Chesterfields."

The store was just next door, but Mom told my older brother to go with me. It was late and New Year's Eve, with everybody drinking and carousing around. She was on edge.

We ran out of the door, across the yard, and into the store.

"Happy New Year, boys." Mamie was always good to us. Sometimes, if her husband wasn't watching, she would slip us a little piece of candy.

Then we saw Art. He lived on the other side of town but would come to Mamie's to get moonshine and beer. Two days before, as he staggered half-drunk down the street, our little gang had followed him yelling,

Gene, Gene made a machine
Joe, Joe made it go
Art, Art let a fart
And blew the Goddamn thing apart.

He chased us but we got away, pelting him with snowballs and chunks of ice. I knew he would remember me, my being the only colored kid in the gang.

I moved to run away. He quickly got between me and the door.

"Art," Mamie cautioned, "leave the kids alone."

"I'm of a mind to let you go." His face was near mine, swaying, stinking from cheap booze. "I might even give you a nickel if you dance a little jig for me."

"I don't dance for white trash." It came out without my thinking about it.

Wham! The stars and whirligigs filled my brain. Mamie's scream and my brother's yelling seemed so distant. I gave up trying to rise and sank into the warmth of the floor.

They told me that Pop first went for his pistol. The men at the party disarmed him. Then he went for the murderous bowie knife. They took that from him, too. Pop saw Art was getting away. I got to the doorway in time to see him run through the snow, slipping and cursing. He caught Art, spun him around, and hit him in the face. When the men pulled Pop away, he was fighting Missouri style, grinding the heel of his shoe onto Art's mouth and nose. The men got Pop back to the house and Art to the hospital.

The party didn't last much longer after that. At midnight everyone sang of auld lang syne. Then they went home, apprehensive and frightened by the fight. Within an hour, Mr. Mason knocked on the door. He and Pop stood beside the stove talking in tense whispers. I heard Mr. Mason say, "Don't be a fool, Ben. Just put the family in the car. I'll go with you to Winona. My kinsfolk will put you up."

"Bert," Pop said with soft resignation, "I'm the only colored man in this town. I can't run. There's nowhere to stop."

They talked a little longer and Mr. Mason left. Pop got the .30-06 and loaded it, then the pump shotgun, then the .38. He was a little drunk and pushed Mom away when she tried to stop him.

The sheriff came to the house. He didn't even try to talk softly. "Ben, this is serious. There's a mob forming. They're talking about a lynching. I can take you up to Reeds Landing, or I can take the family to the jail, where I can protect them. I don't have the men to protect you here."

"Luke, I appreciate what you're doing. If I can't handle this, I want you to take the kids to my sister in Minneapolis. No, Luke, I've got to do it my way. It's my right and its my duty."

The sheriff shrugged. "I can't do nothing until somebody breaks the law. Don't take the law in your hands."

The sheriff left. It was one o'clock and now I was wide awake. Pop started to put on his coat. I crept back into the bedroom and put on mine, got my .22, and went out the back door to the car. I barely heard Pop giving his final answer to Mom.

"I'll come back with respect, or on my shield."

Pop had bought the big brand-new Packard sedan for ten dollars from Mr. Swenson after the bank foreclosed on his pickle factory. It wasn't just that he didn't want the bank to get the car; selling it to the only Negro family for ten bucks taught the bank a lesson. I snuck into the back and huddled on the floor by the time Pop put the guns in and started the car.

There were at least fifty or sixty men standing around the front of the tavern across the street from the Anderson Hotel. They knew Pop's car and they stood silently, facing him as he pulled to the opposite curb and got out on the passenger side. First he laid the shotgun, then the .30-06 across the hood. He stepped under the street light and pulled his belt a notch tighter so they could see the .38. There was a moment of dramatic silence that Pop really enjoyed.

"I hear you sons of bitches are looking for me." The silence deepened. Finally one of them said, "Well, I don't think anybody is going to respect a man who doesn't protect his family. Come on and have a drink. Let's forget it."

He was gone an hour and I didn't wake up until he opened the door. When he saw me with my rifle, he chuckled, "Gonna help the old man out, Laddie Buck?"

I mumbled a sleepy yes.

Half drunk but serious, he shook me gently. When I awoke he said, "Don't let those white cock whollopers grind you down or scare you. They coming for you? Go meet 'em. They got more to live for than you. They'll back down."

★

The plan was forming in my mind. I felt more at ease and slept as the big six-by-six truck growled to the top of Montezuma Pass and began the twenty-mile decline to the fort.

22

IT WAS A bigger effort than we had bargained for. Planning and carrying out a secret operation involving some seventy-five soldiers from three different regiments taxed our ability to the breaking point. We spent the first meeting dividing ourselves into three regimental committees and then talked about what we were going to do. Only at the end of the meeting did Brad raise the issue of how we were going to get it done. After working out a plan, it took three more weeks to get it underway. That didn't hurt us. The Eighth Air Force men and the MPs lowered their guard each day that passed without our retaliating.

By working in the Operations Department of the battalion I picked up the fundamentals of organization and was soon in charge of that part of the job. We set up a communications system based on the battalion message centers. That way we had access to a jeep and a radio if we needed them. Each regimental committee was responsible for its own security. We agreed that no rifles would be taken. We would have to rely on the friendliness of the Policía and the Mexican people.

The plan was a simple one. We would get twenty-five men from each regiment. After arriving at Ranchita, we would fan out in groups of five. Each regimental committee would have a leader. The leader of each five-man committee was responsible for keeping the men together during the fight and seeing that they got back to the safety of the walled area.

Three men would go into El Tecolote bar and order drinks. We could count on the whites to start something. The three men would gang whoever started the fight, knock him out, and hurt him. Then the three would fight their way to the door. A five-man squad would be outside the door ready to go in if they trapped our men. We didn't want to damage the bar. We would need the goodwill of the Mexicans inside. The remainder of our little army, scattered in the alleyways, would join the fighting outside. In Mexico we had nothing to fear from the disarmed MPs.

Lee, Brad, Bunk, Hewitt, and I made up our squad. Hewitt was not one to get into a street fight. He was only five foot five, and his slender body was more accustomed to sitting at a desk than gutter fighting. We told him it wasn't necessary for him to go. Hurt that we might not want him along, he looked at each of us for a moment.

"I don't think a lynch mob will wait to find out that I'm a West Indian student at Columbia."

Punching him on the arm and warning him not to start arguing with the pecks, we welcomed him in. As soon as I could, I pulled Brad aside and told him that the two of us would have to be responsible.

At the end of the third week, we briefed the squad leaders and were ready to take on the Eighth Air Force.

★

Nogales was so peaceful, so unaware of what we planned. The convoy was a little larger than usual and took a little longer to make its way down the asphalt road through the new section of town. As we passed El Tecolote bar we glanced over the area and, satisfied with our strategy, sat back and relaxed. The convoy swung onto the rough-rutted dirt road that led into Ranchita.

The operation was going so smoothly it frightened us. A quick meeting with the regimental leaders was reassuring. As the night darkened we knew that the air force men were already on the way to getting drunk. They would be less alert, less able to fight, and would be getting on the nerves of the Mexican patrons at the bar.

Group by group the squads slipped through the gate and fanned out toward the bar. The men from the 25th and the 368th left and the five squads from our regiment began sauntering through the gate. We were to bring up the rear. Brad signaled to Hewitt, who nodded to Lee and Bunk. With hearts hammering we left Ranchita and headed for the bar. There was no turning back, and sending someone ahead to scout the area was impossible. Everything now depended upon luck and discipline.

Outside the gate, the two men from the 368th who had been beaten up joined us.

"We goin' in. We got some gettin' even to do."

"Only reason we didn't want you all to go in first is that they might recognize you. We got to have surprise."

"I know. We'll keep our heads down. It ain't right that we don't get the first lick in."

It was too late to argue or to change plans. Brad was in charge. His decision came in tense whispers. Brad, the men from the 368th, and I would enter the bar. He explained to them the necessity of staying close together and getting out as soon as possible. They agreed, and we crossed the street into the final block to the bar. Black soldiers hid beneath the trees and in the alleyways. The whites would approach the bar from the other direction, and it was unlikely that they had any idea what was in store.

Parker stepped out of the darkness, rolling his cud of tobacco farther to the side of his mouth and packing it against the molars. The steel-rimmed glasses pressed against his face as he glared at the bar and said to Brad with matter-of-fact finality, "Ah'm goin' in with you."

There was no arguing with him—the plan changed again.

"What ya got in your hand? We can't use a knife or gun in there."

Parker opened his fist to reveal a six-inch piece of broomstick.

"It ain't illegal—make your fist hard. Or you can push it out a little an' swing overhand. Bust a motherfucka's head if they's crowdin' you."

Brad glanced at me as if to say, "If we don't hurry the whole thing is going to fall apart."

"OK. Don't want more than four in there—it'll alert 'em. Nels, you take charge out here. Let's go."

★

Brad stepped around the corner and into the bar followed by the 368th men, with Parker's huge hulking frame bringing up the rear.

A block away a group of air force men passed under the dull street light and came slowly toward us. Our position suddenly became precarious. Caught between two groups, we would lose the advantage of superior numbers.

"What's happening, Hew?"

"They're talking to the bartender. The white guys are looking at them, but nothing is happening . . . they're drinking a beer . . . four white guys are coming over . . . they're talking. He pushed Brad . . . the 368th guys are beating the shit out of him . . . "

The approaching airmen were fewer than fifty yards away. They saw us and slowed their pace. After a moment's hesitation, three of them began walking toward the bar.

The shouts and scuffling inside grew louder. I ran to the window. Fewer than half the white soldiers were trying to get into the fight. Most had backed away, but twenty of them were attempting to surround Brad. The soldiers approaching us were very close and we would have to meet them. I signaled to the nearest squad. They ran from the alleyway to the entrance to the bar.

"Bunk, you guys take care of the door—Lee and me'll go see if these guys want to talk."

They saw that a gang fight was underway. The soldiers stopped to look. Brad and one of the 368th men were backing out of the bar. They held one airman between them, banging his head against the wall and punching him in the face.

"What's going on in there?" one of the air force men asked me.

"A fight." I tried not to sound belligerent.

"'Bout what? Who's fighting?"

"Looks like some of you guys don't want us to go in that bar. We goin' in."

"Jesus fuckin' Christ, what do you mean, 'you guys'? I don't care who goes anywhere . . . "

The fighting was spilling into the street. We had to get back. I turned to the airman. "If you all ain't in it, stay up here. Stay out of it."

Lee and I had to run to get past the airmen who were now spilling into the street. The men from the Ninety-third were doing it according to plan. As those who were fighting retreated past them toward Ranchita, the squads would run from their hiding places and, from a flanking position, jump into the fight. What at first had appeared to be an uneven fight between four black and thirty white soldiers became fifteen against thirty, then thirty against thirty, forty-five against thirty, sixty-five against thirty. Those who called us "nigger" were beaten unmercifully. Aside from that, the fight was mostly shoving and hitting in the chest or arms. They were half drunk, confused, and outnumbered. Some were fighting as white against black, some as air force against army, and we were having fun getting even.

A jeep with a load of white MPs screeched to a halt. The MPs leaped out, flailing their clubs against the black soldiers. They caught a few by surprise and knocked them to the ground. Suddenly the edge of playfulness was gone and we were fighting for our lives. The men began to team up against the MPs.

I more sensed than saw that Hewitt was in trouble. An airman had him in a choke hold while an MP rammed his club into Hewitt's ribs. There was a frightful scream of pain and a rattling gasp for breath. I shoved the airman away from me and leaped on the back of the MP, grabbed his club, and tried to wrestle him to the ground. The man holding Hewitt hit me hard in the face, sending whirligigs and stars spinning through my brain. I fell off the MP's back, rolled over, and, as I was getting to my feet, took a kick in the chest. Now I was fighting on infantry training, and that training, almost an instinct, was to kill. The MP raised his club to hit Hewitt in the face. I got my hands on his wrist as he gouged at my eyes. Suddenly he stiffened and went limp. His eyes widened and his open mouth gasped for air as he fell, blood spurting from a punctured kidney. I kicked at his groin and turned to meet the expected blow from the man holding Hewitt. Then I saw Brad, lips pulled back from his teeth, snarling at the MP in naked hatred.

"That's for the boys in Bisbee, Goddamn you to hell!"

We both jumped at the airman beating Hew. Brad jerked the man's head backward and hit him in the throat. Lips parted, teeth clinched, he was growling over and over, "Turn him loose, you motherfucker—turn him loose."

I saw the blood on his hand and saw where it had stained my pants leg.

"You hurt, man?"

"No, I'm all right. We gotta get out of here."

I glanced at the MP writhing on the ground, holding his side to stanch the blood and unable to cry for help. For a moment my mind flashed back to the Seattle freight yard and I saw Red Anderson lying in his blood. I fought back the urge to kick him in the face and nuts before we left. A tug from Brad and I turned to help him hold Hewitt between us as we made our way through the swirling, cursing, fighting soldiers.

The policía had arrived, and so had two more jeeploads of MPs. Four of the Mexican police officers stood beside the cars holding rifles while the others—using clubs—separated the fighters.

Through some magic communication we learned in the slave pens and the prisons, the Ninety-third men as if on command began to scatter and disappear into the night, making their way back to Ranchita. I looked around. None of our men was on the ground and none captured. No one seemed too interested in following us into the night.

Hew's bruised rib cage gave him trouble breathing as we dogtrotted into the old section of town and to safety behind the walls of Ranchita. I had a big, tender lump below my temple, but otherwise I felt fine. At the public spigot Brad washed his hands and I scrubbed the blood from my pants leg.

As the last of the men came through the gate, we went to meet with the regimental leaders. With all the men accounted for, a carnival spirit evolved as they described their individual fights.

Lee was holding court: "You all see me lay that cracker down?"

"You laid him on the killin' floor, man."

Lee, barely five foot seven, was shuffling through the dust as if he were in the ring, landing jabs and uppercuts on his imaginary opponent.

"I didn't get mad till he calls me a ugly fuckin' nigger. Nobody calls me ugly. I laid a left jab to the guts an' brought a overhand right from the floor."

Lee leaned back as if he were a pitcher, bringing his fist from the ground, over his shoulder.

"I tagged him smack on the chin. He staggered. I tagged him again—" Lee grunted with the effort, "and he fell like shit from a tall bull. PO-LA-AP." Lee threw out his arms and flopped on his back in the dust. The howls of Southern laughter echoed through Ranchita. The next man took center stage, but an undercurrent of apprehension ran through the laughing and joking. We all knew that a gang of black troops couldn't whip a gang of white troops and get off scot-free.

A white lieutenant colonel from the Ninety-third drove his jeep into the center of the compound. Grabbing every noncom he saw, he ordered them to round up the men so he could talk to them.

The noncoms spread out into the bars and whorehouses, rounding up the soldiers. As we assembled, the lieutenant colonel mounted his jeep and informed us that a riot had taken place. Nogales was now off-limits for the Ninety-third. We mounted into the trucks while the Eighth Air Force MPs tried to identify some of the fighters. The trucks formed a convoy and pulled out of Nogales for the long ride back to the fort.

As the convoy gathered speed a soldier began to sing and the rest of the men joined in.

>Sister Mary, don't you weep, don't you moan
>Sister Mary, don't you weep, don't you moan
>Old Pharaoh's army got drowned-ed,
>Oh Mary, don't you weep.

Some rough laughter, and the song died out as the uncorked tequila bottles passed down the row of troops.

"Wonder what they gonna do with us now," Bunk mumbled, after shaking the tequila fumes from his mouth and nose.

"Bisbee off limits, Nogales off limits—don't dare go to Phoenix."

"They can't keep us bottled up in Huachuca. That place is going to explode," Hewitt added between painful gasps for breath.

The following week a division directive alerted us to move out to the maneuver area of Louisiana.

23

UPON RETURNING FROM the Philippines in 1916, the Twenty-fourth Infantry was broken up into three independent battalions that saw duty in California, Wyoming, and Colorado. In these states, the men enjoyed a minimum taste of democracy. They were uneasy about the orders sending them to the Texas-Mexican border. Texas was an area that combined the most violent features of the West with the Negro-hating lynch mob spirit of the rural Deep South.

As tension between Mexico and the United States eased, the generals thought it safe to send the Third Battalion of the Twenty-fourth to Houston to guard new military installations. The whites, especially the police, were furious that an organization of armed black infantrymen should suddenly be thrust among them.

If the whites were irate over the arrival of the troops, it delighted the segregated, militantly proud black community. From 1903 to 1907 they had boycotted Houston's public transportation to protest the segregation. Defeat only deepened resentment over their second-class status. The militant democratic spirit of the men in the Twenty-fourth was quickly reflected in the attitude of black Houston.

Trouble began at once. The soldiers refused to accept segregation. They threw the Colored-White seating signs out the windows of the streetcars and kicked over the No Negroes or Dogs Allowed signs in the parks.

The brutal cops of Houston were expert veterans in the "control" of blacks. They realized they would have to precipitate a crisis and crush the rising democratic spirit before it was too late.

Houston cops descended from the Negro-hating, slave catchers—the Texas Rangers. Some were worse than others. Worst of all was Officer Lee Sparks. He would publicly display the four notches on his pistol, bragging that he didn't count the ones who didn't fight back. Killing blacks was not Sparks's main pleasure; it was beating women. The more public the beating, the more brutal it was, the better he liked it. Houston blues singers had a song that ended "Lee Sparks whup a pretty young woman same as a ugly old man."

On the afternoon of August 23, 1917—during the war to defend the rights of people to self-determination—Lee Sparks decided to arrest a black woman. She hadn't moved out of the way of a white woman fast enough to suit him.

Her protest against arrest was all he needed. A backhand slap knocked her down. Gun in one hand, club in the other, Sparks began beating the woman. Her screams brought a black soldier running over, protesting the brutality. Sparks knocked the soldier unconscious with the club. An unarmed black military policeman came over to protect the soldier. He was shot and brutally beaten. More cops arrived at the scene and hauled the three bloodied, brutalized blacks off to jail.

News of the incident spread quickly to the bivouac area of the Twenty-fourth Infantry. The men assembled in groups preparing to get into town and rescue their comrades before the cops killed them. Sgt. Vida Henry, a professional soldier in every respect, immediately went to his new battalion commanding officer, Major Snow. The major decided to do nothing and let the law take its course.

Sergeant Henry had other duties to uphold. One was to his men, the other to his people. Rebuffed by Major Snow, Sergeant Henry went back to the bivouac, broke open the ammunition boxes, and handed out the rifles. The soldiers headed for the police station, killing five cops and twelve civilians. Sparks hid out and stayed alive to continue beating and murdering Houston's blacks.

As the fighting died down, Sergeant Henry, torn between his duties to the army and his people, put his rifle to his head and pulled the trigger.

The army quickly tried the "mutineers." They hanged twenty-three soldiers in one day. It was a massacre aimed at frightening all blacks into submission. This massacre was exceeded only by the massacre in New Ulm, Minnesota, where twenty-six Indians and three Negroes were hanged for an "uprising." An additional sixty-four brave soldiers stood at attention in chains and leg irons before the court. Not one flinched or begged for mercy as the uniformed sons of slave owners spit out the sentence, "Life at hard labor."

Ideals do not stay hanged or imprisoned. Nat Turner had risen again from the quicklime grave to shout Vengeance. An entire people listened, raised their heads, and turned their eyes toward Houston.

This was the opportunity the generals had waited for. They disarmed the major black combat units and reduced them to labor battalions. The few remaining combat organizations, broken into small, impotent groups and scattered around the country, remained under the gun of the Negro-hating generals.

Political aspects of World War II forced the generals to regroup the disarmed, scattered black soldiers and reconstitute the combat organizations. Violence between the black soldiers and the white authority attempting to keep them in their Jim Crow place quickly reached a new peak.

The commanders, the government, and the police should have learned how to govern a brutalized, enslaved group. The most effective way is to create levels of petty privilege to thwart unity. Mistreat a mass of people equally and sooner or later they stop thinking and acting as individuals. They begin to think and react as a group. The scattered, defensive fighting by the soldiers was beginning to consolidate into a pattern of resistance that threatened to explode into many Houstons. Isolation was the rational solution, but they could not keep the Ninety-third at Fort Huachuca.

Over the protests of the government of the State of Louisiana, the generals sent eighteen thousand bitter, frustrated, armed black men into the heart of the Louisiana Black Belt.

Part Four

TROUBLE COMING

24

DURING THE WEEKS before entraining for Louisiana, we met with the committee leaders of our little group. Violence against us was inevitable. We vowed to fight it out. If necessary we might as well die in America as overseas. We began to secure and hide ammunition. Over the beers at the Long Bar we agreed that two clips—sixteen rounds—was all any of us should try for. We could not easily conceal more than that. With two clips each, we could fight our way to more.

The commanding officers of the division knew of our apprehensions. They knew that we either had or would secure the means of resistance. They attempted to frustrate our plans with unending and often surprise inspections. None of our men was caught. Men who would not join us would warn us when they heard of the probability of inspections. Having set up a communications network around the message centers paid off. A telephone call from Regimental Headquarters that began with "Hey, man . . . " warned of an immediate inspection. The soldiers became more and more resentful of the constant inspections as if we soldiers, not the army, were trampling democracy underfoot. They went so far as to arouse us in the middle of the night and searched over and under the barracks with a mine detector for arms and ammunition. Finally the game ended. The Regimental Intelligence and Reconnaissance Platoon and the battalion staffs entrained for Louisiana.

★

As we approached Many, Louisiana, Captain Akeley came through our coach and told us to detrain at the next stop. At Many, we filed from the train and marched toward a vacant lot next to the station. As we passed the station, I spat on the White and Colored signs. Jeff mumbled, "Fuck that shit," and knocked them down with his rifle butt. Captain Akeley, the only white man among us, pretended not to notice.

We stacked our rifles and lined up to hear a pep talk by Captain Akeley. "Now, men," he began in a soft, embarrassed Southern tone, "We in the South. You all know that. Some things here you all don't like. There's some things that I don't like. We in the South and we in the army. You all know the score. Sergeant Peery."

"Yes, sir."

"Ah done et your ass out about disobeyin' me before."

"Yes, sir."

"Well, you do it down heah and Ah'm gonna get you a court-martial. You understand that?"

"I ain't done nothin', captain."

"I just want you to understand."

The platoon giggled. We were still teenagers or barely into our twenties and still could giggle at the most serious thing.

Everyone knew that Akeley wasn't going to court-martial me. I did a good deal of his work, arranged his papers, warned him when the generals were coming down. When something went wrong, I took the blame. He'd "et my ass out"—dress me down in front of the company and then leave a bottle of whiskey or carton of cigarettes in my bedroll.

"Yes, sir, captain." I smiled at him. It was all part of the way he got the message across to the rest of the platoon.

Akeley turned on his heels and walked toward his hotel quarters. The men, grumbling and cursing, fell to pitching pup tents and digging drainage ditches.

Some of the older whites and scores of black youngsters came to the station to look us over. They had good reason to rejoice or fear. We were the first black soldiers they had ever seen with rifles. They did not see the bitterness—or the ammunition.

That first day wore on with the men playing cards, trying to sleep in the heat, or talking to the people who came by to make friends. A young woman crossed the street and shyly came over to me. Her skin was the rich color of dark chocolate and her face seemed to have been constructed around the biggest, clearest eyes I ever saw. Breasts, too big for such a young body, strained against the starched, pressed calico dress.

"Where you all from, soldier?"

"Arizona—Fort Huachuca, Arizona. Know where that is?"

"No, but I know where Camp Claiborne is. My brother's a soldier there."

"Yeah. What's your name?"

"Sarah. What's yours?"

"Nelson. How old are you?"

"Sixteen. How old are you?"

"Nineteen. Wanna do me a favor? Go across the street and get two red pops—one for you and one for me."

"They don't serve colored there. I'll go down the street."

"They'll serve you." I handed her the quarter.

With a look of apprehension she took the coin. I watched her walking across the street into the sunlight. The youthful, muscular thighs swelling into round buttocks pressed and outlined against the thin dress. She had barely disappeared into the store when she came back out. This time I wasn't looking at her body. Before she spoke, the adrenalin and the rage was racing through me, wiping out any semblance of rational thinking. Somewhere in the back of my mind I could hear Pop saying, "Trouble coming toward you? Well, you go to it—ain't none of them white cock whollopers want to die." I grabbed my rifle and half heard her say, " . . . that they don't serve no niggers there."

The pudgy, cigar-chewing man behind the barlike counter didn't seem to notice the rifle. I suddenly realized I didn't have a clip of ammunition in the chamber. What if he went for his pistol? It was too late to back out.

"What kin I do for ya', soldier?"

"Like two bottles of red pop, sir."

He huffed his way to the cooler, took out the soda, and turned slowly toward me.

"This 'un is on the house. The boys that come to this area are headin' overseas."

"Thank you, sir. I'd like to pay." I placed the quarter on the counter, picked up the soda, and backed out the door. Halfway across the street I turned and walked to the bivouac area.

Sergeant Jackson was barely shaking his head. "You crazy son of a bitch. You're gonna start a riot down here."

"No need to worry, Road Buddy," Brad said. He eased the clip out of his rifle. "I had the motherfucker covered."

Sarah was gone. Brad had told her to go home to get her out of the line of fire.

We made a roster and posted guards every night from then on. I was a little embarrassed, having caused the platoon such trouble, and I worried about the sudden, uncontrollable rage.

★

The next morning we started our task of staking out the bivouac areas for the regiment and checking the accuracy of the maps.

With that task completed, the trains began to arrive. Our platoon provided the guides at the various road junctions to direct the regiments into their respective areas.

The troops began to arrive early in the morning. Throughout the day they marched past my checkpoint. Each soldier seemed to sense his responsibility in presenting the best possible appearance of the Negro soldier to the South. I was tremendously proud of them.

In the early part of the afternoon, a bewhiskered old white farmer came to see the men and matériel of war. They filed past us: the big guns of the artillery, the antitank cannon, the jeeps with machine guns mounted, the weapons carriers and the halftracks spitting dust. Most impressive and formidable of all were the infantrymen. Their clean khaki-and-green leggings contrasted with the many shades of tan and brown and black faces beneath the green of the steel helmets. The M1 rifles, Browning automatics, machine guns, and mortars were slung or perched across their shoulders. On they came—8 abreast—48 to the platoon, 200 to the company, 800 to the battalion, 4,000 to the regiment, 18,000 to the division. The unending stream of healthy young men came to train to defend a democracy more alien to them than the fascism they were to fight against.

The old white farmer stood apart from me, quietly working his jaws over the cud of tobacco—spitting occasionally. Now and then he turned his head when some matériel of combat came by that was of particular interest to him. As the darkness gathered he cleaned his mouth with his finger and shook his head in dismay.

"Gawd damn, I ain't never seen so many niggers in my life."

I shifted my rifle to hit him in the face. He wasn't even looking at me. There was amazement and a bit of fear in his eyes. Instead of hitting him, I smiled at this old man who was seeing his worst nightmare come to life.

25

THE EIGHTY-FIFTH Division, our "enemy" during maneuvers, arrived in the area. We rolled our packs, slung our rifles, and marched out into the bayous and scrub brush to meet them.

The weeks seemed unending as we marched and dug in and marched again while the field officers practiced the skills of battle by moving us back and forth and sideways on their maps. "Hurry up and wait" became the standard operating procedure. While the generals plotted their moves we washed our muddy clothes in the streams, carried on the crap games and the stories, and carefully picked the chiggers and red bugs from our hide.

Getting rid of chiggers requires skill. The first impulse is to grab the filthy little bastard between the fingernails and jerk. If that's done, the head separates from the body and it stays embedded. In a few days the infection sets in. Touch it with a hot pin or the lit end of a cigarette and its legs begin to wave in the air, wildly scraping against the skin, trying to dig farther into the flesh. When, finally, the chigger pulls its head out to escape, it is in a world of trouble. Few were simply smashed. Torturing chiggers became an art of retaliation that never quite compensated for the painful, itching red lumps.

The officers completed their "battle" plans and the orders came down for us to roll our packs and move out.

We knew something serious was up. Lieutenant Hartsfield came toward us walking especially erect, shoulders squared, as if he needed a military bearing to get his message across. We began to rise to our feet.

"Rest—as you were."

We slumped back down. Most of the black junior officers were from the ranks. We had known some of them as enlisted men. The excessive military courtesy that strengthened them in the presence of whites embarrassed them if no other officers were present.

"How ya doin', lieutenant? What's the killin' shit?"

"I'm doing just fine, Corporal Moore. You gentlemen can roll full field packs. We've got forty miles to make."

"God dowg, lieutenant," Parker mumbled between teeth, lips, and cud of tobacco. "We was marchin' all week long. We tired."

There was still a boyish quality to Hartsfield's grin.

"I'm not the chaplain. I'm not the colonel. Let's go, men. Off and on."

We looked at one another—forty miles? Marching twenty miles in the Louisiana heat and dust was our limit. The galling part was that we knew why we had to march. The poop came

down the week before that the generals were admiring Russian
and German elite units that could cover fifty miles and go into
combat. They simply wanted to know if we could do it.

We would sack out early that night.

★

The smell of GI coffee, dehydrated eggs, and potatoes all mixed in
with Jackson's yelping at 4:30 in the morning was enough to make
a soldier puke.

We crawled out of our pup tents, scratching at the red bugs,
stretching out the stiffness of a restless night on the damp, cold
Louisiana ground. First stop was lining up at the slit trench that
served as a latrine. Standing shoulder to shoulder the yawning,
peeing soldiers cursed one another awake. Next, line up for a helmet of water. A cupful to brush the teeth and rinse the mouth.
The rest to wash from the top down—face, neck, armpits, groin,
and feet. Next, line up before the big kettles where Black Jack
ladled out the slop. After a few mouthfuls washed down with the
bitter coffee, throw rest into the garbage pit.

By 5:30 the pup tents were down and we began rolling our
packs. Smooth the shelter half out on the ground. Lay the blanket
on top. Fold it neatly twice, kneel on the blanket and shelter half to
roll them tight. Lay the roll out straight in the pack and pull the
straps tight so the entrenching tool rides high and out of the way.
Hook the canteen, bayonet, and medical kit to the web belt.
Secure the steel helmet to the pack. Attach the straps of the pack
to the web belt and hoist the whole assembly onto the back and
shoulders. Sling the rifle over the right shoulder. The whistle blew
and we lined up for the short walk to the assembly area.

At 6:15 the battalion assembled, platoons and companies
lined up standing at ease. The advance guard moved out. The
colonel entered his jeep. It moved onto the dusty road in second
gear. Captain Harper raised his arm. Cpl. Sam Gaston straightened the company standard on his shoulder. Sergeant Thompson
yelled, "Compan—yeah." We snapped to parade rest.

"Ten—shun!" Rifles snapped to our sides, feet clicked
together.

"Sling—Arms!" The rifles were slung muzzle up over our
shoulders.

"Route step! Forward, march!"

At 6:30 the sun was blazing hot. The battalion moved onto

the road and crossed the line of departure. Captain Harper turned to Sam Gaston, the company guide, and said, "Shorten the stride and step up the cadence."

Sam leaned a bit forward. His big size twelve boot swung out as he increased the cadence. We settled in behind him. We were the infantry and took pride in our misery. Heads up, each soldier mechanically kept step as his thoughts drifted far from the army and Louisiana.

By 12:30 the pace was beginning to tell on the men. Their green fatigues, streaked with sweat, showed white traces of body salt. Each ten-minute break seemed shorter than the one before. The Spam and the peanut butter and jelly sandwiches were washed down with a bit of the remaining precious water. We had marched twenty-four miles. The remaining sixteen would go slowly. The temperature inched up to 105. Louisiana's scorching sun became a glowing ember in the cloudless sky. Canteens emptied and the weaker men began to fall out. They rode the ambulances for a short rest before rejoining their platoons.

The hot, dusty road burned our feet. Erect heads slumped under the broiling sun. Bright young eyes had scanned the scrub brush countryside with curiosity a few hours before. Now, they were listless, half hypnotized by the rhythmic rise and fall of the boots slogging through the dust. The tiring men ahead raised clouds of fine red dust as shuffling became part of the exhausting march. The dust forced the men to breath partly through their mouths and drink the last of their water.

Time took a new dimension. It stood still. The world became the scorching sun, the thirst, the boots in front, the dust, and the red dirt road. The boots went up and down; trees, brush, and fences slipped past. The boots, the thirst, the dust, the road. Nothing changed.

Parker kept a cud of tobacco pressed to the back of his mouth, wedged between his cheek and gums. He swore it kept his mouth moist and was seldom without it. Walking determinedly with head up, he seemed in his element—walking down a dusty country road under a blazing Southern sun.

Big Joe shifted the heavy Browning automatic rifle from shoulder to shoulder. No matter how difficult things became, he never complained. Realizing that I was looking at him, he shifted the cigar stump to the corner of his mouth and smiled his open, friendly, toothy smile.

"How ya doin', Big Joe?"

"Everything is lovely."

Juicy stepped out of the column onto the side of the road.

"You OK, man?" I asked as I neared him.

"I'm not goin' no fu'ther—or I won't be OK."

Lee unbuckled his canteen.

"You can have some of my water, Juicy."

Juicy half smiled at his little antagonist.

"Naw, thanks, man. I just ain't gonna kill myself."

At thirty-six and one of the "old" men, Juicy could get away with falling out. We couldn't.

I glanced back at Brad. Droplets of sweat had left dusty streak marks down his face. The big, hazel, girlish eyes were half closed against the sun and dust. He looked up at me and mumbled, "Fuck this shit."

Up ahead, around the long curve in the road a white man and two girls were handing the soldiers buckets of water. The two girls would run to the well while the man held out the buckets.

"Thank you."

"Much obliged, suh."

The long gulps of cold, clear Louisiana well water was the sweetest drink of my life.

"God, that's good. Thank you, mister."

"Least we can do, soldier. You all boys is givin' everything."

We plodded on refreshed by their effort as much as by the water.

Brad turned to me, half smiling. "That's the trouble with this country."

"What's that?"

"You never know which of these motherfuckers to hate."

★

The sun burned out the day. We stood our test by marching forty-two miles. Tired, thirsty, footsore, and hungry, we were close to our new bivouac area north of Natchitoches. Most of the white officers mounted jeeps and drove the remaining distance with the excuse of inspecting the bivouac area.

We took our final ten-minute break at the crossroad in front of a small store, a restaurant, and the few primitive shacks that made up the community. Ten or twelve of us went into the store to buy sardines, bread, or anything they might have to eat. Disciplined soldiers, we lined up to wait our turn. One of the men called out, "Damn if we ain't got a Mason-Dixon line here."

A crude sign hanging from a string pulled across the center of the restaurant indicated the colored and white sections. The soldier grabbed the string and broke it. He turned to the storekeeper, eyes blazing with hatred. "Looky here, motherfucker. Here's what I think of your Mason-Dixon line!"

The storekeeper, plainly frightened, tried to gain control.

"That's the law here. If you colored boys ain't gonna act right, you gotta get outa my store."

More soldiers, attracted by the commotion or looking for food, entered the store in time to hear the word. One big husky soldier crooked his arm around the storekeepers neck. "We's soldiers, ya bastard you. Soldiers! There ain't no boys 'round here. An' there ain't no Jim Crow."

It was totally spontaneous. The soldiers began to stuff produce into their pockets.

"Clean him out!" someone yelled.

"What he got belongs to us anyway."

"He's a Ku Klux."

With the store stripped in a matter of seconds we walked out laughing. One of the last soldiers yelled back, "You damned peck—we're the foolin' fuckin' fightin' Ninety-third. When we leave, the Ninety-second's comin' in. You better get used to it!"

Lee got in late. The only thing left was a box of Kotex. He walked across the street to the platoon, tearing up the gauze and cotton yelling, "Any ah you gentlemens got the piles?"

We slung our packs and fell in with the company. By the time the police and MPs arrived, we were well down the road on our way to Natchitoches.

26

WE RETURNED TO Many during the final break in the maneuvers. With a few free days on our hands, we set about entertaining ourselves or looking for entertainment in the town.

In the early afternoon, I started to look for Sarah. The town was so small, everybody knew everyone else. The first youngster I asked gave a big-toothed grin and led me to her home. As we

approached the shack in which she lived, he ran ahead shouting,
"Sarah Lee, Sarah Lee—there's a soldier man here to see you."

Sarah came to the door, squinting into the bright sunlight. As
she recognized me, she pushed the door open and stepped out.
The oiled, freshly pressed hair shone in the hot, brilliant sunshine.
She smiled shyly, ripe young body pressing against the constraints
of a brightly colored starched cotton dress. She turned her face,
looking to the ground with Louisiana Black Belt modesty.

Her mother, an attractive, thin, dark brown–skinned woman
in her middle thirties, came to the doorway, wiping her hands on
her apron.

"My goodness, Sarah Lee. Where are your manners, child?"
She turned toward me. "Won't you come in? You must be the soldier Sarah Lee told us about."

"Thank you. If she said something good, maybe I am."

She returned my smile. I knew I was welcome.

Inside the little house, her father rose from a rickety rocking
chair. Brushing away some imaginary dust, he held out a huge,
calloused hand. We talked for a few moments about the war and
the effect of having the soldiers here. The blacks, like the whites,
had never seen so many black soldiers at one time and felt at least
a temporary protection.

Sarah rolled her eyes toward the door. I excused myself and
followed her outside.

"You sure look pretty, Sarah. You got a date?"

"No." She cocked her head coyly. "I was going to look
for one."

"Oh, yeah?" I must have sounded as peeved as I felt, for she
answered quickly, "I knew the soldiers were back. I was going
down to the station and look for you."

"I'm sorry. I was thinking of you out there in the woods. I
didn't want you to go out with someone else the first day."

"You want to ask me for a date—carry me to the dance
tonight?"

"Sure. Can I take you to the dance?"

"You have to ask Mama. But she'll say all right. She likes you.
I can tell."

I had forgotten she was only sixteen. When you're nineteen
there's a big difference.

I received permission from her mother, said a polite good-bye,
and hitchhiked back to the bivouac.

★

"Hey, Road Buddy," Brad said as I passed his pup tent.

"What's the good word, man?"

"There's gonna be a dance tonight in Many."

"Yeah, I know. I'm takin' that good-lookin' brown skin you met at the station."

"You lucky bastard. You like to dance?"

"I ain't never learned to dance, Brad. I couldn't tell her that."

"You introduce me. You dance the slow ones—it's easy. I'll take the fast ones." He began to hum a blues number, grabbed his rifle bending over it, grinding his groin against the butt.

"You crazier than hell, Bradley B."

"Look here," he panted, laying aside his rifle. "Let's get some drinkin' whiskey for tonight."

"Where you going to get that? You know this parish is dry."

"Ain't no place dry. Wet parish, you buy it at the store. Dry parish, you get the bootleg. That's why it's dry. We'll find some."

We left the bivouac, following a partly concealed trail into an area he knew contained stills. Brad would stop, sniff the air, and, smelling nothing, continue to walk. He stopped, sniffed, and sniffed again.

"Damn, if I don't smell some drinkin' whiskey."

I sniffed the air and smelled nothing. Brad was walking quickly down the trail until I, too, could smell the bitter corn mash. We entered a small clearing where an old white man with an unkempt gray-white beard and dirty overalls was quietly stirring the mash.

He must have seen us coming, for he didn't turn around when Brad asked, "You want to sell some whiskey?"

"Yep. That's what I make it for. Five dollars a gallon."

Brad handed him the money and he began to draw a gallon of the crystal clear whiskey.

I walked around the still, trying to discover how whiskey is made. After inspecting the coil I looked into the boiling mash. A huge rat was lying in the pot. The fur had boiled away on the underside, leaving white cracks in its body.

"For Christ's sake, man. Why don't you take that rat outta the mash?"

The man spat a huge slug of tobacco juice that nearly covered the rat's head.

"Hell, it don't make no difference no how. 'Nother'un be there in the morning. Damn things come at night and eat the mash, get drunk, and fall in. Don't hurt nothin'. Nothin' but steam goes up that coil."

I didn't think I wanted to drink any of that whiskey. By the time of the dance, I had changed my mind.

★

Sarah and I had walked slowly from her house, joining up with groups of young people. Most of the soldiers were alone. A few of the lucky ones had dates from the town or the surrounding share-cropping farms.

The civilian men wore scrubbed, starched overalls or zoot suits and broad-brimmed hats. The women dressed to cripple and kill. Tight-fitting yellow, red, or black dresses complemented various shades of their black, brown, or tan complexions. They walked awkwardly on the dirt road in their Sunday-go-to-meeting shoes.

Those of us with dates had to be careful to avoid both the civilian and military police. They enjoyed humiliating the black soldiers and their girlfriends by stopping them and demanding health cards. The cards, carried by prostitutes, had to be presented on demand. The white MPs demanded these cards from white women working in houses of prostitution, and from any black woman accompanied by a soldier. In their eyes, all black women were prostitutes. If she did not have a card she would be taken to jail and forced to submit to an examination. If the soldier protested, he was beaten or jailed or shot. The men fought back individually as best they could. They killed several MPs and were hanged for it. It was part of the unending harassment of the black soldier.

The one dim street light hanging over the crossroad cast eerie shadows on the dance hall. The barnlike structure was set back, half hidden by the giant, moss-covered eucalyptus trees. A line of dim lights was strung across the front of the building. The door was open and the rough tables were lined up close to the walls to provide the maximum room for the dancers.

Brad and Bunk were waiting for us in the shadows before the dance hall. Introductions were made and the jug was passed around. Nearly strangling on the undiluted corn whiskey and gasping for air, I hid the jug in the underbrush. Regaining some composure, we went in. The organizers of the dance asked everyone to leave any liquor outside, because the sheriff might come by.

The dimly lit hall began to fill up. Little groups gathered around the tables, loading them up with 3.2 beer and red pop. The lanterns shone on hair slicked and plastered down with Murrays or "conked" into limp waves. The soft light reflected on gold-capped teeth, some of which held the engraved sword and star of the Prince Hall Order. These were the dandies from De Ritter, Natchitoches, or Shreveport. They followed the dance band circuit into the smaller towns, selling whiskey, running card and dice games, or attempting to recruit fresh flesh for the whorehouses springing up around the training camps.

The combo arrived and set up their equipment. They tuned the instruments to the piano and the dance began. The snare drum, the sax, the trombone, the guitar, and the piano began a fast boogie-woogie introduction.

Sarah looked at me.

"I'm too out of practice for this one."

My head was spinning from the raw liquor. She seemed a bit hurt not to dance the first dance. Southern courtesy meant that she would have to dance the first and last dances with me. I hoped that something slow would be next.

★

Couples began the fast dancing. With snapping fingers and tapping feet they felt the common cadence. Twisting, bobbing individuals merged into a dancing mass. They caught the complex half steps and the steady eight full beats to the bar. This was dancing that I had never seen before—Black Belt dancing. He struts and pecks and spins. Contentiously thrusting first chest then groin forward, transported to a cosmos of boogie-woogie—a world of black fingers flying over the keys, pounding out the intoxication, sweat dripping from a tossing head, the free foot stomping out the beat. Strong fingers jerking up and down the neck of the guitar, chords mingling between and crowning the heavy rhythm of the piano. The trombone and sax court each other, filling with and contrasting to the wire snare dragged across and slapping the taut skin of the drum. Eyes half closed, rocking in rhythm, he dances, excited by, yet oblivious to, his fascinated oscillating partner. She responds, pulling the tight dress upward, unfettering muscular thighs, torquing gyrating hips to the east and breast to the west, strong white teeth glistening between full, excited, parted lips, head thrown back as rhythm captivates consciousness. Arcane Africa smiled and embraced her passionate children.

The music ended abruptly and the crowd left the dance floor sweating, embracing, applauding.

With reed instruments laid aside, the guitar player moved between the drums and the piano. Soft, mournful music of the Delta spread out from the combo. It penetrated the sultry air of the dance hall and brought the entire crowd to its feet, swaying to the familiar tempo. A young woman stood next to the piano, eyes closed, waiting for the proper chord. It was the song I had hoped for. I held out my hand and led Sarah to the floor. She leaned against me, right arm around my waist, left hand against my shoulder blade. Swaying against and moving across my pelvis, she pulled me into the sexuality of the music, the dance, the undulating, closely packed crowd. The woman began to sing the popular traditional blues:

> *Oh, my easy rider*
> *See what you done done.*
> *Lawd, Lawd, Lawd,*
> *Easy rider,*
> *See what you done done.*
> *You made me love you*
> *An' now your gal has come.*

Eyes closed, the world consists of the lamenting, whining soprano, the sweating cheek, the braless youthful breast, the oscillating thighs partially astraddle my leg. Music more felt than heard drifted out of earshot. The crowd, hypnotized by its motions, continued to dance a few moments without the music. There was no applause. Still entwined, the couples made it to the tables and the cool drinks. A few more numbers and the combo took their break. The dancing and partying intensified with the sweltering heat of the hall.

The minute hand moved to ten o'clock.

"Ten o'clock, sweetheart."

"We can stay a little."

"I promised your ma."

She rose, presented a sweaty cheek to Brad and Bunk, and we started the short walk home.

"When will I see you again?"

"I don't know. We have to finish the maneuvers, then I guess we'll go overseas."

"Guess you'd never want to come back to a place like Many."

"I'd like to see you again. We'll still be somewhere around here for another month."

"I'm not hard to find. I'm at home or at the school."

"When do you graduate?"

She laughed the laugh of an adult when a child says something silly.

"I been through school. I teach the little ones."

I was taken aback. Sixteen, through school, and teaching! Jesus Christ, I knew the South was different and poor; I didn't know it was this poor.

Her mother opened the door a crack, acknowledging that we were back in time. We sat on the porch talking about the South until her mother politely offered to make me a pallet on the floor. I declined and, pulling Sarah to the side of the house, kissed her and, pulling her tight against me, told her I'd be back soon.

I got back to the truck stop just in time to catch the 11:00 P.M. convoy to the bivouac. Excited, wanting her terribly, afraid of leaving her with a baby in this god-awful poverty, I lay awake a long time under the mosquito netting, listening to the buzzing of the insects.

I tried to understand this grinding poverty and the inability of the South to combat it. I had seen enough evidence that the Southern white farmers and workers were not any different from people anywhere else. Somehow so many of them had bought the idea that the road out of their poverty lay in pushing the blacks farther down into it. Worst yet, those who didn't believe that seemed helpless to change it. I knew one thing for certain: the blacks had to defend themselves until the whites learned better. Each attack and each defense drove these natural allies further and further apart, so they would never be able to learn.

Bunk and Brad stumbled in and flopped fully clothed on their blankets. Their drunken snores overwhelmed the sounds of crickets and mosquitoes. I rolled over into a fitful sleep.

27

A TIDAL WAVE of antiblack violence swept the nation. Each incident became the basis for an escalation of violence. After the Klan attack on the black troops at Camp Shelby, we knew we would be drawn into the fight. The Ninety-third Division was the largest concentration of black soldiers in the country. The generals had carefully separated the various regiments of the Ninety-second to keep them ineffective. Politicians and generals alike were paying the strictest attention to our restless division. The G-2 department was doing everything possible to keep information from us, and to keep the possible "troublemakers" under surveillance. They enforced the order of the previous year to "reduce and control the publication of inflammatory and vituperative articles in the colored press." They knew, and we knew, that if the Ninety-third went into action—eighteen thousand of us—it would drag all the other black outfits into the struggle. Controlling the Ninety-third was the difference between containing the protests of the small outfits and the possibility of a civil war. G-2 and the Counter Intelligence Corps (CIC), somewhat akin to an internal CIA, operated within the Klan, the police, and the political structure wherever we went, issuing warnings and organizing to prevent any provocation on the part of the Fascists.

The Ninety-third was trapped, bottled up between the Eighty-fifth Division, against whom we were maneuvering, and the Twenty-seventh stationed at Camp Claiborne. G-2 contingency plans were to use both divisions to attack us should any fighting break out. We knew we had to be careful.

Our field problem ended and we marched back to our bivouac area near Many. The following morning Brad, Joe, and I went into town to find Sarah and get what information we could. As we approached the ramshackle, barnlike structure that served as a school, we heard the children's voices proudly singing the Negro National Anthem, followed by a subdued "My Country 'tis of Thee" and a mumbled Pledge of Allegiance.

We stood outside the unpainted door. When she noticed us, Sarah handed her book to one of the students and hurried out.

"Hel-lo! I'm so glad to see you all." She glanced back into the classroom and carefully down the road.

"I'm glad you all come back. I'm afraid there's going to be some trouble."

"What happened?" We moved closer to her.

"Day 'fore yesterday, some white man slapped a colored girl for bumping into him. Mr. Charles saw it and got into a argument with the man, and the sheriff arrested Mr. Charles."

I could see the muscles twitching in Brad's jaws. His eyes were reflecting my thoughts: "Goddamnit, the shit's gonna jump before we can get ready."

Joe was probably thinking, "God, don't let it happen here."

"Is he all right? What's going to happen?" I asked.

"Daddy got some people together and we're meeting at the church tonight."

"Lucky we came by. We'll bring some of the men."

"We were countin' on you all. I was afraid you wouldn't get back."

Sarah looked at me with wide, trusting, frightened eyes.

"It's gonna be all right," I said.

She smiled the half smile of resignation.

"Daddy used to say, 'there's a train comin' and the track's all out of line.' Now I know what he means."

With a surprising militancy Joe said, "Sarah, there are eighteen thousand of us. At least half will fight if we have to."

The smile broadened, and she turned and went back into the schoolroom. We started the long walk back to camp.

★

There was no time to mobilize. We spread the word of the incident and the meeting and hoped for the best. Shaking the wrinkles out of our khaki, we sharpened our trench knives and strapped them inside our pants legs. Thirty-five soldiers showed up at the motor pool. Jinks signed out a truck and in two trips got us all into town.

The church, hardly better than a neat barn, was the finest building in the community. Immaculately clean and freshly painted, it was the only structure in the area that had a basement. The black townsfolk were milling around outside, discussing the latest incident in our centuries of oppression. The railroad workers, led by Sarah's father, and the men from the sawmill were at the center of the group.

Some of the people sensed that we would, of course, support

them if violence should come. There were others who honestly feared violence and wanted to shun that course in favor of one that would simply guarantee that such an incident would not recur, if that was possible. There were the shifty-eyed, who thought and said everything we have is from the white man, that we are living in his country, and should he choose to wipe us off the face of the earth, he could. They placed the blame on the little girl, saying she could have avoided the man if she had tried. Then there were the hard-bodied young soldiers of the 369th who stood apart, .45 pistols bulging under their shirts, trench knives outlined beneath their pants legs. We were sure we were at the beginning of something that would change the South.

The preacher came to the doorway and waved us in. We filled the building, the khaki contrasting with the dull work clothes of the people. Sarah sat between Brad and me. Conscious of the clean smell of soap on her hands and body, I partly covered her hand with mine.

The minister walked to the head of the church and held up his hand for silence. With the congregation quiet, he bowed his head and loudly prayed that the Lord would bless the meeting with wisdom and patience in the face of wrongdoing. Although the prayer asked for calm, an exhilarating sense of militancy crackled in the air and quickened the blood.

Ending the prayer, the preacher said, "Lord, we don't understand everything now, but we'll understand it better by and by." Then in a hoarse, powerful voice, he sang,

By and by when the morning comes

The congregation, startled, joined in:

All the Saints of God have gathered home
We will tell a story how we overcome
We will understand it better by and by.
Though we wonder why the test
When we try to do our best
We will understand it better
By and by.

Hardly pausing for breath, he began to preach. He called on the people to turn the other cheek, shouting, "Vengeance is mine, sayeth the Lord." Brad and I looked around in absolute amazement. The people who had called the meeting to speak couldn't. The religious appeal was wrecking the meeting.

Sensing that the combative spirit was broken, he mopped his face with a huge handkerchief and began to sing again. This time, the demoralized people fully joined in:

> *Oh, Lordy, won't you come by here*
> *Oh, Lordy, won't you come by here*
> *We're sending for you, Lordy*
> *Come by here.*
> *Bring your justice, Lord*
> *And come by here*
> *Somebody needs you, Lordy*
> *Come by here*
> *Come by here*
> *Come by here.*

A few more words, a prayer, and the meeting ended. The people left the church mumbling to one another. One woman asked in a loud undertone, "I wonder how much Mister Charlie paid him for this?"

"No need to pay him nothin'. Just pat him on his head and tell him he's a good darkie."

Lee walked over and joined us.

"Damned shame what that man did."

"It happens all the time. We just can't do anything when we ain't together."

Explanations were not necessary. It was just another sentence in the age-old story of the struggle of black America.

Mr. Charles was released. Some said it was to quiet the Ninety-third. Others said it was because there was no violence and the white man wanted to be fair. One of the women told me two white officers had visited the reverend the day before. Sure it was the CIC, I wished she had gotten the license number. Then I'd "understand it better."

★

The tension increased. A white gang raped a black woman in Shreveport. Some of the men agitated to get up there and take it out on the first whites who crossed them. A third of the men of every company spent their off hours huddled in little groups, talking about the inevitability of a riot and what they must do. Plans were thought out, presented, discussed, and discarded. The frustrations, fears, hatred, and militancy of six or seven thousand young soldiers boiled and intertwined into a bombshell ready to explode.

Army life went on. I was too busy to spend much time talking with the men in the line companies or trying to get our little committee back together. Overlays had to be drawn, maps checked, operations and field orders issued. I could barely keep up with the spontaneous tensions as they moved toward the explosion.

May 30, 1943, a sheriff killed another black soldier at Camp Van Dorn, Mississippi.

June 5, we received the news that twenty thousand white workers had walked out of the Packard defense plant in Detroit when three black workers were upgraded.

June 9. We heard the news from that hellhole for the Negro soldier, Camp Stewart, Georgia. A gang of white soldiers had murdered a black soldier and raped his wife. This was the inevitable and unacceptable next step of brutality: segregation and insults heaped upon the black troops. They broke into the supply rooms and armed themselves with rifles and submachine guns. We were thrilled and excited as we picked up the story from the careless discussion of the white officers. The first attack by the military police was turned back. They left several dead and wounded on the field. The army decided that the swaggering, cursing Klansman in a military police uniform could no longer frighten the black soldiers. Two battalions of white troops, armed with automatic and heavy weapons and supported by half-tracks, launched a full-scale attack and finally overwhelmed the black heroes.

All officers of black units were alerted for trouble. The directive from the General Staff stated that the root of the problem was the "average Negro soldier's meager education, superstition, imagination, and excitability."

June 15, 1943. We received orders from corps headquarters to move out to the Sabine River for a river defense problem against the "invading" Eighty-fifth Division. I finished the necessary map work and was taking the overlays to Captain Akeley. As I approached the command tent I heard the whining, nasal Tennessee drawl of Captain Forrest, the intelligence officer.

"I don't know what you intend to do, but these Goddamn terrapins are fixin' to do something. I been working niggers all my life and when they get too quiet, you'd better watch out."

"Well, Dick," Captain Akeley's heavy Mississippi slur filled in, "that's one way to make it happen. Ah'm afraid something is going to happen. Far as Ah'm concerned, they's soldiers and Ah'm going to treat 'em like soldiers long as they act like soldiers."

I struggled to control myself. Every impulse was to rush into the tent with my trench knife and kill the skinny little white bastard. I knew I couldn't do it, not now. As I knocked at the tent flap I swore before God and on my mother's name I was going to kill him before the war was over.

"Come in, sergeant," Akeley called out.

I went inside, saluted, and handed him the overlays. They both knew I had overheard them. Forrest, flushed, left the tent. Akeley finally returned the salute and I turned to go.

"Wait a minute, sergeant. I want to talk to you."

I was thinking how to deny I had heard anything.

"I want to talk to you man to man."

"Yes, sir?"

"There's a lot of trouble brewin' in this country. Always a small group that pulls the rest in."

"Yes, sir."

"Well, for the past two months your name been sent up to G-2 as one of the people in that small group. We been workin' together for almost two years. I figured I owed it to you to warn you."

My heart leaped into my throat, hammering so fast and hard that I was a bit dizzy for a moment. I didn't know how to answer; I didn't want to be caught in a barefaced lie.

"Must have been because I went to that meeting at the church."

Akeley's eyes narrowed ever so slightly.

"Just watch yourself, sergeant. This is the army."

"Yes, sir." I saluted and left the operations tent.

★

Itching and sweating under the blazing Louisiana sun, I walked back to my tent. How could I be so fuckin' stupid? Must have thought that everybody's a race man. We're like crabs in a barrel. Spend all our energy pulling one another down instead of trying to get out. I know there's a couple of stools in every company.

After the deal in Nogales, of course they're gonna tighten up. It's somebody close to me. I've got to find out who it is.

Brad, Lee, and Jeff were playing Drink or Smell Coon Can. They turned the cards face up. Jeff won. Lee sniffed the bottle of whiskey and passed it to Brad. He took his sniff and Jeff took a long drink.

"What the killin' shit, Road?" Brad hardly looked up from his cards.

"I think the man's on to us. Akeley just told me my name been sent up on the G-2 list for the past two months."

"Shh—it. Then they got our names, too. Somebody in this company is the rat."

"I'm going to talk to Sergeant Henson up at Regimental. If he knows anything, he'll tell me. I'm just telling you guys so you'll be cool."

At the message center, Jinks called Regiment and asked for Henson. After the greetings, Henson told me he was charge of quarters that night and would be glad to see me.

Henson was from Saint Paul, Minnesota, a draftsman who had worked steadily through the Depression. Part of the black "upper class," he was a bit disturbed by what he called my "antics." Nineteen years older than I, he hadn't known me before the war. With fewer than a thousand blacks in Minneapolis and Saint Paul, most adults knew one another. He knew my parents. Assigned to Regimental Headquarters, we had not been close, but he was always warm and friendly.

I entered the headquarters tent. Henson got up smiling. With strong white teeth, tan complexion, salt-and-pepper wavy hair, he was a handsome, self-confident man.

"Well, fella, how the hell ya doing? Gettin' much?"

"OK, Henson. Hell, no. I could go for some of that north woods stuff."

"No lie." He rubbed the back of his hand across his chin. "No lie," he repeated mostly to himself, probably thinking of one of the angels of the saintly city. He pulled himself out of Saint Paul.

"Glad to see you, Nels. What's up?"

"Look, Henson, I wanted to let you in on some thinking."

He settled back into his chair.

"OK."

"I been thinking about all this shit that's going on."

"Guess all of us have."

"It's getting worse, man. That attack by the Klan at Camp Shelby is enough to make you sick. Then last week the Klan grabbed this guy from A Company—tortured him all day long."

"Yeah. I know. He's in the hospital in Camp Claiborne. They're carrying him on the books as AWOL so no one will know."

"Most everybody knows how they fucked that guy up. Those pecks did that for a purpose. It's kill one, scare a thousand. I don't think we dare get scared. All these things happening in Shreveport and De Ritter—there's going to be a riot. They want to make sure we don't get into it."

"Yeah, I know. I have friends in Beaumont. They say things are getting real tight. I'm not much of a fighting man, but I wish I had just one platoon if it happens."

That was the opening I was waiting for.

"We got a whole division here."

Henson rubbed his hand across his chin and then through the thick, graying hair. He was catching the drift. After a few seconds he said, "OK, I get the point. How the hell do you intend to get a whole division into motion?"

"I'll tell you the truth. We've been talking to some of the men in the rifle companies. They're ready to fight. We've even got some sort of a command set up."

"You're playing with fire. These companies are shot full of Toms and snitches. You can't do it."

"I don't think that's true. We did it in Nogales."

"Damn your time," Henson chuckled. "I knew you were in on that. G-2 thinks so, too. That's what I'm talking about. I was in a line company; I found out that they're not going to pull together."

"Henson, these men have learned something since they've been out of basic. I'm not for involving everyone. Just enough people to have a command if something happens. Jesus Christ, man. What if the motherfuckers got ahold of you?"

He turned his hands palm up in a gesture of surrender.

"Yeah, I know. What do you want me to do? You know what this is?"

"Sure, I know. It's mutiny—rebellion—I don't give a damn. Better the army hang us than the Klan."

"You know I'm with you. I can't do anything. If anything starts, these people will really have their eye on me."

"That's just the point. We don't want you to do anything. We need information."

"What?"

"I worked with Major Woods once. I know he's too lazy to do anything he doesn't have to. These reports that come in from the companies on who says what—if Woods don't get them up to G-2, then you must. Anyway, you can find out who the stools in the companies are."

"Yeah. I can."

"Look." I leaned close to him and continued in a whisper. "Can you get to the reports and get the names of the stools in the companies? Then we know who to avoid. If any reports get through, maybe you can kill them before they get to G-2."

"If this sort of thing ever got out, I'd be shot. This stuff is top secret. Christ, they'd break Woods down to a buck private. I don't give a damn—but I'd hate to get hooked on a hummel."

"They're pushing us into a fight, Henson. We ain't got the chance of a snowball in hell if we don't know who is squealing on us."

"Man, I can't do it. I'm too exposed."

"I swear on my mother's name, it'll never get out."

Sergeant Henson glanced at me. "I'm going to the latrine for about ten minutes. Take charge of quarters for me 'til I get back."

"OK, Henson. But think it over."

He laid his wallet on the table. "Watch my wallet—everything I own is in there."

I thought it a strange request but sat down to await his return. After a few moments it struck me. Jesus Christ! How dumb can you get? I grabbed the wallet and opened it. Sure enough, the key was there. I glanced outside and closed the tent flap. With my heart beating against the roots of my teeth, I opened the steel locker and pulled out the envelope. I scribbled down the names, stuffed the report back into the envelope, put it back into the locker, and turned the key.

By the time Sergeant Henson returned, I was still scared but breathing normally.

No calls? Everything's all right?

"Everything's fine. If them bastards start anything—we're going to give them a fight."

"Take it easy, man." It was exhaled as a tense sigh.

"Yeh, Henson—"

"Huh?"

"Lay dead—play crazy."

The list of G-2 spies amazed me. I knew half of the fifteen
names, including a man from Saint Paul whom I considered my
friend and a fighter for our people. I memorized the names I
hadn't known and burned the paper.

I crawled into the pup tent and under the mosquito netting.
How the hell are we going to handle this? One mistake and they'll
string us up as they did those soldiers in Houston.

Half asleep, I remembered that frightful day in September
of 1938.

Pop was on the telephone when I walked into the house after
school. Waving the morning paper, he signaled me to be quiet.
Mom whispered that he was talking to the police. I raised my
hands palms up, as if to say, "What's going on?" He unfolded the
Minneapolis Journal. It had a terrifying one-word headline: RAPE!
Beneath the headline was a picture of a thin-faced white woman.
Her address was only five blocks away. Large type reported an
abduction and rape by a Negro man. Slightly smaller type hinted
that white men might form vigilante mobs to "assist the police."

"Chief," Pop was saying, each studied word separated and
spoken as a hammer blow. "Chief, our legion post has always
worked with your department. This paper says vigilantes are
forming to help you. We are going to help you keep a lynch mob
out of this neighborhood."

A moment's silence.

"I'd be happy if you sent an officer over." He hung up and
turned to us. "We can't take chances with all these kids. This time,
we'll be ready."

Mom, always the peacemaker, said, "Can't the police handle
this? This isn't Mississippi."

"A lynch mob is the same anywhere." He turned to me. "I'll
never forget when they lynched my cousin. Our family had
known the sheriff's family for two generations. After the funeral I
went to the sheriff and asked him why he hadn't done something.
He looked at me like I was crazy and said, 'What do you expect
one Dutchman to do with a hundred drunk Irishmen?' I never
forgot—and don't you forget—when the chips are down, whites
are going to stick with whites and you better be ready to fight
them."

Mr. Ransom, Mr. Elliot, and Mr. Keys came to the door. They
were wearing the caps of their segregated American Legion post
and carried baseball bats. A few more men were approaching the

house. Twenty years ago they were together in the trenches of France. Defending our little community gave back a bit of the pride they had lost in the unemployment of the Great Depression.

A squad car pulled up to the house. The sergeant from the public relations department left the car, adjusted his cap, and walked to the front door. Pop nodded to Mom and me. We went into the kitchen.

The muffled voices filled the room for twenty minutes. Then the doors opened. The policeman was saying, "We've asked the papers to tone this thing down. But you have to help."

After the police left, Pop said, "All right, men. We won't carry guns. In each of the alleys we'll station a car with the rifles and shotguns. We'll be ready."

The men left. I took my .22 from the scabbard, put a shell in the chamber, and hid it near the front door.

The day passed into a night of ominous silence. Reports came to the house of how gangs of white men were crowding the taverns six blocks away at Thirty-eighth and Nicolet. They were cursing and threatening, but no one volunteered to lead the lynch mob.

The taverns closed at 1:00 A.M. The whites drifted to their homes, too drunk to make any trouble that night. A few of the men slept at the house with the rifles. The rest went home.

The morning paper came on time and the headline stated that the woman had confessed that she made up the story. She had spent the night with her lover.

The tension subsided, and that afternoon the men came back to the house to sip coffee and talk about what they would have done if the mob had come. They knew they had won a victory.

Mr. Ransom said, "If we'd have been sniveling and crying for protection, those Paddys would have burned this area down. The only thing held them back was they knew we were ready."

"It went just right," Pop said. "We didn't provoke anything. We let the police know, and they let the mob know. It went just right."

It was then that Pop found my rifle. He showed it to the men, proudly saying that I was his best soldier. They all laughed. They were all combat veterans and the army was still in them. They shook my hand, saying that sixteen was old enough to learn about an equalizer.

That's what we have to do. We have to be ready. We have to

let the Klan know we're ready. But we can't start anything. I felt better. I knew we were on the correct path.

It was way past taps when I finally fell asleep.

28

WE SPENT THE morning of June 16 cleaning up our areas in preparation for the move to the Sabine River. After duty hours, Brad, Bunk, Lee, Jeff, Hewitt, and I got together. The position of our committees was getting dangerous. Once we left the bivouac and spread out along the Sabine, maintaining contact with the committees in the 368th and 25th would be almost impossible. We had to decide on a plan of action if rioting should break out in our area. Whatever was to be done had to be done quickly.

We agreed to try to get together the battalion and regimental leaders of the squads that night. After retreat, Brad and Bunk went to the 25th, Jeff and Lee to the 368th. Hewitt and I wandered through the 369th and found the three committee leaders from the battalions.

The seventeen of us had not been together since Nogales. There was a good bit of backslapping and handshaking. To avoid looking too conspicuous, we spread several blankets and sat together talking. Brad and I met with the regimental committee leaders. Hewitt and Bunk met with the battalion leaders.

We could do nothing to protect an area more than twenty miles away. We were going to have to wait, no matter what happened, until we got the chance to strike. We had to keep our men ready, but they had to be cool.

The meeting had gone surprisingly well. The men well understood the dangerous position of the entire division. We were just preparing to disperse when Moore came running up to us.

"What's going on, White Rabbit?"

"There's a riot in Beaumont. The motherfuckers are burning the colored section of town."

"What happened?" "When did it start?" "Are they fighting back?"

"Wait a minute." Moore held up his hands. "I just heard it on the radio. The whites attacked the colored section. They set the place on fire."

"Well, Goddamn it. They want a war, let's give it to 'em."

"Man, this is what we were talkin' about. We can't get to Beaumont. We can't start a fight here. We got to wait until they attack us, then we can wipe 'em out."

A heavy silence fell over the group. A hundred and fifty miles away a mob with a few weapons was killing our people. We sat here—concentrated, armed, trained for combat, and unable to come to their rescue.

"Men," Brad said quietly. "My home ain't far from Beaumont. I know how every one of you all feel. The stakes are pretty big now. Everything depends on discipline. Military discipline. They're gonna hit De Ritter or Many. When they do, we'll kill every one of the motherfuckers. If we show our hand now, we ain't gonna help nobody."

The moment of tense silence hung on.

"We'd better break it up," I said. "Remember that when we get to the river, you guys are going to have to stay in touch—we won't be able to find you."

The men began to drift away toward their companies. Two of the men from the Twenty-fifth hung back. I went over to them.

"Don't know if you remember me. My name's Sammy Atkinson. I was with you down in Nogales."

"Sure I remember you, Sammy." And I did. He was one of the men who had been beaten by the Eighth Air Force soldiers. He seemed so calm and shy, I'd have never recognized him.

We shook hands warmly.

"I brought my home buddy up to meet you. I liked the way you guys organized things in Nogales. This here is Joe Henry Johnson."

I turned and shook hands with the lanky, smiling, dark-skinned young soldier. I recognized him too. He had taken first prize in the competition for assembly and firing of the water-cooled machine gun. I recalled how he had deftly assembled the machine gun blindfolded, recognizing the parts by touch and putting them together.

"Proud to know you, Joe Henry. I remember you and your machine gun from Huachuca."

He smiled for a moment and then said almost pleadingly, "My peoples in Beaumont. We gotta do something. I gotta do something."

I felt almost like a handkerchief head but I had to say it.

"Joe Henry, I want to fight bad as you do. But there ain't no use fighting a losing battle. We're going to have to wait. How are we going to get to Beaumont? We're going to get our chance. We've got to be soldiers and hold our fire."

"Part of me says you're right, but we can't let these white people drive us back into slavery and we got all the guns."

"Only thing I can say is, we got to have a plan and everybody got to stick to it. The plan now is to fight in De Ritter or Many and not get split up."

"We know you're right," Sammy said. "It's hard takin' low all the time. I just wanted him to hear it from you."

We shook hands again and they left for their area.

Brad had been standing quietly, listening.

"I don't think we can hold it together, Road. The men have had all they can take. If Uncle Sam got any sense, he'll get us out of here now."

"You can see the mother ain't got no sense, or we wouldn't be here."

★

June 19, 1943. The division loaded up into a huge convoy of trucks that deposited us along a twenty-five-mile front on the Louisiana side of the Sabine River. We immediately set about digging our latrines and garbage sumps and setting up the battalion headquarters. The men went about their tasks in sullen, ominous silence.

The rioting spread. Seven more blacks dead and 150 seriously injured that week in ten racial outbreaks. Fifty men and women injured in Mobile, Alabama. A man was lynched near Tampa, Florida. Five black shipyard workers were gunned down by Coast Guard reservists in Chester, Pennsylvania. Four black soldiers were shot in Riverside, California; three shot in Augusta, Georgia. Two more black soldiers were shot at Camp Van Dorn, Mississippi, when they refused to say "yes, sir" to a group of white men. One black soldier was shot dead at Fort Bliss, Texas.

The next morning there was a surprise inspection for ammunition. No one was caught. By limiting ourselves to two clips, we had been able to bury them the moment we arrived at a bivouac and easily dug them up just before we left.

The officers were plainly concerned by the taut silence. The news from Beaumont was horrible. It was impossible to distin-

guish between rumors and fact. We knew the radio and newspapers weren't telling the truth and hoped the word of mouth
from Beaumont was exaggerated.

Rumor had it that the mob pinned the blacks against the river
and a slaughter occurred. The papers stated that the fighting was
dying down as the troops moved in. We knew, in fact, that the
troops had joined the mob, and "establishing calm" meant the
brutal military crushing of the resistance. Wherever men from the
Ninety-third met in little groups, there was an exchange of rumors
and a swearing of revenge.

Unbroken by the brutality of the troops, the scattered attacks by
the Klan, and the constant threat of renewed mob violence, black
Beaumont heroically stood firm and defiantly celebrated June
'teenth [nineteenth], the prohibition of slavery in the territories.

Tension and danger charged the air. Black Jack ladled supper
from the cooking pots. The sun set into Texas. At 10:00 P.M.,
Harold laid aside the GI bugle and took his trumpet from the battered case. The area hushed to a surly, brooding silence as he
played a mournful taps for Beaumont.

★

June 20. The day was especially hot and the humidity oppressive.
We tried to maintain contact with our men through notes whenever a message was sent to their areas. The day wore itself out
with routine chores. At 11:00 P.M. I finally got under the mosquito
netting and went to sleep.

At 12:15 A.M. Lee shook me awake and motioned for me to follow him. When we were out of earshot of the headquarters tent,
he whispered, "The shit is on in Detroit."

"What happened?"

"We turned the radio on in the message center and got a news
broadcast. A riot started on some island near Detroit. They're
killin' every colored man they can find."

"Jesus Christ, Lee. What do you think we should do?"

"Can't do nothin' 'cept what we're doin'. If I know this white
man, they're gonna expect us to do something. They gonna really
search for ammo."

"I think you're right, Lee. See if you can get a message to the
men to get rid of the shit."

"I think Jinks is already doing that. I just wanted to check
with you."

When the sharp sound of reveille pierced the woods and lagoons, I had been peering into the graying sky for several hours.

★

June 21. The rifle companies moved from their bivouac area to take defensive positions along the river. The 25th and 369th were on the defensive line, with the 368th in reserve. The radios switched from clear to code and imposed battle discipline.

There was little more for the operations section to do for a few hours. Captain Akeley was groggy, having been on his feet for eighteen hours. I hated myself for it, but I spread out his bedroll and told him I'd be able to handle things for a few hours if he wanted to sleep. He looked at me in absolute shock that I would do such a personal thing without an order.

"Thanks, sergeant. But wake me up in two hours."

"Yes, sir."

He pulled off his shoes and stretched out. In a few moments I could hear the gentle, deep, regular breathing.

★

True to their word, our committee leaders from the 25th, 368th, and 369th regiments came to the battalion headquarters to check in. It was a good feeling to know that we were maintaining good communications.

Our information was that the white mobs had killed at least twenty blacks and seriously injured many more in Beaumont. As the fighting died down there, it increased in fury in Detroit. Over thirty were confirmed dead and the injured topped seven hundred. The news fired the men into a seething, impotent rage. They wanted to march. Our little group, by urging the men to be cool, found itself in bed with the officers and Uncle Toms.

★

June 22. Sergeant Jackson woke me up at 5:00 A.M. The river operation was to begin. After gulping down the bitter coffee, I went to the operations tent. Captain Akeley was at work. At 6:00 A.M. he mentioned that he was going to a staff meeting at Regiment. He left and I walked up toward the message center, where I could get the reports as they came in.

The river crossing began. From our hilltop headquarters I

could see the assault boats heading across the river and the combat engineers constructing a pontoon bridge.

TUM-TUM-TUM. TUM-TUM-TUM. The sound of the machine gun ricocheted across the river, through the swamps and the forest, and shattered against the hills. Forty-five seconds of sustained firing followed the two short bursts.

Holy Jesus Christ! What the fuck is going on? I ran to the Message Center.

"Jinks, what the hell is happening?"

"I don't know. Sounds like a water-cooled down in the Twenty-fifth area."

"Reckon those white boys want a shooting war?"

"Could be the Twenty-fifth."

The 240 radio lit up. The speed key began to sing. Jinks reached for his earphones when the message broke in clear.

"This is General Leyman. Battalions report!"

"Cobra Red."

"Cobra White."

"Cobra Blue."

We stood breathlessly as the commanding general continued. "All company commanders are to make immediate inspection for live ammunition. I will be in the company areas within the hour."

"Roger!"

"Over and out."

Jinks printed the message on the quadruple forms and called the company runners.

"Get this to the company commanders, but first tell everybody to get rid of the shit."

★

Within the hour General Leyman and several jeeploads of his staff had arrived in the area. They were holding full field inspections throughout the division. I waited in the operations tent, resigned to whatever might happen.

Captain Akeley, a white major, and a lieutenant entered the tent.

I rose and saluted the officers. They returned the salute.

"Rest, sergeant."

"Sergeant Peery," Akeley's face was tight and grim—"Major Thomas, from Division G-2, and Lieutenant Jefferies, from CIC, want to talk to you." Akeley's eyes were almost pleading for me to come clean. While not the target, he knew he was in the line of fire.

"Yes, sir."

The lean lieutenant's snakelike eyes were barely visible behind the air force glasses. He exuded a menacing air.

"Take a seat, sergeant."

"Thank you, sir."

"I'll come right to the point. We're fighting a war for the existence of this country and its way of life."

I breathed deeply to control myself.

"To win this war, we need the army to function as a unified command. Articles of War defend the soldier *and* the army. You understand that?"

"Yes, sir." I had to breathe deeply again.

"We have reports that you may be involved in a conspiracy."

I thought it best to be silent.

"Do you know what that means?"

"Yes, sir."

"This conspiracy now means two men have been charged with attempted murder. I want you to tell me honestly two things."

"Yes, sir."

"Were you in the riot in Nogales?"

Lay dead, play crazy. If they knew everything, they would have arrested you a long time ago. They think you're another stupid jig they can intimidate. I fought to hold back the rage.

"I didn't know there was no riot, sir. My friend and me (don't speak too good English —it'll make them suspicious) we was walking a little ways from what they called Ranchita and some white soldiers jumped us. We got in a fight and got back to where the convoy was. I heard there was other fights that night."

The major was ruddy, paunchy, threatening. He leaned toward me. "You listen to me, boy—uh—soldier. What happened out there is serious. You either tell me the truth or I'm gonna have you arrested and put under oath. You'll tell the truth then." His voice was heavy with rural South Carolina.

It wasn't a question. I looked at the ground and then glanced at Akeley. Our eyes met for a millisecond. He flushed slightly. I sensed he wasn't going to let them mistreat his nigger.

"Do you know a Corporal Joe H. Johnson in D Company, Twenty-fifth Infantry?"

The blood was pounding in my temples. Half truth this time. They know something.

"Yes, sir. I got to know him when he won the machine gun competition in Huachuca."

"You seen him lately?"

"No, sir. Not since we left Huachuca." My back and scalp broke out into an itchy sweat. My God, it must have been Joe Henry.

"Did something happen to Joe Henry, sir?"

"We'll ask the questions." The major's face flushed even more.

"Something's going to happen to him," Snake Eyes said. "He opened fire on unarmed soldiers this morning. You volunteered. Why? You enlisted in the Civilian Military Training Corps. Why?"

"I went into CMTC because my dad always liked army life. I sorta wanted to become an officer in the army."

"That's why you volunteered?"

"No, sir. I believe that I should defend my country. I don't like everything, but it's my country." Snake Eyes was backing off me. I wasn't fooling Maj. Johnny Reb. There was a moment of awkward silence while they figured out how to proceed. Captain Akeley cleared his throat.

"I would like to dismiss the sergeant and speak to you all privately."

Akeley glanced at me. I rose, saluted, and left the tent. I knew what was going on in there. Akeley, from Mississippi, would say he's a good boy. Yes, from the North. Runs his mouth too much, and don't quite know his place. He's learning that the colored people still need the firm and kindly guidance of the Southern whites who know them best. Akeley would say that he was responsible for me and would vouch for me. The other two, being in the white man's club, would have to accept this. They would let me go and keep me under surveillance.

This final realization of a black man's impotence weighed against my chest. I could hardly breathe and tears were beginning to fill the emptiness. Black man will never be anything but a boy in this country. Even if you kill one of these white bastards, you're not a brave man; you're a dangerous, crazy nigger. You outsmart them, you're a sneaky, sinister nigger. I can't even raise a rebellion without the protection of a Mississippi white man.

Suddenly, I realized that this was my birthday! I was twenty and it was the worst day of my life.

29

MANEUVERS WERE BROKEN off. The officials of the State of Louisiana demanded that the Ninety-third leave their state at once. Convoyed back to Many, we were confined to the bivouac area. We simply sat there as if on garrison duty, while the generals and heads of the congressional committees on the military tried to figure out what to do with us.

The black press was increasing its clamor for the army to commit the Ninety-third to combat. Most of the generals and politicians wanted to ship us anywhere overseas. That would pacify the black press. More important, it would eliminate a ticking time bomb. It wasn't that simple. General Eisenhower informed the War Department that he was looking for but found no country willing to accept Negro troops.

When a black anti-aircraft unit was sent to Trinidad to guard the Panama Canal, the British colonial government raised hell until they were withdrawn. The British Colonial Office was deathly afraid that black troops would revolutionize their colonials. Governor Gruening of Alaska believed that the effect of colored troops on the Indians and Eskimos would be "undesirable." The air force demanded that no blacks be sent to Iceland, Greenland, or Labrador. Gen. George C. Marshall issued a directive stating that no black combat troops should be sent to the British Isles.

Australia, fighting the Japanese on Australian soil, refused to accept black combat troops. The *Chicago Defender* ran a cartoon showing two Japanese soldiers on the attack in Australia passing the sign No Colored Races Allowed. One soldier grins at the sign saying, "So sorry, please."

Every country, even states within the United States, feared the effect our militancy and aggressiveness would have on their own second-class subjects. Black soldiers had become engaged in street fighting on the side of the people in Trinidad, British Guiana, Panama, the Bahamas, St. Lucia, and Jamaica. Army Intelligence recommended that no Negro troops be sent to the Caribbean or Latin America.

Patton, as did his predecessor, Pershing, let it be known that it would be preferable to fight for the Germans than have black combat troops under his command. He always added that he would take all the black soldiers he could get as service and labor troops. By the end of the war he accepted a crack black tank battalion. Gen. Bedell Smith dug his heels in on the line that there would be no integrated fighting as long as he was in command.

Southern politicians were worried about the large number of white troops going overseas and the buildup of black troops in the States, especially in the South.

We had to leave Louisiana and there was no place to go. Some smart-ass general solved the riddle.

Dump them out in the Mojave Desert. The generals believed they could resist the political pressures from the black press for at least six months. Then they'd figure out something else. In the desert, there was nothing to rebel against.

Black troops staged an uprising in Camp Breckinridge, Kentucky. Black military police were brought in to quell an uprising at Camp Van Dorn, Mississippi. The black military cops opened fire on the black soldiers, killing three. Uprisings bloodied Fort Bliss, Texas. At March Field and Camp San Luis Obispo, California, the black soldiers took up arms to defend themselves against the oppressive system and its army.

As the decision was being made, the rumor mill began to grind. They were going to train us for desert warfare and send us to North Africa. The division was going to be broken up into labor battalions.

They were playing a cruel game. We knew it, and the generals knew we knew it. Although superbly trained, our division was not combat-worthy. It was cynical, disillusioned, and confused. There was no will to engage the German or Japanese armies. Infantry soldiers must have a high state of morale. Morale is the basis of combat efficiency. A high morale means the troops are ready to fight and die for a national cause they believe in. It never occurred to the generals that we didn't want to die to uphold a system of lynch law, mob violence, segregation, and daily humiliations.

The generals, proceeding from a deep conviction that we were an inferior race, explained the lack of morale as "Negroes lack stamina and aggressiveness." General Spaatz, commander of the air force, was the ideological leader of the pack. He saw to it that black soldiers under his command had the stamina to work twelve hours a day unloading boats and building airfields. He filled the military prisons with blacks as a cure for an aggressiveness he denied they had.

Both sides played the game for political reasons. The generals would send us to the desert for "further training." We knew they had no intention of committing us to combat, and we were glad of it.

★

The official word came down. We were going to the desert and do the maneuvers over. Then we were going overseas.

★

Before anything official had been written, the rumor, with a stamp of truth on it, had gotten to the platoon. The men stood in small groups, commenting on this latest step toward overseas duty. I walked over where Juicy was holding court.

"Man, think about it. These motherfuckers got it all figured out. They can't hold us here. We're trained to fight. They figure if we stay here, sooner or later we're going into action right here. Best thing is to get rid of us. Send us to North Africa and let Rommel kill us all."

"They're not going to send us to Africa. It would be like training a division of Sioux Indians and shipping them to North Dakota," Hewitt said. "We'd find out where and who to fight."

"Shut up, Hew," Lee said. "You wants to get to Africa so you can find a wife black enough for you."

When the laughter died down, Brad said, "The shit is getting deep here. These people are beginning to depend on us. That's why they're shipping us out. Colored people in this area ever get together, there'd be hell to pay. I don't think they ever realized that they're the majority. They got to get us out."

There was a moment's silence. It was my turn to speak.

"I think part of everything that's been said is true. I think the main thing is that after Joe Henry squeezed off on those soldiers, it showed that we ain't afraid of killing whites. The Klan's white, most of the officers are white. The sheriff is white. They got to get us out of here."

"That's just why we got to find some way to stay here. We ain't

lost nothin' overseas. If we're going to fight, we got to do it here."
Harold had taken a new layer of militancy since the Beaumont
riots.

There was little left to say. We wanted to stay. The army was
going to make us go.

"You goin' into town before we go?" Harold asked.

"Yeah. I got an overnight pass, beginning tomorrow
morning."

"Man," Brad grinned, "you the only cat around here getting
overnight passes. You must be getting white around the mouth."

"Fuck you, Bradley. You know I earn those passes. Akeley
don't give me no pass, I don't do his work."

"You a bitch with your shit." Jeff laughed. "You still chasing
that big-eyed gal there in Many?"

"Yeah, she's the only one I know."

"You must be trimmin' her up around the edges." Juicy gave
a stupid, leering look. He knew I was a little embarrassed that
Sarah was only sixteen.

"She's a school teacher. Hell, she's got more sense than I have.
I ain't never touched the woman."

"You think school teachers don't want to do it?"

Jeff, Big Joe, and Juicy were in their middle thirties. They
were enjoying the little game of tease and embarrass.

"You gonna cover a young filly like that 'un, you better know
what you doin'. You half fuck one of these Lous'ana gals, they put
a voodoo on your ass."

"You know how to jelly-roll?"

I laughed; that sounded good. "What's that?"

"You know what a jelly roll looks like. Got a curlicue of jelly
goin' round and round in a spiral?"

"You talkin' about the boar hog grind," Big Joe said. "If you
want to do it good, don't read books. Watch the animals. They all
do it different. The horse is different from the dog. The rabbit different from the bull. They're animals, they can only do it one way.
Study the animals and you can do everything any of them do.
Then you'll be able to kick some sheets and bend some skin."

"If you get buck fever on the firing line, me and Juicy will be
your tactical reserve."

"Pay them old bastards no mind," Lee said. "They too old to
get it up if they could find a woman."

After the laughter died down, the little group broke up and the men went to their pup tents, preparing to break camp.

★

We were scheduled to pull out Monday morning. Wanting to make the most of this last visit, I left camp early. Walking down the dirt road to her little house, I tried to understand the relationship that had developed between us. I had an overwhelming admiration for this young woman. Passing the little barn that served as the school, I thought of the times she had invited Hewitt, Joe, and me to speak to the kids. We had an education. We had gone to brick schools with huge libraries. I knew that the three of us put together could not do the job she was doing. She often told me that the only thing that kept her going was her belief that educating these youngsters would hasten the day when the South would be free.

Approaching her house, I felt a surge of happiness. She was a good woman. Only sixteen, but a good woman. I wanted to hold her close and tell her how I felt.

She walked out from the porch to meet me. The starched bright print dress, the oiled and pressed hair seemed bright and inviting, in sharp contrast to the fixed smile and the somber eyes. News of our leaving had reached Many.

Within the warmth of her embrace I saw the curtain move and knew her mother was watching with apprehension.

Saturday was a day of simple pleasures in Many. After chores, the people sauntered to the open lot that served as a baseball diamond. When the game ended, there was barely enough time to wash up and get to the church social. What a meal in wartime! Chicken, candied yams, sweet corn with collard greens cooked with diced chunks of fatback and stored in an earthen crock for two days. There was corn bread and hush puppies and corn pone. Fresh pork loin set beside ham shanks that hung in the smokehouse most of the week. Sweet potatoes and white potatoes and both kinds mashed and whipped and placed beside the heavy breads and light biscuits were rushed from the oven to the church. It was still a time of small plots and backyard gardens.

After the scrumptious dinner and the rest hour that followed, most of the people returned to the church for the prayer meetings, followed by the Men's Club and Ladies Auxiliary. Church took up the day and tightly knit the blacks into an interdependent community.

At seven o'clock, a projector was set up and a nickel bought a seat on a backless wooden bench to see the movie. This was the alternative to sitting in the filthy Jim Crow balcony of a theater with its outside toilet for the black patrons.

Throughout the long grade B drama, I was terribly conscious of the scent of her hair, the dab of perfume on her neck, the firm womanliness of her youthful body. She momentarily leaned against me for protection from the fires, explosions, and subterranean monsters that leaped from the makeshift screen. My fingertip pressed where the breast swelled full from the rib cage. There was no sign that she felt any of the deepening longings or the rising passion that gripped and shook me. I wished that she weren't sixteen or that I weren't twenty.

The movie finally ended and we left. It was dark. The muffled racket of dozens of types of crickets and bugs filled the warm Louisiana darkness. The night birds were crying in the bayous. The stars, close, shone thick and bright through the clear clean air.

We struggled with our own thoughts in silence. I had received little sex education during the few talks with Pop. The one thing I remembered was, "Don't go to bed with a woman you're not willing to marry in the morning." I wanted her and I'd be willing to marry her if anything happened—if only she were seventeen!

We sat on the flimsy porch, legs hanging over the edge, each wondering how to approach the other. Sarah leaned against me, breathing deeply. If only I had said something before we reached the house. It was impossible now. It was almost eleven o'clock and there was no place to go.

Before long, the gentle scraping of the door let us know that her mother was there.

"Sarah, honey, it's past eleven. Mr. Nelson"—she always addressed me as "mister"—"I put down a pallet on the floor. We'd be proud to have you spend the night."

"Thanks. I don't have any way to get back to the camp."

She closed the door. Sarah, her eyes wider still with passionate questions, looked into mine.

"I hate you're going away." Lowering her eyes, pressing her face against my chest, she mumbled into my shirt, "I love you."

Without answering, I held her tight until the moment passed.

Inside the house, we both glanced to be sure her parents' bedroom door was closed. Assured, she fell into my arms. Her lips, full and soft and warm, pressed against mine.

"Sarah, honey. This is crazy, we're going to get caught."

Breathing deeply, she squeezed my hand and went into the room she shared with her two younger sisters.

The pallet spread out beneath the window in the living room to the front of the little four-room house. I pulled off the boots, took off the pants and shirt, lit the cigarette, and lay down. Inhaling deeply, staring at the ceiling, I opened my mind to the jumble of thoughts waiting at the gates. I sure was lucky meeting Sarah. It's a hell of a lot more than knowing there's a pallet to sleep on while the rest of the soldiers are sleeping in the woods. Or having this big-eyed, pretty young woman to make the guys jealous. I learned from her. If it hadn't been for her, I would've never known what being proud to be a Negro meant. Minneapolis is supposed to be liberal, and underneath it's just as rotten as Many. You can't fight the Jim Crow because of the liberalism. It does something to you. Makes you soft—don't know who to fight. These people got some pride we never had. Guess it's because they're together in a way we couldn't be. Funny how the deal goes down. We're not going to solve the problem in Minneapolis until the one down here is solved. We're like a branch growing off the tree. We're not going anywhere. We don't try to solve the problem where it got to be solved. It's too hard. Better to try to solve it where it can't be solved. It's easier that way. Shit, man, these people got our minds so fucked up it's a shame. Maybe when the war is over, I'll come back here. Me and Brad and the guys—we could stir up some shit. It'd be a liberation army like they've got in China.

My thoughts were shattered by the muffled sound of bare feet tiptoeing across the rough floor. Her white broadcloth nightgown was ethereal alabaster against dark skin. She knelt beside me as I sat up to embrace her. The excitement of full soft lips. Finally, finally the breasts. God, what breasts! Hands hungered to touch those breasts. Firm, full, I believed they could feed more babies than I could ever sire. Her breath was deep and heavy. She pulled her mouth from mine, pressed her mouth to my ear, and whispered, "Confess, honey, first confess."

"I love you, Sarah. I really do." God, it's been over eighteen months.

She lay down on the pallet and, bending to kiss her, I remembered all the reasons we couldn't do it.

"Sarah, I want you so much. But it ain't right. You're only sixteen."

"I haven't had a chance to tell you—I'm seventeen now."

She raised her head to meet my mouth. Lips parted before the slight pressure, the teeth, the meeting of tongues. She gasped and arched against me.

"Your mother. Your mother will—"

"Mama knows. I told her. She won't tell Daddy."

Her hand slid to the back of my neck, fingers grasping at the hair, nails digging into my scalp as I rolled over and against her.

★

After the last good-night kiss she tiptoed back to her room. I lit up, and the thoughts flooded back. How the hell can anybody turn his back on this? Here's where I belong. Here's where the fight is. Maybe Hewitt is right. Fuck everybody else. If the Negroes would only stick together. Jesus Christ, what's going to happen to these people when we leave? The crickets and night birds were singing love songs. I barely had energy to crush the smoke before giving in to the wave of sleep washing over me.

30

SERGEANT JACKSON WAS blowing the whistle and yelping for the men to crawl out of their pup tents for reveille as I entered the company area. We spent the day policing up, covering the garbage sumps and drainage ditches. This was our last day in Louisiana and after duty we were free. With the blankets spread out beneath the trees, the games began. Tonk, coon can, bid whist, and dice games coexisted with prayer meetings and the shit-house lawyers holding court. The day wore on—slapping mosquitoes, torturing chiggers, writing letters, and daydreaming of home.

Night rose from the bayous and the gullies. Brad and Big Joe brought out a five-gallon crock of white lightning. The party was on. A few of the men began laughingly playing the "dozens."

"Hey, Luke, I ain't gonna talk about your mammy, 'cause I heard you got two bald-headed pappies."

"My mammy is your mammy, go on an' talk about her."

"Why don't you all shut up that kind a' talk 'fore you start fightin'?"

The jug made its way around for the third time, and semi-literate men began reciting the half-hour-long "Sinking of the Titanic." The whole group would join in on the good parts:

> *The daughter of the Captain ran across the deck*
> *Panties 'round her ankles, brassiere her neck*
> *Yellin' Shine, Shine save poor me*
> *I'll give you all the pussy that you can see.*

The poem droned on with the white folks begging Shine to save them as he jumped into the icy ocean and swam away.

> *When the news reached New York*
> *That the Titanic had sunk,*
> *Shine was on 125th and Lenox*
> *Dead drunk.*

Harold borrowed a guitar and with a rich Houston voice sang an old favorite Blues. Big Joe stood up, his huge bulk swaying, canteen cup half full of white lightning. He raised his hand for silence and sang:

> *Boys, I'm reelin' and I'm rockin'.*
> *I'm a-spinnin' like a wheel.*
> *If you ever loved a woman,*
> *Then you know how bad I feel.*

> *New Orleans, that's a seaport*
> *Bogalusa is a saw mill town*
> *If you get up to Kansas City*
> *Then you really gettin' round.*

> *I'm reelin' and I'm rockin'*
> *I'm spinnin' like a wheel,*
> *If you ever longed for whiskey,*
> *Then you know how bad I feel.*

Big Joe sat down amid the applause. A few more men sang their favorite songs. When we began to tire, Harold sang our song. We all joined in the chorus:

> *Well now I don't know, but I have heard*
> *From Fort Huachuca came the Ninety-third*
> *They stood a test nobody thought they could*
> *When they started their maneuvers in the Louisiana*
>   *woods*
> *That was a time. My Lord, that was a time.*
> *Great God 'Amighty, now what a time!*

The singing died down and a few of the men continued reciting poems between drinks.

Parker stood up and took a slug of the corn liquor. We all applauded. It meant something for Parker to recite a poem.

> *I'm big and black and bad,*
> *An' my feet don't touch the ground,*
> *I come from the back river country*
> *Where the sun don't never shine*
> *I got a graveyard disposition*
> *An' a tombstone mind,*
> *I'm a mean motherfucker*
> *An' I don't mind dyin'.*

He sat down to cheers and applause.

Harry, from the message center, stood up, took a sip of the white lightening, and said,

> *Any one can plainly see*
> *I ain't meant for this army*
> *I'm sayin' my last good-bye.*
> *Don't none of you soldiers cry.*
> *I'm taking a furlough, fur long*
> *Fur ever.*

Harry staggered through the drunken laughter toward the road. We never saw him again.

Half drunk, fighting a terrible longing for Sarah, I staggered to the pup tent. Rolling up in my blanket to shut out the singing and laughter, I could see her as in the darkness of the room. Big, expressive eyes shone from the dark chocolate of her face. How terrible it is to be away from women, to long for them. They make the whole world good. They make you want to be manly and brave. I slept.

★

At dawn on Monday morning, the regiment lined up on the road for the five-mile march to the train station. The firm, disciplined tramp of the soldiers brought Many's blacks to the roadside to say good-bye to new friends and lovers.

As we neared her house, I saw her on the porch, peering through the ranks as they passed by. She saw me. Jumping from the porch with girlish enthusiasm, she skipped through the communications platoon and grabbed my hand. Captain Akeley turned to order her off the street. Our eyes met. He thought better of it.

"You going away now?"

"Yeah, honey. I have to."

"Think you'll ever come back?"

"I want to—maybe when the war is over—maybe I can find you."

"It's been real good having you boys here. These white folks gonna get even now."

There was no way to answer her. The platoon stopped beside the coach. The men began to climb aboard. I handed Brad my rifle and embraced her, kissing the tears that were welling up.

"Good-bye, Sarah."

"Good-bye, honey."

"I love you."

"I love you, too."

Brad handed me my rifle and I swung aboard the train. I took a seat on the opposite side of the coach, slumped down cursing the war and white folks and the stupid black soldiers who wouldn't take a stand. Looking back would be unbearable.

The engine screamed for the right-of-way and the driving wheels began to turn. I rushed to the other side of the coach as the station began to slip away. She was walking slowly toward her house, head down, crying.

★

Riding across the lush plains of East Texas and into the hot
deserts of the West, I could not forget the sight of Sarah, broken-
hearted, crying, so terribly alone, walking from the station. It
wasn't that I was leaving. She knew I would have to leave. Our
eighteen thousand rifles protected her. We were all leaving. Suddenly thrown back into the age-old dependency, she would cry
and pray for strength until morning. Then she would go to her
chicken coop of a school and call the bright-eyed youngsters to
order. I could hear her contralto, firm and strong above their
childish voices, leading them in the morning anthem:

> *Lift every voice and sing*
> *Till earth and heaven ring,*
> *Ring with the harmonies of Liberty.*

Mama lion of the Black Belt, she would survive. She would
survive until some day, dear God, some day soon, we soldiers
might get half her courage, come back, and finish the fight.

How naive I had been! How quickly I forget Father Thompson's explanation that the Bible isn't so much God's word as the
lessons and experience of all God's children. "Thou shall have no
other gods before Me." A person can't dedicate himself to more
than one cause. How many gods am I trying to serve? Love and
race and the revolution. How stupid to think I could take up one
cause and not lose all the others. Everything is slipping away—
sweetheart, friends, the future—everything fading into darkness
and becoming harder to remember. The only reality is my buddies and the war.

I turned my face to the window. I couldn't stop the tears, and I
didn't want Brad to see.

31

IT WAS A summer evening in July when the train stopped to the
west of Needles, California. There, hundreds of trucks waited to
take us out into the moonscape of the Mojave.

The generals had a new role for us. The divisions going into the North African campaign needed to absorb the lessons of desert warfare. The Ninety-third would be their opponent in training maneuvers.

After building a base camp, which some authority named "Camp Clipper," we marched out into the desert. With two canteens of water per day in the 120° heat and one blanket for the freezing nights, we found the Mojave worse than Louisiana.

Friday evenings we made the long march back to Camp Clipper for a weekend of showers, washing our clothes, and getting drunk. The once-a-month passes to Los Angeles weren't worth the sixteen-hour journey, and few took it. To overcome our almost total isolation, there were more singing circles and bull sessions on the inexhaustible subjects of religion, democracy, women, white folks, and war.

As the sun dropped behind the mountains, we lowered the flaps of our squad tent to preserve what heat we could, lit the candles, and fired up our makeshift stove. Brad, sergeant of the guard at the motor pool the night before, traded a fifty-five-gallon drum of gasoline to a civilian for four quarts of whiskey. What a deal! Steal from the army to cheat Joe De Grinder! Lonnie tuned up the guitar, a harmonica gave the pitch, Harold got out the silvered trumpet, a flint stone for the washboard, a pair of sticks for the tub, and the hoedown was on.

In a few moments the squad tent was crowded. The whiskey was passed around, the singing began—country blues, modern swing, love songs, raucous songs from the chain gangs and prisons. Things were really jumping when the tent flap was pulled open. Sergeant Jackson stepped in, warming his hands above the stove. Something bad was about to happen.

"Hate to interrupt you, gentlemens. Colonel Meyers wants you all to come over and play for the officers for a little while."

"Sergeant Jack." Lee was already drunk. "Tell that monkey-ass motherfucker to get his mammy to play for him."

Jackson rolled his eyes and decided to ignore it.

"Men, you know it ain't me."

Harold laid his trumpet aside.

"Fuck that shit, man. We ain't on duty."

"You all better go," Jeff said softly. "They can make it pretty hard for you."

"Now, ain't this a bitch! They got us stuck out in this fuckin' desert, and they're gonna take the little fun we got away from us."

Harold picked up his trumpet.

"OK, Jeff's right. If we don't, we all are going to hear about it."

"Come back soon as you can."

"Save us some whiskey, man."

The men left. With the guitar, trumpet, and harmonica gone, we turned to our favorite subject.

"Man, this is a crime. That guy wants us to still say 'Yessah, Masta Meyers, Nosah, Masta Meyers.' If I ever get that peck in my sights, damn if I ain't going to squeeze one off on his ass."

"You'll never get the chance—that son 'a bitch ain't never going where there's danger."

"I'll tell you one thing." Big Joe tilted the bottle to his full lips. "Them people better quit fuckin' over Aunt Haggerty's chilluns. One of these days the bottom rail liable to go to the top. They ought to remember, what goes around comes around."

"What I'm talking about is first they say that we simple—all we can do is sing and dance. Then, bless Jesus, they make us sing and dance, and then, Goddamnit, they say that's proof that all we can do is sing and dance." Bunk reached for the bottle in payment for his contribution.

"Man, I know them people—they dirty rotten. White man is the only man in the world who'll screw a woman tonight and not speak to her on the street the next morning," Moore said.

"Shit, that ain't nothin'. They'll get out of bed with your sister to lynch your ass." Parker shifted the cud of tobacco and raised the bottle.

Juicy rolled his big, bloodshot eyes in an effort to sum up the talk. "They're afraid that if you get equal to them, you'll take their women."

"Not with your short pecker, they ain't." Giggling, Lee ducked behind Jeff.

"You all ought to stop peddling that shit," Brad said. "That's the white man's propaganda. They don't give a Goddamn about no women—not even their own. It's money. They got to keep the working class of people fighting each other. They're afraid we'll get together and deal with them. Right before the war, the CIO was trying to organize the oil fields. The company broke it up with that white-fight-Negro shit."

"I didn't know you was in the CIO, Brad. Them Commonists know that organizing shit," Big Joe said.

"They ain't all Communists. I was in the UAW. I still don't know what a Communist is, except they're honest union organizers."

"I don't agree with 'em because they're against God. But I will admit, the best white man I ever met was a Communist." Joe added a touch of seriousness to the discussion.

"Hell, man, there's lots of decent white men."

"The war come along and they need us. They done the same thing before—talk about democracy and equality to get you to do what they want. White people funny that way—let you sleep with his wife —anything to get what he wants. Once he got that, he's comin' down on you. You know it, and I know it. Stick to your own race," Jeff said.

"I'm for race pride. But that ain't enough to get us anywhere. Those people got the land, they got the guns. We got the muscle. Way it's set up, we got to have them and they got to have us," Lee said with studied solemnity.

"Plenty of white people works for a living," Joe said.

Since the catastrophe at the Sabine River, I was very careful about what I'd say except within our inner circle. No telling what new snitch was around. I knew they were with us and I knew G-2 was watching me. I couldn't keep out of the discussion. One of the men turned to me.

"What you think, sarge? You must have been almost raised by the white folks up there in Minnesota. What you think is going to happen?"

"I think some of what everybody said is true. The real problem is there ain't enough jobs to go around. So there's competition for jobs. The Man knows what he's doing. He put the competition on a race basis instead of on ability. Every time they want to keep the white workers in line, they get out the rumor that some colored men are going to take their job. Then they stop fighting their boss and start fighting some Negro guys that's got to eat just like they do. I don't think it's going to end until everybody has a job." How simple it sounded. I'd learned so much from the Communists without even knowing it.

"You going to have to make some powerful changes to get that! There's a man for every job, but there ain't never been a job for every man," Moore said.

"I never saw it so clear until we went to Louisiana. The white man believes that he can get up if he keeps you down. But he can't keep you in the ditch without getting in there with you. We see it. They don't. They're a'scared of us for no reason, and we've got reason to be scared of them." I thought I'd said enough and was glad when the tent flap opened. Harold, Lonnie, and Jinx crowded in, yelling for the whiskey.

★

The months ground on with our maneuvering back and forth across the rocky valleys and snake-infested hills. We lost any understanding as to why we were stuck out in the desert. The idea that this was a trick to keep us isolated seemed more credible every day, making us even more bitter and lowering our combat morale even more. Maneuvers against our new enemy, an armored infantry division, finally ended in December. They loaded up for the invasion of Italy. We marched back to Camp Clipper, glad it wasn't us.

It was good to get back to the base and stretch out on a cot inside a real tent. I was waiting my turn to wash clothes when Harold opened the flap and poked his head inside the tent.

"You guys hear the killin' shit?"

"What's up, man?"

"Lena Horne got a bunch of colored movie stars together and they're coming here this Saturday."

"Sure enough? 'Bout time that fuckin' USO did something for us."

"USO my ass. They don't give a damn about no Ninety-third Division. This is Lena Horne, man. She heard that nobody ever comes near us, so she organized it."

As he started to close the flap, he poked his head in again.

"Oh, yeah. Joe Louis is coming in, too."

Lena Horne! Somebody got out a cheesecake photo of our dancing, singing, smiling beauty and nailed it to the tent pole. We didn't wait for orders to clean up the area and get it looking good for the first women to visit our camp in the Mojave.

Saturday was a perfect day. The engineers completed the big stage. The microphones and loudspeakers were in place. Eighteen thousand strong, we marched to the amphitheater in class A uniforms—khakis, ties, and overseas caps. We watched the approaching big cloud of dust raised by the convoy bringing the entertainment from Hollywood. As the car doors opened, a mighty roar went up from the men. The starlets, feeling the electricity, responded, throwing kisses and waving their arms.

The men shouted and whistled as Lena gave us her radiant smile and led the women to the dressing rooms to prepare for the show.

Joe Louis sparred with our division champ and then gave us a talk about how Hitler didn't intend to fix any of the many things wrong with this country. If we were going to get America straight, we had to finish Hitler off first.

The troops sat politely, listening to the morale booster. We didn't disagree. We just weren't interested. We came to see the women.

The Ninety-third Division band took its place on the stage and tuned up their instruments. A few popular songs by the band, and then the starlets, dressed in short skirts and dancing shoes, filed onto the stage.

White soldiers don't know what entertainment is! Betty Grable, Lana Turner, and all white Hollywood couldn't put on such a show! The singing, the dancing, the jokes that only Negroes fully understood brought us to our feet every few moments, applauding and screaming for more.

Finally it ended. The exhausted starlets, laughing and chattering, surrounded by Negro officers, walked toward the officer's club. The men fanned out across the desert, walking back to the squad tents.

"Ever think about it?" Lee said. "We do all the work, we fight the fuckin' war—the shavetails get the gravy."

"Oh! Them women's supposed to walk you home, huh?" Juicy said in mock surprise.

"No, I don't expect nothing. I'm just saying we's the drones and they's the queen bee."

I stretched out on my cot, half wondering what it was like having a date with one of those beauties, when Brad jerked the tent flap open.

"Un-ass that cot, man, and come out here."

"What's going on?"

"Lena Horne's walking around talking to the men."

It was true. She came toward us with Warrant Officer Mays, leader of the band. With a few words for this soldier, a smile for that one, she came toward us. Suddenly she was in front of our tent—the dimples, the sparkling white teeth, the burnished bronze of her face still aglow after two grueling hours on the stage.

"Hi, sergeant. Did you like the show?"

Brad mumbled something incoherent.

"It was wonderful, Miss Horne," I said.

"Come on, sergeant, I'm not that old." She winked her eye. "Lena."

There were a few more mumbling replies to questions wreathed in smiles.

"Are you going to invite me in?"

"Please come in, Lena." Brad regained his composure.

It was a stroke of genius, hanging her picture on the tent pole. She noticed it and smiled.

"Our favorite pinup girl." Jeff had practiced that one.

She glanced around our neat tent and, gracefully crossing her legs, sat on my cot.

"I want to thank you for coming out here—I mean, talking with the enlisted men," I said.

Her face relaxed from the perpetual smile to a thoughtful seriousness.

"I don't need any thanks. I think I know what you common guys, you GI Joes, are going through. You're the ones who do the fighting and dying. If my singing and talking helps—"

"Would you? I mean, sing one verse—just for us?" Harold's smile was irresistible.

She stood up humming. The Lena Horne on-stage smile brightened the squad tent. "Don't buy sugar." A bump and a grind brought our hearts into our throats. "You just have to touch my cup." She pressed her fingertips to her lips and blew the kiss to us. Dreamlike, she disappeared from the tent, leaving five black soldiers in love with her forever.

★

Christmas in the desert was even more miserable because we knew that our next move would be to the port of embarkation. On the first of January 1944, the company commander handed out furloughs to most of the men. We knew what that meant.

32

IT WAS A long, grueling three-day trip home on the crowded trains. From Texas to Joplin, Missouri, the Negro soldiers were segregated into the filthy old Jim Crow cars. After sleeping in the aisle and standing for hundreds of miles, I needed a full day's sleep before I could enjoy my furlough.

Ben was in North Africa and the little brothers had grown tall and strong. Still, home was the warm, messy, noisy place I missed so much. I wanted to tell Mom how idealistically wrong I was about the army and America. I wanted to tell her about the fight between the races and the classes that would erupt when the war ended. It was too difficult. I kept it inside and went to the corner.

Happy that I was in the army, Mr. Spiegel warmly shook my hand. Getting me out of his drugstore to fight Hitler was truly killing two birds with one stone. In the Dreamland, Mr. Cassius smiled his welcome and came from behind the bar with a bear hug and a pitcher of beer for me.

How things had changed! I hardly knew anyone on the corner. The gang was either in the army or out west working in the war industries. Mac seemed to be the only one left, and he was working twelve hours a day at the tank plant. Afraid of the truth, I didn't ask him about Heidi. The taverns were crowded with menless women. I felt more alone among them than with the womenless men in the desert. No soldier liked "Shorty George," as we called the able-bodied civilians. Loaded with money, they hoped the war would last forever. We loathed Joe De Grinder, the hustler who wasn't even working in the war plants but making it gigoloing off the soldiers' wives and sweethearts.

Looking over the people in the tavern, I thought of an Australian infantryman's song:

> *Where whiz-bangs are flyin'*
> *And comforts are few,*
> *Brave men are dyin'*
> *For bastards like you.*

No one noticed when I left the tavern and walked home. My friends were mostly gone, and I didn't fit in with the people who crowded the taverns, nightclubs, and dance halls. The third day home, I was ready for the desert and a life I hated but understood. I spent most of the furlough visiting relatives, seeing a few friends from school, and just being home. Mom made me take her to see the play *Native Son*. It was great. I was glad I went. Canada Lee, the internationally acclaimed actor, played the leading role. Refused entrance by all the major hotels, he took a room in a private home.

The day before leaving for camp, Mac called. "Hey, man. I thought I'd have to leave without saying good-bye."

"Sorry we didn't have more time together. They got to have those tanks. I just wanted to say, so long."

"Glad you called, Mac. I'll see you when I get back."

"Oh, by the way. I ran into Heidi. I thought you might want to talk with her, so I set up a date—tonight at seven o'clock at the Paradise."

I got off the streetcar at six-thirty and walked the three blocks to the crummy little hotel and bar a half block from the train station. The Paradise was used mainly by the railroad waiters and porters who had a layover in Minneapolis. The rooms, rented by the day or hour, were the only hotel accommodations available to blacks in the city.

I took a glass of beer and a shot of bourbon to the booth with me. Thoughtful of Mac. If things work out, we can get a room without the hassle of taking a taxi.

A few minutes to seven she walked into the barroom. Still a little pigeon-toed, womanly, erect, and balanced on high heels, she smiled and came toward me.

"God, I'm glad to see you, Nels."

"Hello, Heidi. You look wonderful. I'm glad you could make it."

Hungry for her, I embraced her and drew her to me for the kiss. With the slightest stiffening of her body, the slightest turn of her head, she offered her cheek. I pressed my cheek against hers, thinking, "It's really over. I hope she doesn't start that can't-we-still-be-friends jive." She sat opposite me, waiting while I gulped the bourbon and took a long drink of the beer to cool the fire.

"Will you order me a drink, too?"

"Sure. Didn't mean to be impolite. What will you have?"

"Scotch and milk."

Itchy sweat popped out on my back. She didn't have to tell me, I knew. The waitress smiled and returned with the drink.

"Tell me about yourself. Do you like the army?"

"The army isn't something you like or don't like. It's something you do. Something you fight a war with." That sounded unnecessarily aggressive.

"I guess you're still trying to save the world."

"Only because I'm part of it, Lot of people out here don't feel that way. But tell me about yourself. How are you doing?"

"I'm all right. The war makes it kind of difficult sometimes. Lot's of things are rationed."

I steered the conversation into small talk. We caught up on mutual friends and reminisced about shallow, humorous things we'd done. The whiskey and three lonely months in the desert finally overcame caution.

"I'm going overseas when I go back. I don't know when I'll see you again."

"I hope you'll be OK."

I wanted to get up and leave but tried again. This time directly.

"Will you get a room with me?"

"Why, Nels?"

"'Cause I guess I'm still in love with you—because I still want you."

"I don't want to. I'm with Reggie now. I just wanted to see you for old times' sake."

"Old times' sake? Well, I guess that's what it is. We were pretty close for a long time, but maybe it was a long time ago." I didn't want to talk about Reggie, or what being "with" him meant—maybe in his stable.

"Were we close enough for me to ask what happened? Why you broke off with me?"

"You broke off with me," she snapped, narrowing her eyes. "You left me first."

"What the hell you talking about? There's a war going on!"

"You volunteered! I'll never forget that night. You wanted to fight for Russia. You didn't care about me. You wanted to fight for heaven knows what."

I picked up the mug, thinking, marking time, slowly finishing the beer. Jesus Christ, is this the same woman who used to read poetry to me—who helped shape my ideals? My God, what has that fuckin' Reggie done to her?

"When I said I had to fight for Russia, I didn't mean a country. I meant what they stand for. You were always talking about getting equality and all that. What's the use of talking about wanting something, then when the deal goes down, you're not ready to fight for it?"

She looked as if she didn't understand a word I said. I had to finish. If we never meet again she had to know what she had betrayed.

"You're right about one thing, though." I had to say it. I'd never said it before. "Millions of Russians are dying for what I believe in. I'm going to stand or fall with them; otherwise, I can't live with myself. I'm an infantryman, just like them."

How the hell can she look bored, when I joined up to fight for her, for us?

"Well, you made the decision." She hunched slightly. "You went away."

"I didn't think it was a decision. It's the way I am. I spent my life running away from problems I couldn't solve, or trying to run away from them. I've seen a lot, been through a lot in the last three years. I'm through running. I'm fighting now, and I'm never going to be through fighting."

"Then you know why it was over. It was your decision."

Sliding out of the booth, I reached for my heavy olive drab overcoat and overseas cap.

"I guess I'll always love that girl who loved moccasin flowers and Shelley and Keats. You ain't her. I don't know what that motherfucker's done to you, but it's a Goddamn shame."

"You're leaving?"

"I ain't got nothing here. I really hate what happened. Whatever I did wrong—I paid it off with interest."

Tears were forming in the corners of her eyes, but I knew she wasn't going to budge. One last look and I walked to the door, opened it, and stepped out into the bitter January cold.

★

I returned to Camp Clipper just in time to get in on the heavy work of breaking camp. Tents were struck, folded, tied, and loaded on trucks. Kitchen equipment was cleaned, crated, and loaded. Field equipment was cleaned and boxed. Foodstuffs, medical supplies, ammunition—all accounted for and loaded up. Finally it was done. With the last latrine covered, the battalions

formed and marched to the assembly area. Trucks shuttled the
division through forty miles of dust to waiting, blacked-out trains.

Lee looked at the covered and taped windows.

"Shit. This looks like a slave ship or something."

"This is it," Lonnie said. "We're going to bip."

"What the hell you mean, bip?"

"I mean the sound of a motherfucker goin' up aside your
head—bip! We goin' to combat."

We filed aboard for the trip to Camp Stoneman, the staging
area for the San Francisco port of embarkation.

Stoneman was a whirlwind of activity. We turned in our
equipment and received new rifles, tommy guns, camouflage jungle suits, packs, helmets, and boots. We formed long lines and
marched through the medical huts, emerging sore from the shots
and laden with salves, pills, powders, and disinfectants. This was
it! We practiced for hours scampering up and down rope ladders
thrown over the sides of a ship, and took one more crawl through
the infiltration course.

The battle for New Georgia was in its final stages. The Fourteenth Corps stormed ashore on Bougainville. The Russians were
breaking out of the defensive at Stalingrad. The Fascist military
offensive was running out of steam, and the contradictory alliance
against it was beginning to roll.

Army headquarters alerted the regiment after the hundredth
inspection. We marched onto river barges for the short trip to the
warehouses in San Francisco. There we lined up, platoon by platoon, to check off and board the huge liner. The Red Cross
women quietly circulated through the ranks handing out coffee
and doughnuts. It was close to midnight when Captain Harper
called my name.

"Peery!"

"Sergeant, Nelson D. 17051927."

"Check."

Buckling the straps of my pack and slinging my rifle, I walked
up the gangplank and into the USS Lurline for the week-long
journey to Guadalcanal.

Part Five

AN AMERICAN
REVOLUTIONARY

33

THROUGHOUT THE REAR areas of the Pacific, in the more economically advanced islands like Samoa and New Caledonia, the social and legal oppression of the black soldier was worse than in the States. Seventy-five percent of the soldiers receiving the death sentence by courts-martial were black, though we were less than 10 percent of the army. Accusations of rape and mobs of white soldiers beating and killing black soldiers were commonplace. A mob of white soldiers invaded a camp of Negro service troops on Guam. The blacks fought back, taking casualties but wounding several whites. Forty-four black soldiers were rounded up and given long sentences at hard labor. At Fort Lawton, Washington, the Italian war prisoners received privileges and better treatment than the Negro soldiers who guarded them. A riot broke out against these conditions. The army held a mass court-martial for the black soldiers.

Acclimation in Guadalcanal after months in the desert was a physical and psychological shock. We all knew it couldn't happen to any but Negro troops. Acclimation meant endless maneuvering through the humid, stinking jungles. We learned to live with the hordes of mosquitoes and swarms of big green flies, fat from the corpses that still rotted, half covered by the mud and slime. The dehydrated foods and other discomforts of living in the field were no strangers. We unlearned the tactics of desert warfare and learned squad control and combat in the jungle.

Moralewise, the division was unfit for combat. Fight to preserve our way of life? We were fighting to change it! To the generals, this attitude could only mean demoralization. The Ninety-third was placed in Fourteenth Corps reserve. Anything needing to be done was done by us. Boats need unloading? Assign the Ninety-third. Need some troops for mopping up operations? Get the Ninety-third. Assign some infantry to secure an area? Ninety-third's not doing anything anyway.

As the months dragged on, the regiment scattered throughout the Solomons. Some went to Choiseul, some to Rendova, some to Kolombangara, guarding installations, mopping up, or providing security.

There was never a formal surrender of forces in the island battles of the Pacific war. The fight went on until one side was dead or scattered into the sterile hills to die of starvation. The battle for an island would simply grind to a halt. With no chance of reinforcements or supply, the Japanese made a hard fight for each island. Charred by flamethrowers, blasted by heavy artillery, relentlessly attacked by overwhelming American forces, the resistance finally broke and the Japanese scattered into the hills.

★

One by one the white regiments pulled out for the invasion of Sansapore and Morotai. We were left behind to finish the job of mopping up what resistance remained. We were also given the responsibility of securing the island from the Japanese army corps that had been bypassed, bombed to pieces, and starved out at the once formidable base across the bay at Manokwari, New Guinea.

As the patrolling subsided, we set about improving our quarters and strengthening the defenses, and returned to close-order drills. A base postal unit and base hospital were moved to the island to service the anticipated invasion of the Philippines. As the WACs and nurses moved in, it became like a state-side garrison—at least for the white officers.

The Japanese airstrip was too small for U.S. Army aircraft. A new one was built a quarter of a mile away. We converted the old strip into a movie theater by laying out rows of coconut logs as seats. When the movies started, the Japanese stragglers would creep out of their hiding places to sit on the cliff overlooking the theater and enjoy the movie. Some kind of unspoken truce evolved. They wouldn't shoot into the theater, and we wouldn't attempt to ambush them.

I never went to the movies. Along with most of the infantrymen, I had a deep-seated fear of airstrips—they were the nerve centers and magnets for combat. We weren't missed. The white men and women soldiers filled the place every night.

Hollywood saluted the various infantry divisions in the Pacific by having a world premiere showing on their island. Our turn came. The world premier showing of the movie *Rhapsody in Blue* would be in honor of the black infantrymen of the Ninety-third Division. Headquarters made quite a to-do about the honor. Work details manicured the area and prepared for the night as if we were at Hollywood and Vine. Rumor had it that Dinah Shore was going to open the movie with her hit song, "I'll Walk Alone." We all thought a voice like that had to have some Negro blood in it. We liked her.

Time came to take the half-mile walk to the theater. I decided not to go, then, as it began to darken I reconsidered. Apprehensive but not wanting to miss the event, I started down the dirt road. The floodlights were on at the theater and landing lights had just been turned on at the airstrip. A hundred yards from the theater, I instinctively jumped to the side of the road and looked upward as two incoming planes roared by. The first was an American C54 transport. Slightly above and behind the transport was the unmistakable outline of a Japanese "Betty" bomber.

At first I ran toward the airport screaming, "Japs—Japs!" The service troops, scattered along the road to the theater, unaware of the imminent catastrophe, moved away from me as if I were crazy. Then I realized how useless it was. I stood watching the drama. The Betty cut her motors and glided in fifty feet above the transport. The closeness of the planes confused the radar and cutting the motors silenced the approach. The transport touched down; the Betty glided over it, dropping two fragmentation bombs. Bodies, seats, and debris blasted up as the plane disintegrated. The Betty gunned its motors, destroyed the control tower with machine gun fire, and turned sharply, passing over the theater. Two "daisy cutter" antipersonnel bombs and machine gun fire raked the theater. Utter pandemonium took over as the Betty disappeared into the night in the direction of Manokwari.

Shore batteries, informed we were under naval attack, shook the island with their heavy guns firing at predetermined positions. The field artillery opened up on targets in the hills. The anti-aircraft artillery gouged flaming holes in the darkness of the sky. Everyone thought everything else was attacking him. A platoon of tanks churned onto the road, blocking the ambulances screaming toward the theater. A 6×6 truck carrying latecomers to the theater stalled lengthwise across the road as it tried to turn around. A commandeered tank pulled it away. Everywhere soldiers were running from the area. Inside the theater was a scene of carnage—nearly three hundred people dead and wounded from the ten-second attack.

I made it back to the company area and spent the night in my foxhole.

The next morning the regimental commander called the reconnaissance men together. When he passed out the shot glasses of whiskey, we knew we were in trouble.

"Men." The uniform hadn't changed him. The white man boss always puts on an air of friendly equality when he wants something difficult or dangerous done.

"The general has determined the air raid last night was directed by radio. The Japanese up in those hills must still have an operational radio. We have been assigned to find and destroy it."

We all knew better. The Japanese had patched that plane together out of the scrap left from the bombings and hit it lucky. The general was under sharp criticism from corps headquarters. It sounded better if there was an organized force to deal with, rather than a lucky punch. We were going to pay the price for someone's fuckup.

★

A World War II infantryman can never forget the sound of a Japanese rifle. Unlike our M1s, with their husky, semiautomatic bam-bam-bam!, the Japanese .25 has a sharp, cracking pow! It is followed by a pause while the bolt is pulled back, the spent cartridge ejected, another round shoved into the firing chamber, and then another pow!

The point man had passed the banyan tree and looked back, signaling that it was safe to move forward. The men stepped from their hiding places—Jeff, Bunk, Brad, and then Lonnie.

It wasn't like the movies. There was nothing dramatic. The pow! ripped the eerie silence and ricocheted into the jungle. The earth paused as each set of eyes darted into the underbrush and up into the banyan tree. The sound seemed to have come from all around us. Then I saw Lonnie. He took one step back and sat down, feet apart, rifle held firmly in his right hand. Slowly he leaned forward until, yogalike, his face pressed against the ground between his ankles. There was no scream. There was no blood. The bullet that hit the center of his heart ended his life before the brain could react.

Our years of training beat back the terror of death in the jungle. We fanned outward, firing a few shots at likely hiding places. Big Joe, kneeling behind a scrub bush, squinted into the tree, his teeth clamped tightly upon the cigar stump. He raised the B.A.R.

as if it were a carbine and squeezed the trigger. The clip of shots tore into the tree, sending the leaves floating downward in peaceful incongruity.

We all heard the gurgling moan. The Japanese soldier fell the fifteen feet to the ground, his chest torn by bullets. A rifle fell and we could see another dead soldier dangling from the tree, his leg stuck between two branches, the blood running from the rips and tears in his body.

Then we saw the third soldier. The wet red splotch on his shirt widened as he struggled for balance. Looking down at the six rifles pointed at him, he pushed his rifle away. It fell to the ground. Weak and unsteady, he slithered and inched along the huge branch. The rifles were lowered. The men were pulling for him to make it. Somehow, we didn't connect this man to Lonnie's death. Reaching the trunk, he leaned to grasp the next-lower limb. Pain was etched in his face as, branch by branch, he half crawled, half fell toward the ground. Five feet from the ground he attempted to hold on to the trunk and find his footing on the huge, twisted roots. Too far gone, too weak for the effort, he fell. He rolled over onto his back, eyes half closed with pain and death.

I was nearest and stepped over to him. My mind focused on the stories of wounded or supposedly dead Japanese soldiers using the last grenade to kill themselves and anyone near. I thought of the slogan—"If they don't stink—stick 'em." Half afraid, half compassionate, I lowered the barrel of my rifle, the bayonet tip inches from his chest. He couldn't have been more than twenty-three. His mouth moved slightly. He closed his eyes, thin lips clamped between his teeth. Suddenly he moved as if to turn over. Instinctively, I lunged against the rifle. The bayonet point disappeared into his body. Kill the bastard—kill him—kill him! The weight of my body pinned him back to the ground. The mouth opened and gasped. The eyes opened and glared at me. The body relaxed, the death stare fixed into the branches of the banyan tree. I answered him, "You made me do it, you motherfuckin' Jap bastard—you made me do it."

I felt Brad's arm around me—I was still pushing against the rifle. Together we pulled the bayonet from his rib cage and wiped it clean on his pants.

"I think he had a grenade," I said almost defensively.

We rolled him over. When he fell, a stick had punctured his

body. That caused the look of pain and biting the lips. That's why he tried to roll over. Brad knew what I was thinking.

"He'd a' died anyway, man. We couldn't a' taken him back. We got to find that transmitter."

We spread out the poncho and laid Lonnie on it. Red, the medic, closed his bulging, staring, sightless eyes. Three minutes before he had whispered to me. It was hard to believe he was dead. None of us had done this before, and we mechanically followed the instructions from the medic. Lonnie was securely tied into the poncho. A pole was cut and the body tied to it. Jeff and Bunk hoisted the pole to their shoulders and, with Lee acting as guard, they started back to camp.

Harold put a bullet into each corpse to make sure. Big Joe shoved a fresh clip into the B.A.R. Brad moved up to become the point, and the patrol moved out.

★

Out of rations and having covered the assigned area, we returned to the perimeter the following day. We did not find a transmitter. There wasn't any, and the colonel knew it. We were bitter about Lonnie's unnecessary death. After the reports were made, we held a little memorial for him. Below the camp, on the beach at the base of the cliff, we built a small campfire and the fifteen or twenty of us who knew Lonnie the best sat or squatted around the fire. Harold took his silver trumpet from the battered case, attached the mouthpiece, and pushed nervously against the three plungers.

As he raised the trumpet to his mouth, we automatically rose to stand at parade rest. The melancholy of taps mingled with the frustrations that we, as Negro soldiers, bore in silence.

As the last note was smothered by the murmuring of the incoming tide, Joe turned and whispered to Harold. Then, with the calm dignity of the Negro preacher, he softly stated that he would sing a song. Harold provided a soft background for Joe's rich, well-trained voice:

> *Were you there when they crucified my Lord?*
> *Were you there when they nailed him to the cross?*
> *Ohhh, Ohhh. Sometimes it causes me to tremble—*
> *Lord, I tremble.*
> *Were you there when they crucified my Lord?*

He paused and the tear-sodden silence cried for him to sing again—to ease the pain we bore for Lonnie, for ourselves, and for our people.

> *My God He calls, He calls me by the thunder,*
> *His trumpet sounds within-a my heart,*
> *Lord, I ain't got long to stay here.*
> *Steal away, steal away, steal away home,*
> *I ain't got long to stay here.*

Joe sat down among us. The worn Bible was passed around the circle. Each soldier read his favorite passage or verse. I quoted my little verse from memory.

"When I was a child I spake as a child, I understood as a child, I thought as a child, but when I became a man I put away childish things."

It was Brad's turn; he closed the book and simply repeated from memory:

"Man that is born of woman is but a few days, and full of trouble. He cometh forth like a flower." He paused and looked briefly around the circle. "And he's cut down like a motherfucker. For what? For nothin'."

Each soldier lapsed into his individual thoughts. We knew that we were finished as a fighting force. Lonnie's death and the endless news of the ongoing racial violence at home wiped out the last bit of combat morale.

★

After the last prayer was said and the last verse read, after the last toast was drunk and the whiskey bottle went dry, the men drifted back to the bivouac area, to their cots and mosquito netting.

The fire began to die. Brad and I sat quietly watching the embers. He knew I desperately wanted to say something.

Finally he spoke softly, still looking into the fire. "What's eatin' ya, man? You still thinking about that Jap?"

"Yeah," I answered. "It ain't really bothering me—I guess I learned something."

After the moment of awkward silence I went on: "I think I know why white people hate us—why they treat us like they do."

"'Cause they're fuckin' rotten. That's why. There's something wrong with 'em," Brad interrupted, vomiting out a bit of the latent hatred.

"Naw, I don't think that's it anymore. After I stuck that guy, for a minute I felt like Jesus looked at me and talked to me. You know I don't believe in God anymore, but I've been taught that it was a sin to kill. I might'a killed somebody else in a firefight—I don't know—that was different. They was shootin' at us and we was shootin' at them. I was sure of this one. It was like Jesus was lookin' at me and said to me, 'Thou shalt not kill,' and I knew that this fuckin' guy had sent me to hell. He made me do it—and I hated him for what I done.

"Later on, I got thinkin' those white people go to church and pray and listen to the preachers. They know right from wrong. Then, when they go out an' lynch somebody, or rape some woman, they know they're wrong. They know they've sinned. They believe they got to answer for it sometime. They hate us because they know they're goin' to hell for what they done to us."

I paused for a moment, getting it all out.

"So then, they got to pretend we're not human. It's different to burn a nigger than a human being. Or rape a nigger bitch instead of a woman. When I stuck that fuckin' guy—I called him a Jap bastard. If I'd of thought 'soldier' or 'man,' I'd of fixed him up and got him to the field hospital."

When the silence became oppressive, I tried to draw some conclusion.

"We're in for a long hard fight, Brad."

"Yeah, I know. Do you think we can ever live together? I don't think so. We ain't equal—that's the only way we can live together—when we're equal. They won't let us become equal. We can't get together because we ain't equal. We can't get equal because we ain't together. It's set up where we've got no win. Maybe we should fight to get a state to ourselves. Maybe, if we had our own government we could get up on our feet."

"I don't know," I said. "I don't see how we can separate. They made us what we are, we made them what they are. I don't think we can really get together until we get even with them for what they've done—I know I can't. I don't know. I know it can't go on like it is."

"It ain't right. It don't seem real. We out here killin' these people to protect something we hate. Lonnie gettin' killed while they lynching our people in his backyard."

"Brad?"

"Huh?"

"If we can kill and fight and die here, for nothin', let's keep on fighting and killing when we get back home. They kill to scare people. If just once we could kill every motherfuckin' peck in a lynch mob—that would be the end of lynching. Let's keep the group together. They're only about 125 men—but they're ready to die and go to hell. We could begin a secret army."

"I thought about it. There's too many handkerchief heads. Too many Toms and long coats. We'd have to kill half the niggers in the United States before we get to the white man."

"We gotta do something. We gotta stay alive. We gotta figure out a way to fight when we get back."

"I know. Right now they figurin' on how to stop us. We gotta figure out how to keep goin'."

The fire settled into embers. The glow turned gray and cold. Gripped by the call to a new kind of war, we went up the hill to our cots.

34

The Negro press finally got its way. In a political gesture of little military significance, elements of the Ninety-third were committed to battle.

The struggle for Bougainville was already essentially won, although the Japanese resistance was far from broken. Reinforcing the Twenty-fifth Infantry as a regimental combat team of the Ninety-third Division allowed for the withdrawal of a regiment of marines for the giant pincer movement aimed at Leyte in the Philippines. Aside from lives, there was not too much to be won or lost on Bougainville. The generals came to heel at Roosevelt's order. We rolled our full field packs, and our platoon boarded the landing craft for the choppy ride back to the Solomons.

★

We moved slowly down the narrow coral road. On one side a column of marines moved toward the beaches, and we, on the other side, moved forward to take their places along the perimeter. As we passed them, some of the marines would say quietly, "Take it

easy, Mac. It won't be bad when you get used to it." Or sometimes, when eyes in a black face would meet eyes in a white face,
the black soldier would say, "You boys take it easy."

While we were taking our ten-minute break, one of the
marine sergeants came over to me and, after introducing himself,
asked if this would be our first night in combat. I told him it was.
He squatted in front of me and stroked his chin for a moment,
then said, "Well, soldier, if you want me to, I'd like to tell you
something. Nobody ever told me anything, and I wish they would
have."

"What is it?"

"Our first night up front was hell. I just want to give you some
advice."

I smiled at the white face in the jungle darkness.

"If it's something that's going to save my life—I want to
know it."

The marine looked around for a moment. "We're getting
ready to move out." He held his hand up, palm outward, like a
lecturer: "Keep your ass down—lots of guys get hit in the ass
when they're crawling forward. Take the Atabrine pills. We've lost
more men to malaria than to the Japs. Wash your feet every
night—else you'll get jungle rot."

On the opposite side of the road, the marines were falling into
a single column, pushing their jungle packs high up on their
shoulders, slinging their rifles upside down. A light, warm, pene-
trating rain began. My new friend glanced over at his platoon and
said hurriedly, "Whatever you do, don't fire at night. They'll see
the flash and shower you with mortar fire. I've got to go."

He held out his hand. I shook it warmly. The sergeant turned
and smiled, saying, "Take it easy, dogface."

The marines moved out down the road and we got to our feet
and sloshed through the shallow puddles and the slippery mud.
We silently passed the artillery emplacements. The crews were
stacking shells near the 105s and 155s. They were firing scheduled
fire—perhaps more for practice than for any effect. We flinched
when one of the big guns fired, blinking our eyes in awe of the
twenty-foot flame that belched from the piece.

"This jive is sure 'nuff now," Lee said, nodding his head in
the direction of the artillery. I didn't answer him. In the darkness I
was watching the boots ahead of me and I felt a real kinship
with the millions of men who before me had marched through the

rain, through the darkness, toward the front lines, toward battle.

Occasionally, we could hear a rapid burst of a heavy machine gun and sometime the sharp crack of a rifle. As we passed one of the artillery emplacements, a young black lieutenant stepped over to me.

"Where's battalion headquarters?"

"Right here is the most of it, sir," I said, slapping my kit of maps and pencils.

"I'm going to be the artillery officer with you. Where is the S-3?"

"He's up ahead, sir. Captain Akeley."

"Oh, well, I might as well walk with you."

"Fine, sir. You can have all of this island you want."

The lieutenant smiled and fell in alongside me.

"Well, don't want any of it. Now, if the Japanese were in Los Angeles where they could hurt those pretty little brown-skinned girls, I guess I'd want to fight."

"I hate moving up, too. In a way I'm kinda anxious to see if we can stand up to it."

"The officers in the American and the Thirty-seventh are betting that we'll break and run."

"Doubt it. It's different in Africa. You can run there. There ain't no hiding place down here. We'll hold, I'm not worried about the men."

"I hope so." After a few moments he went on. "The next twenty years might depend upon tonight. If we fight and win, the folks back home will have something to point to. These white people, the generals and the politicians, don't think a Negro can stand and fight a modern war. If we break—" He left the sentence dangling in the night.

"I think everybody knows that. We ain't gonna run."

Somebody was going to die tonight. I knew that. Every foot-slogging dogface in the line knew that. Each was equally sure it would be someone else.

At the next break, the artillery officer left me and walked on. After ten minutes we got back on our feet and pushed quietly through the darkness. We passed the regimental headquarters, passed the battalion headquarters, and, squad by squad, began to relieve the marines in the bunkers on the main line of resistance. (This was a defensive line that took the brunt of the enemy attack. It was backed up by a final defense line that held at all costs.)

Those of us who were not so lucky formed an uneven skirmish

line and, sifting through the MLR, crawled to the outpost line. (This line screened the MLR and prevented the enemy from using the element of surprise.)

The marines, happy to leave the front, crawled out of their bunkers and holes, leaving huge quantities of ammunition, chocolate, and K rations.

From the bunkers, the blackout tents, and the holes that served as company command posts, I collected overlays, fire plans, routes from assembly areas, routes for counterattack and withdrawals. They were put together on the battalion map and given to a messenger to take to the regimental headquarters. Satisfied that my job was done and done well, I rolled up in my shelter half and slept the listening sleep of the infantry.

★

The night had been too peaceful to be real. We gathered at the message center late in the morning. Lee walked into the area, unbuckling his helmet and leaned his carbine against a tree.

"Combat ain't shit. I slept like a baby."

"Don't worry, you ugly little sonofabitch," Juicy said. "Let's see how you sleep tonight."

I had heard the rumor, too.

"What's the killin' shit?" Brad asked.

"Wasn't told to me—I only heard."

"What's up? What's the rumor?"

"Well, Akeley said that the Japs found out we're green troops and from their patrolling last night, looks like they plan to try us on for size."

"Ain't no use comin' near me, I don't fit none of 'em," Lee said.

Juicy started to say something to Lee, gave him a dirty look, and said, "What you think, Bradley?"

"It's got to come sometime. Fuck it. Let it come."

"Yeah," Jeff said with resignation.

Most of the men slept during the day. The rifle companies hauled ammunition, finished clearing fire lanes, and improved their foxholes. The pioneer platoon was busy inspecting and repairing the barbed wire entanglements in front of the outpost line and the main line of resistance. Communications set about stringing a dual telephone system. Reconnaissance poured over the maps and aerial photographs, and back at the command post the intelligence officer—the S-2—and operations officer—the S-3—read aloud the information they received from the rifle companies during the night. They studied reports from the Thirty-seventh Division that was anchored to our left flank, and from the Fiji scouts who had spent the night behind the Japanese lines.

At the staff meeting that afternoon, the colonel gave his estimate of the situation. He concluded that the Japanese would launch an attack that night with the main effort directed against the Ninety-third Division.

The tension increased as the quartermasters brought up extra ammunition, and troops that slept during the day relieved the frightened, weary men on the outpost line.

The sun set toward New Britain and Manus. The darkness rose from the swamps and engulfed the front. On the outpost line, the men laid their rifles across the firing stakes and, one by one, slithered out of their holes. With their little entrenching tools, they dug holes in the earth to squat over. Hanging onto the underbrush for balance, they pulled the little container of toilet paper from the K ration packet. After their outpost toilets were covered over, they slithered back to the safety of their foxholes. Until morning, the only latrine available would be their helmets.

Along the final defense line, soldiers hooked the searchlights to generators and loaded and locked the antitank guns. The mortar crews locked into position on specific targets. A few self-propelled 75 mm cannon wheeled into position and cut their motors. The men in the reserve company loaded their canteens with fresh water and sat with tense faces in the assembly area. They would not sleep tonight. With bayoneted rifles between their legs and mosquito netting draped over their helmets, they were to be thrown forward to plug any gap in the main line of resistance.

At the message center, the radio operator strapped a speed key to his leg and the messengers checked their pads for carbon paper and sharpened their pencils.

Tension and anticipation crackled in the air. At midnight the front was deathly, unnaturally still. After the artillery bombardment of the day, this strange quiet, louder than the bombardment, frayed the nerves.

At two o'clock the front erupted, the night shattered by flame and the flash and roar of the big guns. The searchlights illuminated the front and any movement brought a rain of high explosives, phosphorous, jellied gasoline, and antipersonnel artillery. The Japanese were brave, disciplined soldiers, and although it was little more than a probing assault, they fought as if it were a main thrust. Again and again, they charged through the minefields and tangled themselves on the barbed wire, disemboweled by mortar and machine gun fire.

It ended with the suddenness with which it began.

Someone along the line was calling, "Get a medic! A man's hurt bad."

The corpsmen were bringing back a few wounded and carrying up supplies of plasma and bandages. A Japanese soldier was brought in, his arm dangling loosely from the elbow and blood dripping from a wound.

The outpost line had withdrawn to the main line of resistance in an orderly way. As the attack was broken off, some of the men were eager to pursue. The scent of victory, the blood lust— the savage instinct to kill, to hate, to destroy—became a material force as the Japanese retreated back into the darkness of the jungle.

No one slept that night. In the morning, when heads were counted, one man was missing. A patrol, sent out to keep contact with the enemy, found the missing soldier hanging by his thumbs from a banyan tree, his body pierced by fifty bayonet wounds.

Kill the bastards. Trapped like two wild animals on the island, only one could survive. We began to act accordingly.

As the morning sun drew the fog from the swamplands, I finished the overlays and went to the message center. Lee's arm was bandaged. He had been running a message to regimental headquarters when a mortar shell had fallen close to him. He dove for cover in the darkness and cut his arm. The rest of the men were unhurt—if tired and nervous.

"Kinda tough night," Lee muttered.

"Don't feel too bad. It'll get worse."

"I guess the boys in the rifle companies caught hell."

"We're pretty well protected here. I don't think we had twenty men wounded—and that one guy killed."

"Them cats in the artillery was doing good."

"An' them motherfuckers said a colored man can't handle artillery."

There was a moment's silence. Each was thinking how many

times they said a colored man can't do this and can't do that, until there was nothing left but mopping floors and cleaning toilets.

"Ya know," Brad said, "Texas ain't much to fight for. But the boys did good last night. They ain't gonna forget it. I know if I can do this, I ain't gonna take no shit off nobody from now on."

Big Joe and Parker came toward us. Parker shifted his rifle to his left arm and dug the tobacco out of his mouth.

"See all you mammy jammers is still alive."

"Yeah," I said. "You goin' back to the outpost?"

"Yep."

"Get any pressure last night?"

"I kilt a mothafucker. Got right up to the foxhole before I saw him. Found out last night we's all men. The mothafucker that don't understand that can give his soul to God, 'cause his ass belongs to me."

Parker and Big Joe moved on to the outpost, Brad headed for the regimental S-2, and I went back to the command post. I watched the men until they were out of sight. I swear there was something new and proud and defiant in the way they walked.

In a thousand subtle ways, in a thousand brutal ways, we were taught that we were not a part of American culture and history. Here, we were *making* history. We were part of the vanguard of a new revolution—part of the struggle of the colored nine-tenths of humanity to gain democracy and dignity. This was the ramrod that straightened the shoulders and lifted higher the heads of the young Negroes who made up the ranks of infantrymen in the Ninety-third Division.

★

The well-equipped, battle-trained Japanese garrison on Bougainville had expected the invasion to hit the eastern shores of the island. The landing on the western side caught them by surprise and met with relatively weak resistance. As the Japanese troops crossed the mountains from east to west, the fighting intensified. Aerial photos and reconnaissance patrols confirmed that the Japanese were hand-carrying light artillery and assault weapons over the mountains in a final attempt to push the Americans into the sea.

We strengthened the defensive perimeter and in some places expanded it to force the Japanese to cross the Torokina River directly into our machine guns. The artillery of the Fourteenth Corps, the Ninety-third, Thirty-seventh, and Americal Divisions was synchronized with the firepower of a cruiser.

During the week, the probing attacks became stronger. Our lines pulled back to the river. The Japanese army slowly fought its way into the death trap.

Lieutenant Olsen, artillery observer from the Fourteenth Corps, was a pleasant young man from Fargo, North Dakota. He entered my dugout (which served as an observation post) as the opening skirmishes began to give way to full-scale fighting. As the Japanese crossed their lines of departure and began the assault, the artillery boxed them in against the river and into the guns of the perimeter. Then the slaughter began. The artillery barrage was the greatest of the Pacific war. The island shook and trembled. The rains came and turned the battlefield to mud. The dead mounted and the rats came—huge rats, bellies bloated with the organs of the dead. Packs of rats, in the tens of thousands, left troughs where they had dragged their full bellies through the mud.

The artillery compressed five thousand Japanese into a mile-square area that shook and trembled with belching fire and scalding phosphorus and hot steel that hurled body parts into the trees to rot in the putrid air. Plotting on the maps each suicidal assault, we called for yet another barrage of hell to hurl them into the river and blast them into rat food.

Night settled in and I realized that rations had not been sent up. I had long ago drunk the last of my water. Sections of the outpost line had caved in and passed through the main line of resistance. Our observation post was cut off for at least the rest of the night. As the firing died down, Lieutenant Olsen hinted that I might crawl the twenty yards to the river and fill the canteens so we would at least have water for washing. The tension made the thirst overwhelming. I crawled the short distance to the river, filled the four canteens, put in the water purification tablets, and crawled back to the dugout.

After the hour had passed, I drank in long, full gulps and then poured some in my hand to wash the sweat and grime from my face. I did not realize that the river looped through the middle of the fire zone. It had turned red with the blood of carnage. The pink hue of the water made me retch.

★

The battle for the Torokina perimeter broke the back of Japanese resistance on Bougainville. They were sure to lose, but they were capable of holding on and extracting more American lives as the price of victory.

A week before Mother's Day I wrote a long letter to Mom and waited for the mail orderly to come up with the rations. Along with the rations he brought a form for sending flowers. I printed our home address and gave him a ten-dollar bill.

"The flowers are five bucks, man. I don't have any change."

"Neither do I."

Then I thought of Miss O'Leary. She gave so much to me, this childless teacher, who nurtured hundreds of young men and women.

"Never mind. I want to send another bouquet as well." I printed Miss O'Leary's address.

Later Mom wrote that Abigail McCarthy (Miss O'Leary's niece) and her husband, soon to become Senator Eugene McCarthy, came by to tell her Miss O'Leary received the flowers the day before she died of cancer. Abigail McCarthy mentions this in her beautiful autobiography, *Private Faces, Public Places*.

I was saddened by her death but happy that she was thinking of me and knew that I, swallowed up by the jungles of the Solomons, was thinking of her.

As the fighting subsided, life behind the perimeter began to take on a garrisonlike quality. A post exchange opened and we built a theater. We began some regularity of work hours at the headquarters. Captain Akeley and I reentered our old relationship. I began to attend meetings with or for him. As the routine settled in, Akeley called for me.

"Sergeant, they're holding a meeting for the information and education officers and noncoms at division headquarters of the Forty-third. It's going to be tomorrow at ten o'clock. You go over there and get the poop."

"Yes, sir. Be glad to go."

★

The meeting took place in the assembly area of the division headquarters company. I got there early and took a seat on a coconut log in the first row. No one challenged me once he noted the French blue helmet shoulder patch. Our Twenty-fifth Infantry combat team was doing a good job and earned the respect of infantrymen who knew what it meant to be green troops thrown into jungle combat.

The assembly area filled up and a major from Fourteenth Corps opened the meeting. He said a few words about the importance of morale and how it rested upon information about our allies and the general course of the war. The major described the war on the western front in Europe. When he finished, a naval officer hung a huge map of the central Pacific and described the strategy and fighting in the Marianas. I was still scribbling notes while the major introduced the next speaker. This was going to be the central report of the meeting. A huge map of the Russian front was hung up and covered with an acetate overlay. The battle for Kursk was entering its second month. It was clear that if the Germans broke through the Kursk salient, they might take Moscow.

"Sergeant Bob Thompson is going to give you an extended report on the war on the eastern front."

Sergeant Thompson climbed upon the stage. Lean and sandy-haired, he had a Distinguished Service Cross ribbon pinned to his shirt.

New York Communists had a way of saying "Soviet Union" that identified them to every other Communist in the world. They said "Sov-yet Chunion." I smiled to myself. "Hey man, that's Bob Thompson, from the YCL." Bob had been a commander in the Canadian battalion that fought in Spain. He won his DSC in the battle of Buna Mission in New Guinea. Infantrymen in the South Pacific knew that if he hadn't been a Communist, he would have been awarded the Congressional Medal of Honor.

It was a wonderful report, full of details of the Red Army men hiding in their deep foxholes while the giant Ferdinand and Panzer tanks rolled over them. It explained how they would then leap upon the tanks with acetylene torches, cut open the locked peepholes, and destroy the Germans with a blast from the flamethrowers.

Bob described the Russian defense-in-depth tactic. There were several, not one, main lines of resistance. There was no such thing as a final protective line. If they pierced one line, the Germans confronted another. Tanks, dug in as artillery during the defensive phase of battle, rolled from their dugouts to cover the infantry in the counterattack. The two million men locked in combat seesawed through the ravines, gullies, and foothills of Kursk for thirty-eight days. We knew that the Red Army was bleeding the Nazis of their last offensive power.

Bob described the role of the partisans in blowing up the supply trains and attacking the flanks and communication lines of the German army. His love for the Red Army, his respect for the firm, correct leadership of Stalin was accepted by the soldiers. It flowed from a fighting man's respect for the Russian heroes in the great fraternity of the infantry.

Bob finished his report. The major answered a few questions and dismissed the meeting.

I made my way over to Sergeant Thompson.

"Hey, sarge, are you from New York?"

He smiled, glancing at my division and regimental insignia.

"Most people know that the minute I open my mouth. Yeah, can't wait to get back. You from New York?"

"No. Minnesota. Minneapolis. I was wondering if you weren't the same guy I met three, four years back. A guy by the name of Carl Ross introduced us."

That did it. Bob broke out in a grin so big it wrinkled his forehead.

"You were in the YCL? Glad to see you. Not many of us over here."

After the small talk was over, Bob suggested that I come meet another comrade, Herman Boettcher. All of us old-timers in the South Pacific knew the story of One Man Army Boettcher.

★

During the campaign for Buna Mission, in New Guinea, the 126th Infantry was attacking over impossible swamp terrain to gain control of the one existing supply route. The Japanese soldiers, experienced in the battles of China and the Philippines, held them at bay. A desperate attack by the American forces broke down. The Japanese counterattack broke through and the Americans retreated in disorder. A catastrophe was in the making. Skilled by years of warfare in Spain, Sergeant Boettcher set up a machine gun and poured flanking fire into the attacking Japanese. Single-handed, he broke the attack, killing the majority of the attacking Fascist troops. Then, gathering his scattered platoon, he led them in an attack that broke through Japanese lines and straddled the supply route. Having broken the Japanese forces in two, he held out against all counterattacks, winning the bloody battle for Buna Mission.

Setting aside the ban on Communist officers, the U.S. army awarded Boettcher its second-highest decoration, the Distinguished Service Cross and the commission of captain. He took command of his company.

Those of us around the Party or the YCL knew the German refugees from the Spanish Civil War. We knew about Herman Boettcher of the Thaelmann Brigade. As a teenager, he got his baptism of fire in the battle of Berlin, when the Communist met the Nazi storm troopers and left twenty-seven of them dead, completely upsetting Hitler's timetable for the seizure of power. His dramatic journey to Spain followed his dramatic escape from the concentration camp. During the Spanish Civil War he rose to the rank of major in the Eleventh (International) Brigade.

When German and Italian troops finally crushed the Spanish Republican government, Boettcher made his way to England and then to the United States. He joined the army as a private and was among the first to see combat in the Pacific.

With all his relatives killed by the Nazis, Herman was the last of his family. He lived to kill Fascists and defend his beloved Soviet Union.

Bob introduced us as simply "Comrade Nelson, Comrade Herman."

The bear hug that German Communists reserve for their comrades followed the handshake. In a short time comradeship overcame the awkwardness of rank. In a serious but warm voice, he inquired about the few comrades who had made it from Spain to the United States. I knew so little, but he appreciated every bit of information. He was especially happy to know I had heard that his comrade-in-arms, Gerhardt Eisler, had been in Minneapolis just before I went overseas. A few more beers were passed around. We spent the afternoon talking about the conduct of the war and the prospects of world socialism.

Before we left, we toasted the International Brigades and stood and sang the battle song of the German Communists. They sang in German; I awkwardly followed them in the English version: "Spanish heavens spread their brilliant starlight/High above our trenches in the plain;/From the distance morning comes to greet us,/Calling us to battle once again."

I had memorized the words so long ago. There was a good feeling in singing the song with these revolutionaries on Bougainville.

Captain Boettcher's battalion was moving up to the front in the push to finish off the Japanese in the area. We made arrangements to meet the following week and after the bear hugs, we parted.

When the meeting day finally rolled around, I went over to Bob's company. The first sergeant, figuring that I must be a Communist too, told me without emotion that Bob had been evacuated to a base hospital with a severe case of malaria.

I bummed a ride to the 126st area, where a lieutenant told me that Captain Boettcher was killed in action two days before.

During the hour-long walk back to my area my thoughts were of Comrade Herman Boettcher and his seventeen years in combat against fascism. Berlin, the concentration camp, the mountains and valleys of Spain, the gates of Madrid, the swamps of New Guinea and the Solomons—his adult life had been one of killing Fascists and spilling his blood for socialism, for the Soviet Union. I felt almost guilty about not having fought in Spain. There was something almost holy about Spain. The first out-and-out war against the Fascists. And we had been so close to victory. I guess this is the way Herman wanted it. *Freiheit! Auf zum Kampf!* Freedom! Off to battle! He died like a Communist—leading his troops in combat. Not so much that he died. It's that Herman did so much, gave so much. Herman had given it all—himself, his family, his comrades. All gone. It was as if an important moment of history had passed unnoticed with his death.

By the time I reached the camp I resolved to go to the graveyard and leave a flower or something to let him or the rest of the world know that in the Solomons there was a soldier who mourned the death of Herman Boettcher, hero of La Guerra Civil, captain of infantry, commander in the Thaelmann Column, defender of the Soviet Union, warrior of Democracy. Herman Boettcher, my comrade.

★

Laid out in straight military rows, the little graveyard was on the high ground near the mouth of the Torokina River. The distance between the crosses, front to back and right to left, was as if the dead stood at attention and the sergeant shouted, "Dress right! Dress!" and each dead soldier raised his right arm to touch the left shoulder of the next and stand at the precise distance right to left and front to back. Then they lay down in their graves in a military manner.

I easily found the grave. Away from the river, toward the back, the fresh dirt discolored the green grass. A detail of black soldiers was digging new graves. I walked over near them and looked at the name plates. Name, rank, and serial number. That's all we were at the port of embarkation. That's all we were in the graves of Bougainville.

The little wooden cross and the name plate were so new. Tears welled up in my eyes as I knelt to place the little bunch of flowers at the foot of the cross.

Flowers for a guy that had killed a couple of hundred Fascists in Germany and Spain and New Guinea and the Solomons? Half smiling, I unhooked my trench knife. Warriors are buried with their weapons. Bows and swords and muskets are found under the crossed arm bones. The earth was soft, and with my hands and the knife I dug down eight or ten inches, put the knife in the sheath, laid it above his chest, and covered it over with dirt.

I heard it only once, but the stirring words of the burial song dedicated to the comrades who died in the Spanish Civil War were clear in my mind: "Rest well, beloved comrade, the fight has just begun, The fight will go on 'till we've won."

I turned and walked away. I knew I had crossed another threshold of my life. The black guys leaned on their shovels and half waved to me. The white officer looked, too, wondering why a black soldier knelt at a white soldier's grave in the Solomons.

36

THE WAR GROUND ON. Each new island looked like the last. The white soldiers went back to New Zealand or Australia for short periods of rest and recuperation. These countries would not accept Negro troops on their soil. There was no rest for the Ninety-third. Unloading boats and clearing the jungle constituted our rest periods.

Green Island and Manus lay behind us. Our "rest period"— securing the island of Emiru—ended, and we boarded an attack transport for the three-day journey to Morotai.

The rumor was out that we would relieve the Thirty-first "Dixie" Division, complete the mopping up operations, and stage for the invasion of Japan. Aboard ship, the few Negro sailors added more rumors to the heap.

"The Thirty-first is the Goddamndest set of Ku Kluxers ever seen."

"Honest to Jesus, they know you all are coming and they aim to fight it out."

"They been beatin' hell out of a Negro water supply company there."

"A field hospital just moved onto the island. The Thirty-first said they gonna lynch any nigger look cross-eyed at the women."

I didn't put much stock in rumors, but I oiled, loaded, and locked my rifle.

The third day at sea, the lush green island of Morotai rose out of the mist. Skirting the huge island of Halmahera, we landed at the southern tip of Morotai.

Sure enough, a hospital was there. Two groups of soldiers and a few nurses stood watching as our landing craft nosed ashore and lowered the ramp. A group of disheveled white infantrymen stood to one side. Some carried rifles. On the other side stood the most forlorn group of Negro soldiers I had ever seen. A group of nurses stood back near one of the big tents.

The ramp settled on the sand and I stepped out to assemble the platoon. Two of the Negro soldiers walked over to me. One grabbed my hand and then hugged me.

"Jesus Christ! I'm glad to see a black man with a rifle."

"What's the matter, man?"

"We been catchin' hell here. These white motherfuckers got all the guns—they're the military police and they been beating us up."

So the rumor was true. So they want to lynch somebody. I turned to the men filing out of the landing craft.

"Looks like the Dixie boys been giving these men a hard time."

Our men, on edge from rumors, stepped quickly onto the beach, rifles in hand, keeping an eye on the white soldiers. Parker screwed up his black face and spit a huge cud of tobacco onto the sand.

"Mothafuck them motherfuckers! Let 'em say something to me!" Parker's snarl carried over the area.

"Parker!" Captain Forrest yelled, "Shut yo're Goddamn mouth!"

Parker glared at Forrest, released the safety catch on his rifle, and stepped onto the beach. The nurses, standing near the white soldiers, turned to one another. The white soldiers shifted about restlessly. On deck and on the ramp a few more soldiers released the safety catches. A few more soft clicks and then at once, every one released the catches.

I stepped quickly up the beach toward the Negro soldiers, my heart in my throat. This was worse than combat. We greatly outnumbered them, but we were bunched together for a slaughter. The officers on deck talked together nervously. Behind them, the sailors glanced around for cover. The white soldiers shifted their weapons. We were more than they had bargained for. I turned my back on them and called to the section, "OK, men, fall in here."

They moved cautiously across the sand and formed ranks. The landing craft carrying Company C nudged ashore and the men began to disembark. A white soldier started toward us, unbuckling the holster of his .45. The men stood quietly, their rifles at the ready. The white soldier stopped twenty feet before the landing craft.

"Who's doin' that Goddamn cussin'?"

His hand slid toward the pistol.

"Ah'm tellin' you fuckin' niggers . . . "

The clack of bolts shoving bullets into the firing chambers drowned him out. Five rifles snapped to shoulders aimed at the half-drunk white man. The nurses screamed and ran for the hospital tents. The white soldiers scattered for cover. Men from Company C ran from the landing craft. The unarmed black soldiers from the water filtration company fell over one another getting out of the line of fire. Captain Williams, the Negro commander of Company C, ran between the groups. Pulling his .45 from its holster, he shouted for attention. Our men lowered their rifles and snapped to. The terrified white soldier did not move.

"All right, soldier. That means you, too."

The soldier came to a sloppy attention.

"You get the hell to your own area. That's a direct order!"

The soldier staggered back to his group. Colonel Meyers walked toward Captain Williams. An exchange of salutes and Captain Williams went back to his company. Two jeeploads of white MPs drove onto the beach. Meyers went to talk with them. We knew what was happening. Meyers, a gutless white supremacist from Oklahoma, wasn't going to look bad before these Southern whites. He wasn't going to let anyone mistreat "his" Negroes. The MPs and the white soldiers left and we marched to the edge of the swamp that the commander of the Thirty-first had designated as our bivouac area.

Tension rose immediately between the white MPs and our soldiers. Arrests and fights between them occurred almost daily. Just as the tension reached the flash point, our division headquarters moved to the island. General Johnson, our new commanding officer and the senior officer on the island, took command. Our military police replaced those of the Dixie Division and the bottom rail went to the top. A few cracked heads and the Dixie boys accepted the black MPs. Before any serious trouble developed, the Thirty-first left for the invasion of the Philippines.

★

For us, it was the same old story. Japanese resistance was broken on Morotai, but the perimeter had to be manned and mopping up operations continued.

Morotai bottled up the forty-five thousand soldiers twelve miles to the south on Halmahera. Because small raiding parties from Halmahera still attacked the island, we maintained beach patrols.

I hit the jackpot. The colonel assigned a section of our platoon to lookout and patrol duty. He ordered me to establish an outpost on a lovely stretch of white sand beach far from the main troop concentration. After building the fortifications, we slung our jungle hammocks and began catching up on our reading and letter writing.

"Man," Harold mumbled. "We finally got it made."

"Yeah. I think I'm going to sleep for a week." Jeff turned over in his hammock.

"This is better than Bougainville or Biak, but it's still the war. I don't think it'll ever end," Harold said.

"Naw, man," I said. "The war is coming to an end. There's a lot of fighting yet—but it's ending. I been reading some stuff in this magazine, *Success in Combat*. That battle of Kursk, in Russia, broke the German army. The Russians are fighting in Poland, Italy's about done. It's coming to an end."

"I don't know," Brad said. "We keep taking these islands and it'll be a long war. We'll take the Philippines and then down to Java. Then we'll get together and hit Japan. By that time we'll have about half as many men as we do now. Then the Japs will move to Manchuria and we'll land there and have to fight the Chinese, too. It'll go on until all us old-timers are dead."

Nobody answered. He was expressing our collective thinking. We were weary of war and malaria and jungles and bad news from home and canned food and bugs and the stink of death and missing a dead or evacuated friend.

As the sun sank into the Pacific, we sat wrapped in our individual thoughts, wondering when and how it would end. Although it was going well in Europe, we were still in the same meat grinder of a war—nothing to win but tomorrow—and nothing to lose but our lives.

The next day the mail orderly walked over to me, smiling.

"If you act nice, I'll give you something."

"Gimme my letter, man."

"I see you're getting your sugar ration again."

The thought of Heidi flashed through my mind—no, that wasn't possible.

"Man, if you got a letter for me, give it here."

"I wonder who it's from?" He grinned. Ever since Huachuca, he had teased me about my mail.

"Might be from your mama. Gimme my letter."

Brad laughed. The mail orderly shook his head.

"Lord, you done throwed shit in the game. Here's the damned thing." He tossed the blue envelope to me. My heart skipped a beat. I knew it was from her. The same neat hand-writing.

"Got one from your old lady, huh? Guess she just forgot your address for two years. Or maybe Joe De Grinder put her down."

"Man, kiss my ass, will you?" I wanted the willpower to tear it up, to let the dead stay buried. Instead, I turned my back to the rest of the men and, with trembling hands, opened the blue envelope. I glanced over the two neatly written pages and then slowly read the heartache.

"My Dearest Nels . . . Can you forgive me enough to at least try again? I realize that I do love you and always have. . . . I have been such a fool . . . I cannot visualize the rest of my life without you."

The same neat signature.

"Get a letter from your old lady in Minnesota?"

"Yeah."

"Well, make out the insurance policy to her and then get your ass blown off. That's all she wants."

"Fuck her. The war's almost over. I'll live."

"I wish it was almost over."

"It might be almost over for you."

"Why don't you guys shut up? I've got a letter to write."

"Are you going to take her back?" Brad asked.

"I don't know. Would you take Ruth back? You're still in love with her."

"Yeah, I still love her. She's like this Goddamn tooth. Hurts a little all the time, but I'm better off with it than without it. I wouldn't take her back. I'd fucking die if I had to go through it again."

"Take her back?" Lee grinned like a gargoyle. "Joe De Grinder done wore her ass out, now she wants back."

"Why don't you shut your fuckin' mouth?" Jeff said. "That fat heifer of yours is doin' the V for victory right now."

"Screw you, Jeff."

"Listen, Nels," Jeff went on. "I'm older than you, and I'm going to tell you the truth. I know you love the girl, don't make no difference if she's white. If she's been selling her ass for the last two years, it don't make no difference. If you love her, take her back— or later on, you'll never forgive yourself. Don't listen to these damned fools and don't listen to your pride."

I laid back on the cot, the almost forgotten days floating

before me. Six, brushing his long blond hair from his eyes. Heidi at fifteen, the tiny lines at the corners of her mouth dancing as she smiled. The sweet, sweet kisses, the acid tears, the frustrations, the shared, secret dreams. How long can a person dream? When you become a man you put childish dreams aside. God knows, I've dreamed enough. She was a childish dream of happiness and love. A dream like the freight train that was going to take me to a place where being black didn't make a difference. Last thing I told her was that I was through running and dreaming. To go back to her would be to run from everything I've got to face and fight when I get back. Old Shoeshine Joe was right. Taking low is natural to a dog, not a man. I can't take low anymore. If I go back to her, I'll take low to her and this system for the rest of my life. I'm not going back. It isn't just that she hurt me so. The hurt was part of the process—it sped up the inevitable. I want something different now. One thing I learned in the infantry, if you want that hill, you got to bleed for it. When I get back, there's a hill I'm going to take, and I'm ready to bleed for it. I guess she's part of the bleeding.

I sat down with the clipboard and began to write. It was a harsh, bitter letter spelling out the hurt. Its ending was even more callous. We were on different life paths now. She could live with what I had to fight. I knew her one decent point was that she never compromised with discrimination; she just wouldn't fight it. That was the dagger to make the meanest cut. After I'd puked it all out, I wanted to tear it up. I knew, though, I could never go back. She'd changed; I'd changed. Should I lack the will to go on, this letter was the torch to burn the bridge.

Sealed and stamped, it fell from my hand into the locked mailbox, and I went back to my cot.

Jinx walked over to me.

"Hey, sarge, want to take over the radio for a few minutes? I got to get something to eat."

"I'm not very fast with code."

"It's on clear."

"OK." I got up and walked over to the radio tent. I had just made myself comfortable reading a magazine when the radio began to hum:

"Come in, Saber Lookout. Come in, Saber Lookout."

"This is Saber Lookout."

"This is Charlie. How you doing, Jinx?"

"Sergeant Peery, Charlie. What's the good word?"

"There ain't no good word. We just got word that President Roosevelt died."

"Cut out the bullshit."

"I just got it shortwave from the States."

"I can't believe it. How'd he die?"

"I ain't sure. Wore out, I guess."

"Am I supposed to tell the men?"

"Sure—let them know. Some guy by the name of Truman—he's from Missouri—is taking over. The colonel said the detachments could hold memorial services."

"I'll spread the word."

"Roger and out."

The red light dimmed out. I sat for a moment in the thickening darkness. What did he say? Roosevelt's dead? He was like a father to the whole fucking country. He's the only president I remember. He was beginning to see that those four freedoms had to start with us Negroes. Eleanor made him see it. Who the hell is Truman? From Missouri. Can't be no damned good.

Jinx entered the tent.

"What's the matter? Any calls from Regimental?"

"Yeah. Roosevelt's dead."

Jinx half smiled. "That guy will live a long time yet. Christ, he's been president since 'thirty-two."

"No, it's no joke. He's dead. It came from Regiment."

Jinx stood quietly for a moment, blinking his eyes.

"I guess I'd better go tell the men."

I should call the men together. We should say a word—he was the commander in chief.

The men were in the squad tent carrying on the endless game of tonk. As I walked in, they knew something was wrong.

"What's up, man?"

"The president's dead. He died today."

"No joke. Is he really dead?"

"Yeah—he's gone. Let's fall out for a little service."

The men filed out of the tent and formed uneven ranks in the darkness. After putting them at ease, I said, "Men, President Roosevelt is dead. I don't know what else I can say except he was a friend to the Negro and the working man. We're going to miss him." I turned to Josh. "Will you lead us in prayer?"

"The old days are gonna come back," someone whispered loudly.

Like most jackleg preachers, Josh could pray for hours without stopping. He surprised me by saying, "Blessed Jesus, another man done gone. Be merciful to President Roosevelt, Jesus. He was a good man. He was a Christian. He didn't want this war, an' it weren't his fault. We, your servants gathered tonight on Morotai, we humbly beg your mercy on his soul."

Josh couldn't go on. There was a moment of silence.

"Harold, will you sound taps?"

Harold got the trumpet and came back wetting his lips. Etched in the brightness of the moon, he stood before us facing the sea. A deep breath and he slowly raised the trumpet to his mouth. Note by note the melancholy of taps rolled out across the sea and through the jungle. As the last echo faded into silence, I dismissed the men and they quietly went back to the tent.

Lights went out early that night.

37

JEFF WAS ON lookout duty in the coconut log watchtower.

"Hey! There's a landing barge coming in!"

I rolled out of my hammock, grabbing the field glasses.

"It's OK. It's ours."

As the landing craft came closer, I could make out Lieutenant Hartsfield and Moore.

The craft wallowed through the surf and beached.

"Hello, Sergeant Peery. Hello, Josh. How are you all doing?"

We exchanged salutes.

"OK, lieutenant. What's happening?"

"I've got some good news for you. Have the scouts fix a combat pack with four days' rations. Take an extra pair of shoes and whatever else you may need."

"I don't have to go, do I?"

"The colonel said you have to go. It's a raid. You're not going as a scout. You'll be operations for me. You have some knowledge of the territory and the maps of the area. Let's go to the tent."

I followed him into the command tent. He reached into his bag and pulled out a carefully rolled map and overlay. Orienting the map, we adjusted the overlay and secured it with tacks. About seventeen miles up the Tjoe River was a neatly drawn red battle flag designating the headquarters of the 221st Imperial Infantry Regiment, the Fascists who had carried out the rape of Nanking.

"So, we've finally found their regimental headquarters."

"Yep. Division Recon captured a lieutenant and he told everything. One of our artillery planes photographed and verified it. That's where he's hiding out. Colonel Ouchi is still alive. Recon is going in to try to capture him. General Johnson told them that if they didn't bring him back alive, they needn't come back. There has never been a Japanese officer of that high rank captured, only a few lieutenants, and damned few of them. I guess General Johnson will be showing MacArthur what he's worth if he can turn Ouchi over to him."

"If Recon is going out, what the hell do we have to go for?"

"A small task force will go in, engage the headquarters security, and withdraw, pulling them out toward the sea. Later that day, Recon will grab Ouchi, and his adjutant if possible, and get them the hell out of there."

"What are we supposed to do?"

"We're coming over the ridge, down the river, hit the headquarters from the rear, burn it, and kill or capture whoever we can. That ought to finish off the 221st."

"We've done some patrolling in this area, and looking at the map, it's rough terrain."

"Yep. But if we follow this stream as far as possible, it will help. Then we'll have to go the rest of the way by azimuth. That's your responsibility. That's why the colonel chose you."

If that was meant as a compliment, it didn't move me. I shrugged my shoulders.

"When we cutting out?"

"We're going to rendezvous with a squad of infantry from Company C and a few men from battalion headquarters at 06:00. We can get there in an hour. You've got some shellac, haven't you?"

"Sure. I brought some up with me."

"Fix the map, burn the overlay, and prepare to move out at 04:30."

"OK, sir. I'll be ready."

Hartsfield left the tent. I shellacked the map to waterproof it and hung it out to dry. When the map dried, I traced our route on it with China marking pencils and burned the overlay. The next task was the pack.

I laid out five pairs of socks and an extra pair of boots. I liked
the tommy gun for the jungle, but I couldn't carry enough ammo.
Besides, those shells were heavy as hell. I chose the carbine and
cleaned and oiled it. The camouflage jungle suit looked good in
the movies, but it was too heavy. I chose two pairs of fatigues. Take
the pancho instead of the shelter half, but take the ropes; they
come in handy. Four days of K rations were twelve boxes—
couldn't carry all that. First day, I'd be hungry and eat three. The
second day I wouldn't be able to eat more than two. The third and
fourth day I'd only eat one. Seven would be plenty. I'd take the tin
cans and the biscuits out, and leave the rest. Take the cigarettes.
One pack of crap paper is enough—damned K rations constipate
you right away. Mosquito lotion, sulfa powder, eight Atabrine
pills, medical kit, bayonet, canteen, water purification pills. I
stuffed it all in the pack; whatever I'd want would be at the bottom
anyway.

The radioman woke me at four and I fixed my breakfast of
dehydrated eggs and powdered coffee. Lieutenant Hartsfield was
already up and helping the sailor start the cold motor of the landing craft. It chugged to life and we started the hour-long trip to the
rendezvous with the patrol.

As we neared the rendezvous point, the other landing craft
drew alongside us. The two craft swung together and beached. A
few of the riflemen ran into the brush to secure the place. As the
officer in command of the patrol, Lieutenant Hartsfield gathered
the rest of the men around him for the briefing.

"How ya doin,' Big Joe?" I shook his hand warmly and threw
my arm around his shoulder.

"Everything's lovely." It was always lovely with Big Joe.

"Yeah." Lee smiled, slurring his words to mimic Joe. "It's
about as lovely as the ass of a wild bear."

We all shook hands around, backslapping and happy to see
one another. What times we had had together! We loved one
another in a comradeship that we would never know again. God,
I hoped we'd never bring another one of us back in a bloody shelter half. Lost in such thoughts, I hardly heard Hartsfield until he
said, "If there aren't any questions, let's move out."

We fell into the loose diamond formation of the patrol, Hartsfield and I in the center for the moment.

"Peery."

"Sir?" I looked into Hartsfield's lean, brown, intelligent face.

What a studious, moral guy to be in the infantry. Yet, I thought, he's just the best example of most of the Negro officers in the division.

"You know we're depending completely on you to keep us on the route."

"Don't worry about a thing."

"I do worry—I worry all the time."

For an hour we walked swiftly and comfortably along the banks of the river. Close to the equator, it was hot and the men were beginning to sweat. I felt especially sorry for the medic. In addition to his rations and clothing, he carried a huge medical pack that made it difficult for him to keep out of the way of the slapping branches and low limbs.

The river was beginning to narrow and the banks rose steeply from the edge. The point man of the patrol hesitated for a moment and then stepped into the water. A few muttered curses and the men filed into the stream. Walking in the water was slow and tiring for us. Worst yet, the map, made from aerial photographs, showed cliffs farther ahead. By noon the men had stopped talking; the only sound was the splash and swish of boots in the muck. Occasionally, caught by a vine or stumbling over a hidden rock, one of the men would curse.

Hartsfield held up his hand and motioned to the bank. We pulled ourselves out of the water. Four of the men crept into the jungle as guards, and we flopped down in the thick underbrush, unbuckling our ammo belts and packs. We were beginning to feel the strain of the march. Some of the men lit their cigarettes; others opened the K ration boxes. I knew Hartsfield was forcing us along as much as possible to gain time that we would lose climbing the rugged hills.

After half an hour he said, "Smoke for two more minutes, bury the ration boxes, and cover each other going back into the river."

We ground out our cigarettes, hoisted our packs, and filed back into the water. Tired, and with the disregard for danger that weariness brings, we slung our rifles, eyes on the pack ahead, and let the flank guards worry about the Japanese.

During the next break, I plotted our position on the map and made a mark where we would bivouac for the night. Hartsfield pursed his lips, measuring the distance, and asked me to call the noncoms together.

"We're falling way behind schedule. I know you've been pushing the men, but from here on it's going to be worse. We're going to leave the river and travel by azimuth through the bush. We've got to make the top of the hills before we bed down. Are there any questions?"

There was a moment's silence. We knew it would be suicide to sleep on the low ground.

"OK, tell the men no more breaks. We've got to scatter ass from now on."

The noncoms went back and talked to the men. By ones and twos the weary black soldiers rose, slung their packs, and filed across the stream into the dense underbrush. Occasionally stopped by bush too thick to penetrate, a few of the men would unsling their packs and with machetes hack a path for the rest of us. The jungle began to darken except for the shafts of light from the setting sun. Time passed with the slow certainty of the muddy combat boots that moved up and down ahead of me—eating up the yards that separated us from the bivouac area.

For a moment I had to think where we were. The Canal? New Georgia? Morotai? It was all the same glamorous war—mud, hunger, death—and worst of all, the indescribable weariness.

How different it was at Fort Huachuca when we marched through Montezuma Pass. The 369th Infantry! Three thousand of us—mostly in our teens and early twenties—singing the traditional songs. How we bubbled with morale, marching through those majestic mountains along the border with Mexico. From sugar to shit. Ending up like this. Lee slipped in the mud, cursed, and regained his place in line. Mud caked our pants all the way to the crotch. God! Was there ever a war without mud—the sucking, stinking, slippery mud! We had left the glamor at the pier in San Francisco, and in its place were the mud and the bone-aching, gut-wrenching weariness.

I took an azimuth shot on the bivouac area at the last of the twilight; the sun vanished and darkness set in immediately. Our only guide now was the phosphorous needle of my compass. We pushed on slowly. Someone muttered, "I'm so Goddamned tired I could cry."

His buddy answered softly, "It's just a little farther. I know you ain't fixin' to fall out."

"No shit." Muffled laughter.

At the top of the hill we scratched out foxholes in a defense perimeter and made a guard roster. It began to rain. Some of the men didn't bother to unroll their packs. They curled up and fell asleep, the rain washing the mud from their faces, plastering their stinking, filthy fatigues against their exhausted bodies.

I tossed and turned until Lieutenant Hartsfield shook me awake. We plotted our course on the map. Already close to our objective, Hartsfield figured if we moved out at 06:30 we could easily reach it by noon.

After our K ration breakfast, Hartsfield stood up and simply said, "Let's go, men."

It was easier on the downgrade, and we made good time to the river that ran beside the headquarters. We spotted the thatched hut that served as a command post and living quarters for Ouchi. The riflemen were assigned objectives. Tightening our rifle slings, releasing the safety catches, we prepared to storm the post. Hartsfield surveyed the area with field glasses. Satisfied that we had not been seen, he raised his hand and pointed forward. We rose and ran, sliding and stumbling through the mud and underbrush toward the cluster of huts.

We reached the command hut. Jeff threw in a grenade. After the explosion we rushed into the foul-smelling emptiness. We were in Colonel Ouchi's living quarters. His personal belongings had been scattered around the room by the explosion. An accurate map of our defensive positions hung on the wall. We sacked the place, stuffing our pockets with trinkets. A sharp burst of machine gun fire and we ran outside, diving behind the scrub trees that lined the Tjoe River.

Across the stream, two Japanese soldiers behind a light machine gun raked the area with fire. Men in battle are the ultimate proof of evolution. The veneer of civilization crumbles. Blood lust—fanaticism or courage, depending on which side you're on—jars the body like a gulp of Louisiana corn liquor, paralyzing the brain. Hot blood pumping from an expanded heart tingles the palms and sets legs trembling. Sight sharpens, and hearing, more animal than human, senses the chirp of crickets within the thunder of guns.

The Japanese soldiers didn't have to fight. Division Recon had annihilated the headquarters security force and captured Ouchi yesterday. They could have hidden in the brush and lived until the war ended. They never thought about dying—only killing. The river, thirty yards wide, separated us from them. We didn't have to rush across the open water to kill them. Our high-powered rifles could have done it from a quarter mile away. An animal closes in to kill. A sergeant screamed, "Kill the mothafuckas!"

The men rushed by ones and twos to the bank of the river. A small drainage ditch separated me from the riverbank. Across the ditch a finger of land, covered by tall grass and brush, jutted out into the stream. From that point I could pour flanking fire onto the machine gunners.

"Let's get across the ditch."

"I'll cover ya."

A crouched run and jump carried me across the ditch. I saw him before I landed on him. The bulging eyes, the arms and legs spread rigid in death were forced slightly upward by the gases that decay generated as he lay rotting in the jungle humidity. A moment's resistance and my boot sank into the bloated corpse. Green, slimy gobs of phlegmlike intestines and vital organs splashed up and onto my leg. I had smelled death before, but nothing like this. The horrible stench was overpowering. Thousands of flies swarmed up from the chest cavity and escaping gasses made gurgling sounds. I leaned against a scrub tree, puking and retching. Using sticks, I unbuckled the boot, kicked it off, and got out of my pants.

A rapid tinny-sounding burst from the machine gun and the answering wham wham wham of our rifles brought me back to reality. I grabbed my rifle and ran through the underbrush to the curve in the river, where I had a good view of the Japanese machine gunner. I brought the carbine to my shoulder and lined the head of the Japanese soldier in the sight, held my breath, and squeezed the trigger. As the hammer fell, Bradley's brown face and green helmet entered the sight of the rifle. For the first time, my rifle misfired. I laid it down and closed my eyes for a moment to stop the trembling. I had come close to killing my dearest friend.

Cigar stump clamped between clinched teeth, holding the automatic rifle to his shoulder, Big Joe waded out into midstream, his 220 pounds rocking with the recoil of the weapon. Sweet, gentle, lovable Joe—hell spitting from his shoulder. It was over. The men dragged the wounded soldiers to the riverbank. One was a lieutenant, the other a private. Blood gurgled through a hole in the officer's chest; the private, eyes half closed, was dying. The officer gestured for us not to kill them. Sympathetically, Hartsfield looked down at them for a moment.

"Jesus, we can't take them with us. We can't leave them here to suffer." I shuddered as Big Joe's automatic rifle blasted away the twisted, pain-racked lives.

Fuck 'em. That's what they get for what they did in Nanking.

I put on my extra pair of fatigues and boots while the men sacked and burned the command post. I couldn't wash away the smell of death, and took a lot of kidding as we ate the last of our rations.

The patrol filed back into the stream and marched swiftly to the sea and the rendezvous with the landing craft. We climbed aboard, unhitched our packs, and sat back smoking fresh navy cigarettes. One of the sailors sniffed in my direction.

"Jesus Christ, something stinks!"

"Whole fucking war stinks."

"Yeah—yeah. But I smell something dead."

"There's only about forty million so far," Lieutenant Hartsfield said.

The sailor gave up, muttering, "Jesus Christ! It's enough to make you sick."

Big Joe smiled faintly and nodded ever so slightly. I knew what he was thinking—what we were all thinking. We were all sick. We could not express how sick and tired we were of the whole Goddamned war. I dragged hard on the cigarette.

"Fuck—I'm going to ask the colonel not to send me out for awhile."

"I don't reckon you're going to have to worry about that anymore. I don't reckon none of us have to go out anymore," one of the sailors said.

"What do you mean?"

The sailors looked at us with puzzled expressions.

"How long you guys been out? They done dropped a bomb on Japan that wiped out a whole damn city."

We looked at the sailor.

"One bomb? What kind of bomb was that?"

"A new thing—an atom bomb. One bomb took out a city. The war ain't gonna last very long with that thing."

We couldn't believe one bomb could destroy a city. We talked about it for a few moments and, only half believing, dropped the subject.

★

General Johnson met us at the dock and congratulated us. He pinned a Silver Star on Sergeant Dillon of Division Recon, who captured Ouchi while the colonel was bathing in the river. We were aghast when the general then assigned a black private to be the orderly for the Japanese colonel.

I thought back to a book I was reading. Maybe Saladin, the great Kurdish warrior, was right—kings don't kill kings. Maybe someday, us stupid soldiers will get the same idea.

As we received news confirming the bombing of Hiroshima, the discussions immediately became political.

"Sure, they'll use that bomb on the Japanese. Know why? 'Cause they're colored. That's why! They didn't use it on the Germans. Know why? 'Cause they're white. That's why!"

"I don't believe Roosevelt would have used that bomb. Burning up all those little children ain't right."

The Russians declared war on Japan and knifed down through Manchuria and Korea, thrusting aside the resistance of five million crack imperial troops.

"Hey now! Uncle Joe done started kickin' ass! It ain't gonna be long now!"

The Chinese Communist armies battled their way to the sea. Japanese resistance on the Asian mainland was broken. The United States dropped another atom bomb, on Nagasaki. The commander of the garrison on Halmahera surrendered his eighteen-foot silk flag and forty-five thousand troops to us. It was the first big surrender of the war.

The island went wild with the news of the general surrender. That night I slept in my foxhole. The joy of the anti-aircraft artillery, machine guns, and cannon was as deadly as their anger.

The war was over. We could go home. We walked around slapping one another on the back, cursing one another—silly happy that we could lay down our sword and shield and study war no more. Party after party rolled around the island until all the money was concentrated in the hands of the airmen who flew the whiskey up from Australia.

The rumor was everywhere: "We're going to the Philippines and from there, home." In a few days the order came down. We set about policing the area, removing mines, and striking the tents.

"Ohhhh Goddamn!" Jeff shouted. "I'm gonna make a beach-head on Chicago and dig in in my own bedroom. Gonna place my hand firmly under the piece, place the butt in my shoulder hollow, line up the sights, and squeeze off!"

We all laughed at Jeff burlesquing the rifle manual as he grabbed Lee, trying to force him onto the cot.

The colonel called a battalion formation. We assembled on the sloping hill in front of the chapel. Chaplain Watkins stood up before us dressed in a brilliant white vestment. He led us in a short prayer of thanksgiving for peace, and then he added, "Men, we have finished our course. The men of the 369th have lived and fought like soldiers. I'm proud of each of you. We have won the military battle for democracy, but the fight is not over. Don't be satisfied with the way things were. Remember, for the rest of your lives remember, how brave you are——how much you gave for your country. Soon we'll be home again. Don't be satisfied to follow a mule from 'kain see to kain't see.' Don't let anyone ever again tell you you are inferior because you are black. We fought on the side of the Lord. Don't desert Him when you get home. Be a man! We owe it to ourselves."

I glanced at Major Akeley. He was nervously drumming his fingers against his knee. I got the feeling that he at least partially agreed.

The next morning we embarked for the comfortable trip to Mindanao.

38

THE FIRST FEW days in the Philippines were a furlough to heaven. The combat teams that finished the war in Jolo, Tawi-Tawi, and Zamboanga arrived in the bivouac area a week ahead of us. They completed the most difficult work of setting up the camp.

The feudalistic practice of "renting" an emergency, or temporary, wife for two hundred dollars still existed in the southern islands. Most of the soldiers looked upon the practice as something smacking of slavery, or at least prostitution, and would have none of it. Some of the men who had the money and purchased wives fell in love with them. Somehow they brought their emergency wives up to the camp with them. We were envious as they stood in the chow lines with two mess kits and ate and slept with their "wives" in tents at the edge of the area. The newcomers, tossing their dice in the air, announced their intention of getting two hundred dollars, divorcing Mary Palmer, and purchasing a "wife" for the duration.

The day after our arrival in Mindanao, passes were issued and the soldiers flooded into Cagayan looking for women, rice wine, and the milky whiskey that left you sucking wind and calling on the Lord.

Those of us who pulled duty and were confined to camp were surprised by a group of young women. Laughing and talking together, they strolled through the camp on their way to wash clothes in the river. They rolled perplexed eyes up at us, wondering why we were staring at them as they disrobed and stepped into the water.

We chuckled to one another. It was a furlough to heaven.

★

Scores of civilians began wandering through the camp in search of food. The cheerful "Hello, Joe" greeting to the soldiers could not hide the desperation of their unending quest for food for their families.

At first it appeared that Mike and his little brother, Jimmy, came to the camp as hundreds of civilians did. He was perhaps nineteen and light-skinned for Mindanao. As did most of the Philippine youth, he dressed in an assortment of civilian and military clothing. Sandals cut from tires and tied with leather thongs served as shoes. GI fatigue pants, a flowered Philippine shirt, and an overseas cap that had once belonged to the Philippine Scouts completed his attire. His smile was constant and genuine. As he came near, I noticed that there were only stumps of fingers on his left hand. There was something different about Mike. He seemed to be searching out seemingly friendly faces before he spoke. He would laugh and say expected things, and if he got the expected replies, he would walk on to the next soldier.

I watched as he approached me. I always felt a little embarrassed that such brave people had been reduced by imperialism and then by war to such abject poverty.

"Hello, Joe. You like Philippine Islands?"

"Yeah. I like it. Pretty country. Nice people."

He had laid down the mortar and seemed to like the brick I had put there. He decided to stay awhile.

"Hey, Joe, you got a cigarette?"

I handed him the pack of Camels.

"Thanks, Joe." He pulled one out and lit up, dragging the smoke deep into his lungs. With obvious reluctance he handed them back.

"Keep 'em. I get them for a nickel at the PX."

"OK, thanks. My name's Mike. What's your name, sergeant?" That was a long way from "Joe," and I knew he knew more about something than he was letting on. He stuck out his hand.

"I'm Nelson. Glad to know you, Mike." His fingerless hand made an effort to grasp my upper arm. "What happened to your fingers?"

Mike feigned a look of surprise and for a moment seemed not to know the answer.

"Japanese cut 'em off—Japanese no fuckin' good."

"I'm sorry, Mike. What happened?"

"Somebody tell them that I carry messages to the squadron. Japanese beat me up and cut off a finger. Four times somebody tell, four times they beat me up, four times they cut off my finger."

There wasn't much for me to say. After an uncomfortable moment, I said, "Well, Mike, we couldn't have won the war without people like you. Sorry that happened, but—"

The smile returned.

"I got more. Some people here had one life and it gone."

He wasn't going to lay down any more mortar, so I just asked, "You were a guerrilla?"

He thought for a moment for an answer. "No. We were the ones who got the food, and carried the messages, and spied on the Japanese."

"And got your fingers chopped off."

"You like the Ou Sa Fee [USAFFE] guerrilla?"

That was real mortar. I realized then what he was searching for. This guy was political and was trying to find some political soldiers. I had nothing to lose. I laid the appropriate brick.

"No, I liked the Hukbalahap."

Mike glanced around to see if that "somebody" might be listening.

"I am with Hukbalahap. The United Front."

It was my turn to glance around.

"I am a Communist."

Mike tilted his head a shade to look straight into my eyes. "Maybe—we should talk." He glanced around again. "Not here. Maybe in Cagayan."

"OK, you come back. It's Headquarters Company, First Battalion, 369th."

I glanced around. No one was paying us any attention. After the disaster on the Sabine River, I knew that G-2 and Counter Intelligence had me on their list of soldiers to be watched.

"Good-bye, comrade," was said softly, deliberately. It sounded good. No one had said that to me since the chance meeting with Bob Thompson and Herman Boettcher on Bougainville.

"So long, Mike. Come back."

Mike touched his little brother. Jimmy had been squatting half-turned from us all along. He was the lookout.

39

AS THE WAR ground to an end, the United States moved to crush the new Philippine revolution. The State Department, the Office of Strategic Services, the General Staff of the Asian Command, the Counter Intelligence Corps, and Naval Intelligence swiftly and ruthlessly put into effect the year-old plan.

They moved in the same way they had done when they crushed national liberation forty-five years before. Utilizing a phony independence plan, they rallied the patriotic middle-class intelligentsia. Then they invited the comprador class of bureaucrats headed by MacArthur's friend Manuel Roxas to return. This gang had served the prewar colonial government and then the Japanese invaders and was prepared to serve the United States colonizers again. They rallied the big landlord class by promising to reverse any land redistribution that had taken place in the areas liberated by the Hukbalahap. Worst and most decisive, they were moving to quickly reestablish the Philippine Army and create a base for a huge, Fascist, privileged officer corps to protect the investments and control the islands for the United States.

At the surrender of the Philippines to the Japanese, groupings of Philippine soldiers went over to guerrilla activity. Led by U.S.

officers and the Philippine military elite, they had been designated United States Armed Forces Far East [USAFFE (Guerrilla)]. Popularly known as Ou Sa Fee, they did none of the fighting except to ambush Huk patrols. Their main purpose was to maintain a legitimate presence of the defeated government. In this way they hoped to prevent the takeover by revolutionary forces after the defeat of Japan. USAFFE (Guerrilla) would become the core of the reconstituted army. Using high pay, privileges, and promises of commissions and noncommissioned officer ranks, they began incorporating the scattered guerrilla groups into the army.

They had a real problem with the largest segment of the guerrillas, the Hukbalahap. Hukbo ng Bayan Laban sa Hapon—the Philippine People's Army to Fight Japan—had grown out of the revolutionary peasant unions, labor unions, and the merged Socialist-Communist Parties. Basically a peasant army, it could not and did not skirt the question of land reform. The breaking up of the huge estates was to be the necessary foundation for the new Philippine democracy.

During the days of the Communist International, the Philippine Communist Party had been a section of the Communist Party of the United States of America. During the war, the OSS saw to it that the CPP (Communist Party of the Philippines) received books published by the Communist Party, USA, such as Earl Browder's *Teheran and After*. These books advocated class collaboration and proposed that United States imperialism would lead the colonial world to socialism. The apparent growing unity between the Allies seemed to uphold that thesis. The leaders of the Huks became seriously disoriented regarding the intentions of the U.S. government. On the basis of this class collaboration theory, hundreds of agents were sent into the leading bodies of the Huks. Only after the postwar counterrevolutionary slaughter began did the Huk guerrillas understand that American imperialism had not changed its spots.

The Huks killed over twenty thousand elite Japanese troops, mainly with bows and arrows. Now, as the war ended, the islands were littered with abandoned Japanese equipment. Worse for the government, American infantry weapons were available for whiskey or a few dollars.

Revolutionary, nationalistic Indonesia restated its claim to the southern islands of the Philippines. Rebuffed by the United

States, they retaliated by shipping tons of arms to their Muslim brethren, the Moros.

Faced with a two-pronged rebellion, the U.S. Army moved to contain the Moros and deal with the Huks. First, whomever they could win over, they incorporated into the Philippine Army. Neutralizing the wavering elements of the peasantry with promises of homesteading land, the colonial government collected and destroyed their weapons.

The offensive against the Philippine people began with throwing six thousand Huks who led the struggle against Japan into concentration camps and murdering most of them there. Then, the U.S. Marines and the Philippine Army moved to liquidate the revolutionary core.

As the slaughter began, the Huk guerrillas became aware of the extent of the betrayal and the plan to slaughter them. They moved to counteract it. Hundreds of their best fighters were sent into the Philippine Army and into the towns to build a base of support. Luis Taruc, leader of the wartime Huk resistance, ran for senator and was elected. Taruc, former leader of the Socialist Party, leader of the united Socialist-Communist Party, became the military and later political leader of the Huks. He would be jailed and tortured for years. Finally, like the imprisoned Aguinaldo before him, he pledged allegiance and endorsed Marcos's martial law.

Penetrated from top to bottom with spies and agents provocateurs, the old organization was dissolved. A new organization—the Philippine People's Liberation Army—the Hukbong, rose in its stead.

40

IF THE AMERICANS had never committed genocide against the Indian; if they had never incited wars of annihilation between the native peoples of this land; if there had never been a Trail of Tears; if America had never organized and commercialized the kidnapping and sale into slavery of a gentle and defenseless African people; if it had never developed the most widespread, brutal, exploitative system of slavery the world has ever known; if it had never held carnivals of torture and lynching of its black people; if it had never sundered and fractured and torn and ground Mexico into the dust; if it had never attacked gallant, defenseless Puerto Rico and never turned that lovely land into a cesspool to compete with the cesspool it had created in Panama; if it had never bled Latin America of her wealth and had never cast her exhausted peoples onto the dung heap of disease and ignorance and starvation; if it had never financed and braced the Fascist dictatorships; if it had never pushed Hiroshima and Nagasaki into the jaws of hell—if America had never done any of these things— history would still create a special bar of judgment for what the American people did to the Philippines.

★

The Philippines were starving. Hewitt and I established a "Self-Sacrifice" club that soon took in the entire regiment. We could not bear to look at the starving little ones and the old folks who stood patiently beside our garbage cans while we gorged ourselves on huge army meals. Joining the club meant pledging to eat two or, if possible, one meal a day and give the other(s) to the children. The word spread about the generosity of the black soldiers, and more and more people came to our mess halls. No matter how little we ate or how much we gave away, the same number of people was always standing with empty buckets when the food was gone.

They went to great lengths to show their appreciation. The little ones shined our shoes and shook their heads when we offered payment. At a second offer they generally changed their minds. The grown-ups seemed to reserve a special "Hi, Joe— Americans good, Japanese no fuckin' good" for us.

They were very much aware that they were colored and we were colored. Their stories of the rebellion led by Aguinaldo in 1900 never failed to include heroic tales of Cpl. David Fagen, who, with five other black soldiers, deserted the invading U.S. Army and went over to the side of the revolution. Within a year, Fagen became a captain in the Philippine Revolutionary Army. The U.S. Army would have never allowed this talented black soldier to become an officer. Captain Fagen, with his black comrades, fought to the death for Philippine independence.

Seventeen other soldiers were captured attempting to desert. Two black soldiers were executed and fifteen white troops had the death sentence commuted to life imprisonment.

Happily, the story of these revolutionaries outlived the brutal reality. During 1899 and 1900, one hundred thousand U.S., mainly Southern white, soldiers invaded the Philippines. They slaughtered well over a million Filipinos while crushing their fight for freedom. They introduced the water treatment to prisoners. This torture was carried out by tying the arms and legs of a prisoner to stakes, pressing a stick across the throat, and pouring water over the mouth and nostrils so the prisoner goes through the horror of drowning several times before actually dying. They established the first concentration camps. These Southern white soldiers routinely brutalized the black troops. Nevertheless, the black Twenty-fourth and the Twenty-fifth Infantry murdered right along with them. The Philippine people would not surrender. In 1914, black troops were sent in to crush the Moro rebellion. This time, however, the black soldiers refused to fight their black Filipino brothers. The people of Mindanao never forgot that.

Defenseless and dependent people always appear to be forgiving and forgetting. It seemed quite natural that the Philippine people and members of their army should circulate among the American soldiers, making friends and exchanging souvenirs. The politeness and easy laughter was for many a veneer over a deep hatred and fear of the Americans.

★

As we finished bringing our quarters up to regulation, the Sixth Philippine Infantry Division moved in between our bivouac and Cagayan. They were still in the process of building the division. Cadre from the Scouts and USAFFE provided the core of the Sixth and stabilized the various recruits.

A few days later, the Thirty-first Dixie Division moved in upstream to our south. I couldn't believe that the army was stupid enough to put us together again. The trouble started immediately. Gang fights broke out when these Southern whites tried to Jim Crow the prostitution houses. The black gangsters used guns when the white gangsters made a determined effort to gain control of the whiskey racket.

The vast majority of both outfits had no ties to prostitution or whiskey. When the fighting started, everyone on both sides was pulled in on the basis of color. It was a microcosm of America. Objectively, we were striving toward a common goal. A few fast friendships developed between the black and the white soldiers when they were together in work or administration. The vast majority of both groups knew very well that they had no interest—vested or otherwise—in the developing struggle. Yet, at the critical point an appeal was made to color. Forgetting all reason, the herds grouped together to defend God knows what against "them."

By this time there wasn't an enlisted man in the Ninety-third who believed that reason could ever prevail against the call of color. Once again we began carrying pistols and trench knives when we went into town. Once again we were forced to travel in groups capable of defending ourselves. And once again the whites believed we traveled in groups because we were gangs looking for white stragglers to beat or kill. There was no communication between us, and someone's death was only a matter of time.

★

Three divisions added up to fifty-five thousand men along with all their trucks, jeeps, half tracks, tanks, and cars. This concentration of idle, restless soldiers shared the little river that wound through all three division camps. The river provided not only drinking water but also a place to bathe and wash clothes for the civilians as well as the soldiers. It was the only place to wash the vehicles. The Thirty-first camped farthest upstream. We got the dirty water from their bodies and their trucks as well. We were furious. The Philippine Sixth got the dirt from both divisions. We came to agreement with the Sixth to wash vehicles and clothes on even-numbered days. We didn't even try to talk to the Thirty-first.

The friction increased. We imagined the men of the Thirty-first laughing as they sent their filthy water down into our area. The resentment broke out in a wild night of firing into each other's areas.

Fourteenth Corps MPs were brought in to calm the situation while the island commander threatened to bring the Twenty-fourth Division up from Davao and arrest both the Ninety-third and Thirty-first. The next day, new regulations were issued ordering all vehicles to be washed below the Philippine Sixth area and clothes to be washed on alternate days. The soldiers of the Sixth believed that we fought for them, and this strengthened our friendship. It proved again that the color discrimination stops when the firing begins. Whenever we met men of the Thirty-first, we always yelled the unofficial slogan of the 369th, "Shit on me— and the undertaker will wipe your ass."

★

Mike returned to the camp after a few days and gave me directions to his house in Cagayan. He suggested that I meet him there and then go for dinner and a beer with "friends." He also dropped a broad hint that his family was starving.

The daily convoy dumped the soldiers in the middle of town. I drifted away from the groups that headed for the booze and women. On the way to Mike's house, I detoured down to the dock. For a few moments I watched the port battalion crew unloading and stacking a shipment of flour. When I felt safe, I walked over and said a few words to the Sergeant of the detail. After a few insinuations about how much nookie a hundred pounds of flour is worth, he tossed his head for me to get in the stevedore line. A bag was thrown across my shoulder. Bent over from the weight of the hundred-pound bag and sweating from the heat, I walked away. It was half a mile up the hill to the tin-and-thatch hut that served as home for Mike, his mother, Mike's little brother Jimmy, his sister Daisy, and their cousin, Carie.

At seventeen, Daisy had somehow missed the worst of the war. She was plain, shy, and delightfully, childishly sweet. I couldn't help but treat her as my little sister and ignored the hurried glance and smile that offered more.

Carie, like most Philippine women, had been raped by the Japanese. She resisted them all the way. They taught her the price of resistance by splitting each breast with their bayonets. Carie's melancholy challenged description. She convinced herself that she could never marry or have children. That crushing sadness became a reality she drowned each night in a sea of tears.

I soon found out that in a country where so many young men had died, the idea of liking instead of loving a woman was almost an insult. But I learned to like Carie. She was a daughter of Mindanao, tall and dark-skinned with black eyes that smoldered when she talked. Sometimes, she spoke of her squadron, the guerrilla grouping for which she found food and nursed, and to which she reported the Japanese movements. Then, the wistful smile that formed at the corners of her mouth would, for the moment, overcome the sadness and brighten her pensive face. Even the most doleful moments could not completely hide her youthful beauty. Little Jimmy was a child of the war, quiet and observant. He would sit balanced on his heels, ready to bolt at the first sign of danger. He seemed happy when he was near his big brother, who had fought the Japanese and was a hero in the town.

★

Mike came home, his face alive with a smile that brightened as he smelled the bread and saw me sitting on the ground at the side of his shack. After the handshake and the embrace, he disappeared into the shack. In a moment he was out again, wrapping a piece of tough chicken in fresh Philippine bread. He ravenously devoured it after I had politely refused. After wiping his mouth with the back of his hand, the hand was wiped on the pants leg.

"I want you to meet my friends."

"Good. Let's go."

Halfway between Cagayan and the camp, we left the road for a trail that led into the brush. Twenty yards from the road, we were suddenly confronted by an armed Filipino. Mike smiled and grabbed his arm.

"Comrade Nelson, this is Comrade Marco." We shook hands, exchanged hellos, and I followed Mike as the trail turned and ended in front of a very large thatched building.

Mike held aside the blanket that served as a door. Inside sat two soldiers, one a lieutenant, and two civilians.

The introductions were made. The soldiers, formerly Huk guerrillas, belonged to the Philippine Sixth Division. Lt. Jose Sosa, whose round face smiled easily, was almost chubby. He came from Panay to Mindanao to lose any identification with the Huks. Five foot nine inches tall, his heavy frame towered above the other comrades. Drawn by the warmth of his smile and the firmness of his calloused hand, I liked him immediately. I liked the seriousness that lurked within his brown eyes, the relaxed, alert way he stood with feet apart, right hand always near the Colt .45 hanging from his belt. He was a warrior, no question about it. Jesus Ruiz, from Cagayan, formerly with the political section of the United Front, had recently joined the army. Quiet, intelligent, and efficient, he disliked the military but understood the importance of his work. He went about his duties with the businesslike attitude of a serious Communist. Martin, a teacher before the war, left the classroom for the life of a full-time leader of the

United Front in Mindanao. Forty years old, lean to the point of being skinny, his large eyes showed the ravages of life in the underground. Cultured, morally and intellectually committed to the revolution, Martin was one of the indispensable Communist cadre that guided the organization through a difficult period.

The other civilian, Guillermo, could only be described as beautiful. His dark skin was a Melanesian mixture of copper and black with a golden hue. There are many black-skinned people in the Philippines, but I had never seen the golden highlights. His skin shone at the high cheekbones. The coloring seemed to contrast with the straight, thin-lipped mouth and the pronounced Asian folds of his eyelids. Absolutely black pupils looked, without blinking, straight into my eyes as we were introduced. His wiry five-foot-two frame was solid. Thick black hair was combed straight back with a hint of pomade.

It was more of a little party than a meeting. San Miguel beer from Manila was available again. Sosa found a few bottles. The other comrades brought chicken and bread. We ate and drank, carrying on a studied but informal conversation. They took careful note of what I asked and answered. I thought the Soviet Union would be expanded to include the Slavic states of eastern Europe. The center-left coalition died with Roosevelt and the war. Truman could not be trusted. I had heard he was once a Klansman. The depression was sure to return as the war industries were phased out. The revolution would probably take the form of proletarian uprisings in the North and Negro uprisings in the South. Anglo-American imperialism was over. The United States would now dominate the French and British. The British could not hold on to India and Burma, and the French could not hold Indochina. The defeat suffered by the Dutch in Indonesia awaited weakened European imperialism everywhere. The United States first conquered the Philippines to dominate China; that was still the strategy and it would fight to hold the Philippines. I warned about underestimating the CIC. The comrades seemed to have taken the mechanical steps of security but were very casual about their relations.

They spoke of the struggle in the southern islands and their fears of massive U.S. military intervention. They considered me important. They wanted a commitment from me to go back home as soon as possible and help form a movement against such intervention.

They were pleased and in agreement when I told them I did not believe that the Ninety-third, or any other group of Negro soldiers, could be used against them.

When they asked me my opinion about the expulsion of Earl Browder and the reconstitution of the Communist Party, I was dumbfounded. I did not know much about the party. I was a communist with a small c. Shocked that the party had been disbanded, I couldn't imagine it without Browder. They finally understood that I was more of a contact than a party member and had learned most of my communism in, through, and during the war.

Martin spoke to Guillermo in Tagalog. He nodded his head slowly and then said to me, "Perhaps it's better that way."

I warned them that I was on the G-2 suspect list and they should be careful about seeing me in the camp. It was agreed that Mike or Guillermo would be my contact for any further discussions.

Lieutenant Sosa carefully explained that General MacArthur was protecting and regrouping the traitorous feudal elite around his friend, Gen. Manuel Roxas. Roxas was running for president with the backing of the U.S. Army. With Roxas as president, the Philippine Scouts could be used to crush the independence movement and safeguard American corporate interests. Sosa looked at me grimly and explained that if Roxas won the presidential elections in April of 1946, they would regroup the squadrons and return to the hills.

Sosa went on to explain how they defeated the Japanese by mastering Japanese tactics. The Philippine Army was trained by the U.S. Army, and the guerrillas would now have to master U.S. tactics. The question was asked obliquely.

"It is important that we get training manuals."

I felt the prickly heat crawl up my spine to the back of my neck. A trap? That's not possible. If I did this, I would be compromised into doing other things. But these people were fighting while I was getting drunk. They're real Communists. I felt ashamed that I even hesitated.

"I'm operations sergeant of the First Battalion. We can get them."

We spelled out the plan. I spent all the next day gathering and boxing up manuals from the regimental and division operations sergeants. The U.S. Army has manuals on everything under the

sun. Several hundred manuals on operations, tactics, nomenclature, first aid—everything I thought they might need—were
boxed and stored in the operations tent.

The following day Lieutenant Sosa and Freddie came to the
battalion headquarters and asked for the operations officer. After
the salute, Major Akeley extended his hand in welcome. Sosa
explained that he was S-3 of his battalion but had no training
manuals. Was it possible for the major to lend them a few for the
training of the recruits? With perfect Mississippi politeness and a
noblesse oblige reserved for all colored people other than
Negroes, Akeley assured him that it was. He called me over and
asked me to give the lieutenant whatever he wanted. Salutes were
exchanged, and, as I knew he would, Akeley retired to his
screened tent, the fan, and iced Coca-Cola.

Freddie and I loaded hundreds of boxed manuals into the jeep.
The knowing smile and the twinkle in Sosa's eyes said I was in with
the Huks like white on rice. I saluted Sosa and they were off.

I felt good. I had helped the comrades at the expense of my
enemy.

41

"**GET ON UP!** Get on up—Let's piss on the rock. It ain't quite
day, but it's five o'clock!" Sergeant Jackson strode between the
tents yelling to the limits of his lungs.

"Off yore ass an' on yore feet. Goddamnit—get on up or we'll
start havin' reveille again."

"Shut the fuck up, you army-happy son of a bitch—"

"Who the fuck said that?"

"Come an' get it 'fore I throw it away," Black Jack yelped,
banging the big ladle on a pot, adding to the noise.

It was the original you-can't-beat-city-hall. The men got up,
scratching backs and hair. Mosquito netting and blankets were
thrown back in disarray; piss hards poked against olive drab
underwear. First stop was the latrine, where we stood for various
moments, leaning against the two-by-four in front of us.

"Awright, Big Joe, quit shakin' that thing."

"Ain't what your mammy said."

"Last drop fall in your pants anyway."

We filled our helmets with water, brushed our teeth, washed our faces and hands, and scraped dull razors across our faces. Still half asleep, we lined up in front of the big pots of dehydrated eggs, dehydrated potatoes, and bitter coffee. After Black Jack shook the spoon until most of the decent-looking food fell back into the pot, he plopped the eggs on top of the pancake, the potatoes on top of the eggs, and a ladle of syrup on top of everything.

We passed the neat little screened-in tent that served as the officers' mess. The delightful smell of fresh eggs and delicate coffee with real cream and hot biscuits soaked with real butter drifted outward.

"Motherfuckers livin'," Parker mumbled.

Behind me Lee yawned and muttered, "'Notha day, 'notha dolla."

★

Worse than the rest of them, this day barely dragged on. Fatigue duty hardly ever included the Battalion Headquarters Company. Sometimes lying around was worse than working.

I hadn't heard from my new friends for over a week. Then, yesterday, Mike, full of enthusiasm, had stopped by to make sure I hadn't been moved out. He said I should get a pass and he would come back, maybe with something important to tell me.

By eleven it was too hot to read. It was never too hot to gamble. I lay back on the hot, scratchy woolen blanket, listening to the game.

"One I shoot. Can I go?" It was Lee, trying to recover his three dollars.

"Faded."

"Five."

"Ya don't bar it."

"Bet."

"Five up and stop."

"Ten lookin' for five."

"Seven."

"Next man."

I stepped outside and went over to the headquarters tent. As the afternoon dragged on, I plotted checkpoints on maps and consolidated reports from the patrols hunting down and killing the Japanese diehards. With the day's work done, I signed Major Akeley's name to all the reports, writing the initials "n.p." behind it. It was time for the work details to start coming in. I stepped outside just as the major came in for a quick checkup.

"Good afternoon, major."

He halfway returned the salute. "Afternoon, sergeant. Everything in order?"

"Yes, sir."

★

December's huge red tropical sun shimmered atop the hills, sending its last searing blast into the jungles of Mindanao. Six hundred miles north of the equator, the bivouac area roasted in the heat. The men stopped their work of building latrines and mess halls and digging drainage ditches. Their fatigues were wet and droplets of sweat trickled down the brown faces and collected in the tiny depression where throat joins collarbone. They looked up at the ember in the sky and mumbled everything from "mothafuckin' sun" to "Thank you, Jesus." With dirty sleeves or dirtier GI handkerchiefs, they mopped their faces and squinted into the heat waves of the western sky.

The sanguine sun sank slowly behind the mountains of the peninsula and into the Sulu Sea. Dark gathered in the gullies and ravines and spread out into the valley, pursuing, enveloping, annihilating the scattered remnants of the dying day.

Generators were cranked up and points of light appeared within screened officers' quarters and the tents that served as recreation rooms. Anxious to get out of there, I glanced around the tent that served as battalion headquarters. The patrols had completed their reporting in. Along with the Philippine Army, we still maintained a series of protective checkpoints. With our checkpoints marked in blue and the suspected Japanese hideouts in red, the marked acetate overlays showed our relative positions. I marked the orientation coordinates in my notebook and erased them from the overlay. Then I rolled up the maps and locked them in the footlocker with the grease pencils and patrol roster. Major Akeley had signed my twenty-four-hour pass. There was no operations work scheduled for tonight and I was free to go.

"Goodnight, major, sir."

He turned to me and smiled knowingly.

"I had to argue with Colonel Meyers to get you that pass. Ain't supposed to be no twenty-four-hour pass. I told him that after two years courtin' Mary Palmer, I 'spect you'll need twenty-four hours."

"I wish I was as lucky as you think. I made friends with some of the Scouts at the checkpoints. They're having some sort of a party and invited me along."

"Yeah, I know. Just get a prophylactic."

"Hope I'm gonna need one, sir."

I glanced at my watch. It was time to wander over toward the road. Sure enough, Mike was coming toward me, kicking up the dust, smiling and raising his fingerless hand. After the embrace, he quickly gave me the news. There was going to be a meeting. Comrades were coming in from Panay and Zamboanga to make a report and analyze the electoral situation. I would be picked up just north of the Sixth Division at 7:00 P.M.

The Philippine comrades were the only Communists I have ever known who were always punctual—probably a hangover from the underground, where seconds meant the difference between capture and mission accomplished.

At a few minutes to seven, I stepped out of the underbrush onto the road. Jesus pulled up and I jumped into the jeep beside him. He drove a half mile past the meeting place and let me out to meet up with Guillermo. I knew from the genuine, enthusiastic handshake and embrace that he knew about the manuals. We turned and started walking back toward the meetinghouse.

Guillermo looked straight into my eyes. I shifted mine slightly.

"Do you have a pass? Can you stay out late?"

"I have a pass—but there isn't any bed check. I just shouldn't let the MPs catch me after eleven. Why?"

"We're going to have a short meeting. We all know the situation. Mostly we want to have a party. Filipinos like to have parties. We know the people coming in. They'll want to sing and dance, too."

We walked single file to stay out of the dust of the convoys bringing the soldiers into Cagayan for a night of booze and whoring. Guillermo finally turned off the road onto the trail to the thatched building. The guard stepped from behind a tree. A few words in Tagalog. The guard grinned. "You go in, Joe."

A bamboo curtain replaced the blanket at the door. A red flag with a golden sickle was tacked to the wall behind the table. People from the surrounding area filled the room. Some had been

fighters in the Hukbalahap. Some were from the political arm of
the United Front. Some were from the "mass" section. Most were
members of the Communist Party. I was introduced to those sitting on the floor near me. Handshakes and smiles and nods. I felt
good. I was a Communist, they were Communists. That's all we
needed to know to be warm and loving to one another.

Martin came in carrying a Thompson. He acknowledged me
with a smile and nod of his head.

"Comrade Martin has been in Zamboanga for a week. The
chairman came back with him."

Two more comrades came in. I glanced up at the man and
woman as they passed by. The man carried a carbine slung over
his shoulder and a GI map case. As my glance shifted to the
woman, Guillermo got to his feet, hopped over my legs, and
grabbed her by the shoulder. She turned to look at him and threw
her arms around his waist. There was no question that they were
brother and sister. The black-golden-bronzed skin, the thick black
hair, the pronounced epicanthic fold to their eyes showed it. Her
right hand gripped her left wrist to hold him tight. He stroked her
hair and patted her back. She could not have been more than four
foot ten and was so perfectly formed in face and body that some
artist surely had created her. Everyone in the meeting smiled
benignly at the warmth and love between them. Martin and the
chairman waited at the table until Guillermo released her and sat
down.

"My little sister, Carmen. I haven't seen her since I left Panay
three years ago. We've both been here in Mindanao all this time
and we didn't even know it." He caught her eye and smiled. She
glanced at me just as I was thinking like a stupid soldier, "Goddamn, that fuckin' woman is beautiful—gorgeous." I had the feeling that she had read my mind, and embarrassed, I thought the
thought again: "His sister is beautiful."

Her catlike smile spread upward, nearly closing eyes molded
from a classical Chinese painting, making the exotic face of this
exquisite warrior of the Hukbalahap even more fascinating.

I realized that Martin was talking, introducing the man
responsible for all the guerrilla squadrons in Mindanao. The
comrade, who had taken the nom de guerre "Andres Bonifacio,"
spoke rapidly in Tagalog. Occasionally, Guillermo would lean
over and translate the essence of the report.

"We have just finished a meeting with Comrade Luis Taruc in

Luzon. . . . The big landowners are reversing the reforms won in the anti-Japanese war. . . . Especially in central Luzon, the reactionaries are resorting to force. . . . Peasants who support the candidates of the Democratic Alliance have been murdered."

The talk lasted almost an hour. I applauded when everyone else did and felt as if I were part of the meeting.

The speaker's ending statements drew an enthusiastic round of applause. Martin held out his hand to Carmen. She rose to speak. Nodding approval of every sentence, Guillermo translated for me.

"The policy of the Philippine Communist Party of not surrendering the armed people to MacArthur has proven correct. . . . The reactionary offensive is transforming the People's Army against Japan into a People's Liberation Army. . . . We protected the people against the Japanese and we will protect them against the Roxas-American butchers. . . ."

Another round of applause and the meeting was over. Daisy, Mike, and Carie came over to exchange embraces and talk about the meeting. The musicians set up their instruments and the dancing began—Spanish dances, American songs and dances, and finally, Filipino dances. Despite the urging and the laughter, I declined to break my ankle trying to dance the tinikling.

Two men knelt, holding the ends of two bamboo poles that they brought together and parted to the steady beat of guitar and drum. Holding their skirts halfway up shapely young thighs, the women danced gracefully between and out from the bamboo poles. I was content to sip my beer and watch.

Guillermo and Carmen were sitting to one side, catching up on their lives. Sometimes I would glance at her and our eyes would meet. Like Guillermo, she would not avert her eyes. I would lower mine.

Some of the older folk went home. Some of the soldiers returned to their camp. The musicians put away their instruments and the young folk took over. Someone handed Mike a guitar. He adjusted the bridge, laid the guitar across his lap, and, pressing down on the strings with his finger stumps, played beautifully. After a few chords he sang,

> Serenade in the night,
> In the jungles of Mindanao.
> The soldiers were creeping,

Positions were seeking
That night.

There were planes in the air,
There were tanks in the jungle,
Singapore and Bataan will soon be recaptured
And the Allies return.

Soldiers, send me bullets for battle,
Soldiers, the fuckin' Japanese surrender
All their planes in the air,
All their tanks in the jungle.
Singapore and Bataan will soon be recaptured
And the Allies return.

Jesus took the guitar and everyone joined in singing a few revolutionary songs in Tagalog. Carmen glanced shyly at me and took the guitar. It seemed that everyone in the Philippines could play. Barely touching the strings, creating a melodic whisper to mingle with and guide her soft voice, she looked down and sang to the guitar. Then, sure of the chords and of something inside her, she looked at me and sang the ending of her Philippine love song:

I'm waiting here to give you all my love,
That's my promise to the stars above.
I want to fill your heart with happiness,
I surrender my heart and my song.

She laid the guitar aside. First Guillermo applauded, then Sosa and then everyone. I joined in. Sosa and Mike were grinning and looking at me. Embarrassed, I looked at Guillermo; he smiled. I glanced at Carmen. Half closed by the smile, her eyes shone black.

It was so clear. Guillermo had told her good things about me. Sosa had said more. Mike had added on.

From the commonly held love of the people, a special love exists between revolutionaries. It is but one small step forward to individual passion. In the two seconds that our eyes met and locked, I understood this and so did she. What does it matter if it is one hour or one year? I was deeply and wholly in love.

The remainder of the night was filled with glances and the touching of hands. Finally, I sat beside her on a coconut log, listening to the songs and watching the dance until Martin came near. He stood respectfully aside until he caught her eye.

They exchanged a few words and she walked slowly back to my side.

"I must go," she said simply.

"I know."

"If things go well, I will return—the world is not so big—"

"Come back, Carmen. I—"

"Huwag mo akong iwanan." It was a quick embrace, her cheek against my chest. She turned and without looking back vanished into the jungle with Martin.

42

WE SEEMED STUCK in the Philippines. Alerted regiments prepared to move out to the replacement depots and embark for home. Then orders would change. The soldiers would grumble, unpack, and anticipate new orders to hurry up and wait. Morale, already low among the troops, was disintegrating into anger and resentment.

The days dragged by, each one birthing its own new set of rumors. The sergeants in the Combat Intelligence and the Operations sections were the main conduit for rumors. From Corps Headquarters to Division, to Regiment, to Battalion, to Company, to Platoon, to Squad, to the individual soldiers, the flow of "poop" was unending. We heard that the Ninety-third would go to French Indochina and disarm the Japanese. The Fourteenth Corps was going to invade Manchuria as the Soviet Red Army pulled out to prevent the Chinese Communists from taking it over. The entire Pacific command was going to Korea to invade Siberia.

One thing was clear. Somebody in the high command was talking of fighting the Soviets, or at least blocking any expansion of the Communist-held areas of China. There was talk of invading Vietnam and crushing the Vietminh. Roosevelt had promised to assist them in their struggle for independence from the French. We saw pictures of Hanoi with its streetcars painted with American revolutionary slogans like Give Me Liberty or Give Me Death. We could see no reason to fight them. We didn't like French, Dutch, or American colonialism and felt that one of the aims of the war was to give everyone independence.

Rumor had it that some of the generals were arguing that we had used the bomb on Hiroshima and Nagasaki as a warning to the Russians, and because they weren't heeding the warning we should follow up with military action. Others pointed out that we had invaded Siberia some thirty-five years earlier and had not been able to sustain the effort politically. They claimed that the Russians would immediately destroy the U.S., French, and British armies and occupy all of Europe and thereby neutralize the bomb.

The so-called Left-Progressive forces in the States were also aware that the Fascist senators, the gang led by Dulles and Byrnes, and the generals led by Patton were rapidly moving to confront the Soviet Union and if possible go to war. They responded by launching a massive bring-the-boys-home campaign as the only way to frustrate these plans.

We soldiers had only rumors to go on. But we knew, if the generals didn't, that if they intended to fight the Soviets, they would have to get a different army.

The GIs knew very well that the Russians won the war. Our total losses in the Pacific were less than the losses for individual Russian battles that had hardly been reported. If it came to war with the Soviets, our affectionate respect for GI Ivan, coupled with war weariness, made the combat efficiency of the South Pacific troops near zero.

The seesaw effect of preparing to go home and then being ordered to wait strengthened the widespread belief that the generals were at least discussing war.

No matter what the individual's ideology might have been, all the soldiers were united on one thing. The war was over and we wanted to go home.

Perhaps it will never be known who coined the slogan "Home by Christmas!" It was a perfect piece of agitation. This simple, understandable slogan was in the immediate interest of the troops and at the same time hit at the core of the generals' hopes of attacking the Soviet Union.

Soldiers in the Ninety-third, Twenty-seventh, and Thirty-first divisions, along with men from the various service organizations, began to raise the slogan. It was painted on the latrines. It was scratched onto the directional posts at the crossroads. It appeared as if by magic in the recreation rooms and the mess halls. Sometimes it was even painted on the screened-in officer's quarters. It became a matter of daring pride to find a new and secure place to paint the demand. Wherever Kilroy poked his nose over a fence or a plank, his crossed eyes were looking down at "Home by Christmas."

Spreading like the flu, the slogan filtered into and seized the consciousness of the troops. No American soldier stuck in the Philippines in December 1945 could quietly accept the seemingly endless and senseless delay.

We were spurred on by articles in *Stars and Stripes* and statements and songs on the GI radio, the Mosquito Network. Soldiers stuck in the replacement depots on Leyte built a huge coconut log raft and erected a sign that declared "Home by Christmas or Bust."

The deal that allowed the CPUSA to be a clandestine, unacknowledged, but influential force within the Roosevelt coalition prohibited party members from forming cells within army units. This directive was rigidly adhered to. No directive, however, could stop Communists and pro-Communists from meeting, recognizing one another, and carrying out the inevitable political discussions. If the Communists didn't invent the slogan "Home by Christmas," they immediately grasped its significance to their campaign to "Bring the Boys Home."

★

Joe opened the screen flap of the operations tent.

"Hey, man—there's a couple of white guys askin' around for you."

"Oh, shit—it's the G-2 or CIC," I said half aloud. Then I realized they don't ask for people—they walk in and take them.

I glanced at these two white enlisted men as they approached the tent. The eyes of every black face in the company were following them. They were plainly Communists. Two Jews with New York accents were coming to talk to the one person in the battalion who was on the G-2 list as a suspected Communist. Thank God, neither Akeley nor Forrest was there.

Dressed in clean, pressed khaki, overseas caps at the correct angle, they did not look like combat troops. One of them was a sergeant. The other soldier wore round, steel-rimmed glasses over his slightly bulging eyes. His mouth was stretched thin and tight over the slightly protruding bone work of his jaws. He nervously pressed his lips tightly together and looked like a man who spent too much time poring over books or solving mathematical problems. I got the feeling he was the type of person who thought for a long time and then gave detailed answers to any question. He was a portrait of the Jewish Communist intellectual who joined the army to kill Germans and ended up in the Pacific fighting a purely imperialist war. I probably was going to deal with the other one. He was thin, almost gaunt-faced. A widow's peak of short, nappy hair looked almost like a ski cap pointing down toward an oversized, thin nose and narrow nostrils. Steady, inquiring eyes gave the impression that he was used to convincing people of things. Probably a union organizer.

Where could we talk? I figured it better to talk at the headquarters than to be seen in the area with them—at least I could lie about the purpose of their visit.

Quite businesslike, they told me their Filipino friends said I was interested in getting the boys home as soon as possible. I carefully admitted that was true. Then these New York soldiers asked me where my home was. I told them Minneapolis. Oh, they said, Minneapolis—they had friends there. Did I know Carl Ross or Gus Hall? I stated that I didn't know them personally but knew of them. I knew that Ross was a leader of the YCL. I knew that Gus Hall was a Communist big shot from Minneapolis. I knew now for sure they were Communists. I would have to tell them what I was.

I related the story of when they put Gus in jail for some small thing back in 1938. I was walking with two friends into the downtown area. As we crossed Fourth Avenue and Sixth Street, a paddy wagon pulled to the curb near a small group waiting for it. The doors were opened and amid the protesting screams and yells of the crowd, the man was dragged out and hustled into the jail.

Construction workers building the new armory a block away came running over and joined the group, yelling for his release. A coal truck slowed for the crowd. In a few moments the truck was stopped and everyone started throwing lumps of coal at the jail. We joined in. At fifteen, we didn't know, and cared less, what the issue was. If we could throw coal at a jail or a cop, we were for it. That was the first time I saw Gus Hall.

When the polite chuckles were over, and they had assessed the story as a statement of friendship and trust, the cards were turned face up.

"Our Filipino friends think very highly of you."

"Well, thank you."

"They told us we could speak frankly to you."

"If you're friends with my friends—I think we understand one another." I didn't want to elaborate any further.

The soldiers glanced at each other and the slender guy took a deep breath and plunged in.

"There are a number of us—Communist and non-Communist—who support the Philippine revolution and are struggling to carry out our internationalist responsibilities."

I had already learned that New York Communists always sounded like they were in a meeting when they talked politics.

"I sure think that we ought to stick together. I think it's important we do everything we can for the Philippines," I said.

"The most important thing—yes, comrade—the key revolutionary task today," he went on, "is not simply to support the Philippine revolution but to defend the Soviet Union. The Soviet Union is the socialist base for all revolution."

I nodded my agreement.

"It is becoming clear," the other soldier said, "that with Roosevelt dead, the reactionaries are beginning to feel their hands are untied. There is evidence that they are connecting up with the clique of anti-Soviet generals around Patton in Europe and MacArthur in the Pacific. They believe that the Soviet Union has been weakened to the point that it could not defend itself from further aggression."

"Didn't they see how fast the Red Army cut through the Imperial Army? Shit, man, the Siberian Eighth could hold off our entire Far Eastern Command."

The two looked at each other, and the slender sergeant said, "We're not combat soldiers. We don't know about the operations part. We know something about the struggle. We were both party organizers before the war. The point is exactly what Comrade Stalin has stated. That is, the peace-loving forces must strive to consolidate the peace. There aren't going to be any more declarations of war. War will simply start."

"I don't think that they can fuck with Russia without rearming the Germans and rebuilding Britain. Besides, I don't think the American people would buy it. I think they're going to beat all the little guys like the Philippines into line, and then try to hang on to China. Seems to me that's where we have to make the stand."

"You might be correct, comrade. But what if you aren't? We are trying to convince the progressive soldiers, especially those with some party or YCL background, of the importance of them getting into the bring-the-boys-home campaign. It's probably the only chance we have to hold off another war. 'Home by Christmas' is becoming a very important, spontaneous mass movement that we must enter and stabilize."

"Well," I said, "I agree with all of that, but I don't know what you think I can do."

The guy with the thin, gaunt face looked at me, sizing me up while he got his thoughts together.

"We're in contact with comrades in Leyte. They have raised the necessity of stabilizing 'Home by Christmas' very sharply. Part of the problem is that we have not had any participation from the Negro soldier. Here on Mindanao there are eighteen thousand Negro combat soldiers in the Ninety-third. Counting up the port battalions, the quartermasters, engineers, graves registrations, and other service units, there are thirty to thirty-five thousand Negro soldiers. There hasn't been any significant participation from them."

I could feel the surge of adrenalin and the hackles began to rise. White folk look out of their blue eyes at the world and they can see only a reflection of themselves. They don't see that there is a white army and there is a black army and they are equal only on payday.

The whites, in the military as in civilian life, would ask us to unite with them on issues that concerned them a lot and us a little. They would never unite on issues that concerned us a lot and them a little. More ominous than that, we knew we could expect no more assistance should the military authority move against us than they gave when the Klan moved against us.

Yes, we wanted desperately to go home. But the men could not be convinced that the way home was through mutiny. The last black regiment to try that in the Philippines spent the next twenty years cleaning the white soldiers' toilets at Fort Benning. The white soldiers were glad they didn't have to work the "sugar run," and most of them figured it proper that blacks clean their toilets anyway.

The white Communists I had known were dedicated to the

struggle against discrimination. The problem was, they seemed to think that we would become equal if they individually treated us as equals. They had to get the sheriffs and the generals to do that too. Instead, they constantly preached to the believers. We were too sophisticated to go for that.

Now it was my turn to size up my comrades and get my thoughts together. How can you tell a person that he is being strangled by an evil he is too decent to see? It was sad and frustrating and insurmountable. It was a Ring Lardner story: "You kids just don't understand."

"We're strapped in the Ninety-third. We can't move. The outfit is chock full of agents. I'm sure I'm on the G-2 list."

Both faces reflected a glum acceptance of the reality.

"I really don't know what we can do," I said.

There was nothing more to be said by either side. The soldier with the gaunt face and calculating eyes was searching for the correct words.

"We know the difficulties you face, comrade. We know you are contributing all you can. We just wanted to give you our thinking. We're in agreement that defending the Soviet Union and struggling for world peace means forcing the government to bring the soldiers home and disband the wartime army."

"That's the important thing, the key thing," the other soldier said.

I agreed.

Hands were shaken all around. They didn't invite me to visit them. Although I wondered, I didn't ask what outfit they were from.

★

Watching them walk back through the company area, I felt more than understood something new. For the first time I got a muddled and disturbing sense that the merging of antifascism with communism produced two kinds of Communists. Communists had led the fight against fascism in Europe. The anti-Fascist war was the practical side of the European and American Communist movement. In the euphoria of victory they were emerging as the social vanguard of their nations.

In Mindanao, in Alabama, in Rhodesia and Brazil and Shanghai and Calcutta, the war had just begun. The practical side of this communism was anti-imperialist war. Freedom, national freedom, the self-determination of nations, the unity of the colored colonial peoples—this was the new war. The tactic of one brand of communism was the struggle for peace. For the other, the task was preparing for war.

43

THE REVOLUTION SEEMED to be as mired in limbo as the U.S. Army. Sporadic assassinations of key Huk and Democratic Alliance figures began. There was considerable pressure by the Huk soldiers not to rely on the elections and not simply to go underground but to fight. The movement back to the hills halted when President Osmeña accepted the support of the Hukbala-hap. The party, the Huks, and the front entered the campaign.

★

President Osmeña's opponent in the elections, Manuel Roxas, had been the main Japanese collaborator. Captured and imprisoned by the U.S. Army, he might have faced the firing squad had he not been pardoned by MacArthur. He was restored to his rank of brigadier general in the U.S. Army and placed on MacArthur's staff. Roxas gathered together the collaborators of the Philippine elite, rearmed the Fascist gangs, and set about winning the election for MacArthur through murder and intimidation.

★

Thousands of troops collected from the scattered island bases arrived daily in Leyte and northern Mindanao. General Johnson was senior commander in the area, and the Ninety-third took over military police responsibilities for Misamis Oriental.

Peace disrupted the memorized routine of war as surely as war had disrupted the routines of peace. With peace, the soldiers began going through a general psychological letdown that, coupled with the boredom of waiting to go home, was too much for many of the troops. Unlike the troops in Europe, most of the South Pacific soldiers had served almost two years in the jungles, totally cut off from civilian life. Dumped in the Philippines, they now had only one thought in mind—to catch up, to live it up with women and whiskey. They couldn't make the rotgut fast enough or recruit enough women into the prostitution houses.

There was friction on the "cock lines" from the beginning. Most of the fights came from cutting the line or selling one's place in line. Then, some of the white soldiers began agitating for segregation. Fighting began to break out between the white and Negro soldiers in front of the whorehouses. Club-swinging MPs could not contain the fighting. Squads of armed infantrymen were sent in to keep order.

The soldiers, blacks and whites, soon found out that the Ninety-third was in control and that any fighting meant arrest.

Several times I pulled duty as sergeant of the guard in the prostitution area. Three, four, five hundred soldiers would form a line stretching for blocks up to the whorehouse. A steel-helmeted Negro soldier with bare bayonet and M1 loaded and locked was stationed every twenty yards along the line.

Soldiers are used to, and rely on, discipline. As discipline was imposed, everyone calmed down and the lines became a place where a soldier could spread the latest rumor or joke while he waited his turn.

Soldiers too sensitive for the lines roamed the streets, propositioning every woman they met.

"No touch Philippine girl, Joe" became the standard opening defense of the women as soldiers approached them.

Other soldiers, running drunk, staggered through the streets of Cagayan, vomiting the rotgut and crying out their loneliness to an uncaring world. Relations between the Filipinos and the soldiers began to break down. Youthful gangs roamed the streets defending their women. The soldiers felt the Filipinos were ungrateful and the Filipinos were sure the soldiers held them in contempt and did not understand the sacrifice they made. Cagayan became a dangerous place and I decided that between the Counter Intelligence Corps and the patrols of young Filipinos, I should stay at the camp.

★

The Communist Party of the Philippines set about rebuilding its infrastructure as the election campaign got underway. With all their available people thrown into the effort, certain comrades were being brought back from the hills to assist. Though very busy, Guillermo and Mike kept in touch with me. I asked that the others stay away until I found out if I was still under investigation. They understood and were concerned when I told them about the visit from the two Communist soldiers. It was embarrassing that comrades who had fought for years against incredible odds would give my name to anyone.

"These breaks in security are becoming more common. Our whole set of relations will be known to the enemy if it continues." Guillermo looked steadily into my eyes. "The problem is that too many of the comrades believe that imperialism has changed and the U.S. is going to give us real freedom."

I knew. No one had to tell me. I knew that America was going to beat us back into line when we got home. The Negro troops got a taste of racial equality in foreign lands. As they came home, that had to be beaten and lynched and terrorized out of them before they would go back to building levees and picking cotton. I could see no reason to expect that the Filipinos, also referred to as "niggers," were going to get any better treatment. It was the reason I felt such a deep sense of unity with, and loyalty to, the islands and their people.

★

The days dragged on at the camp. Gambling, reading books, and storytelling whiled away the hours. The area command tried to get a sports program going. Men from the Ninety-third took almost all the trophies and the white soldiers lost interest in the competition. We slid back into lying around, sweating out rotation.

As December 20 rolled around, we gave up any hopes of being "Home for Christmas." Instead, we set about making a Christmas on Mindanao. A soldier painted a beautiful sign saying "Peace on Earth, Good Will Toward Men." We raised it high above the road to battalion headquarters.

I was stretched out on the cot in the squad tent when I saw Mike coming. Everyone in the company liked him. Although he came to see me, he always spent time laughing and joking with the other men. Everyone knew the story of his fingers and welcomed him as a soldier. Mike was an experienced messenger, and no one suspected him of being political.

By the time he got to the tent, I secured a bottle of beer for him. I was glad to see him, and after exchanging greetings and embraces, he sat down on the cot.

"You work tonight, Nels?"

"No, maybe go to a movie. Want to come along?"

"Maybe you'd like to come with me."

"Why not," I said. "What's going on?"

"Somebody made me promise not to tell you that she wanted to see you tonight."

My heart leaped to my throat.

"Carmen. She came back."

"I cannot break my promise," Mike laughed. "But I know this person needs shoes and something to make a dress from."

My mind was already working on how to get the material.

"I'll be at your house at eight o'clock."

"OK, Nels. Adios."

Mike left and I headed for the supply room. There wouldn't be any shoes in the army that would fit her tiny feet. Filipinos were the most ingenious craftsmen I'd ever known. I was sure that if I got the leather, someone would make the shoes.

Hank, the supply sergeant, was from my hometown, Saint Joseph, Missouri. We weren't related and I doubt that his family knew mine. Nonetheless, I was "home boy" and treated with privilege when it came to supplies.

When I shoved him my last beer, he knew something was up. We talked about Missouri mudcats and possum hunting. We talked about sellout blacks and ornery white folk. We told stories about what "Uncle Luke" had done to both of them. Finally he turned to me and said, "What you want, Home? I know you're after something."

Back in the tent, I wrapped up two soft leather rifle scabbards. There was enough leather to make five or six pairs of shoes. Next, I went to the bottom of my barrack bag and took out the Shinto religious pieces I had taken from Colonel Ouchi's quarters. Just in case, I took the murderous Japanese trench knife I had secreted away in Biak.

The air force supply sergeant looked at that knife with its engraved hilt as if he were a bear eyeing a jackrabbit in the springtime. The air force men lived well and had plenty of money and whiskey, but they couldn't get battlefield souvenirs.

"I can't give you no parachute, sergeant. They'd have my ass in a sling."

"I nearly lost my life over this knife. I got to have a parachute and a fifth to boot."

A few more weakening protests and I left the air force base with the chute and a bottle of Australian Panther Piss.

★

Back at the camp, I spread out the brand-new, billowing white nylon chute and cut away the straps and harness. With my treasures neatly wrapped in canvas and stored under the cot, I went to find the sergeant of the motor pool.

No. Absolutely, no. There is no way to sign out a jeep, unless it is done in person by an authorized officer.

Yes, he could find a way to get me into Cagayan and I could grab the eleven o'clock convoy back. Meet Harold with his jeep at the motor pool at 7:30? OK. Save me a swig of that rotgut. Hell no, man. The booze ain't for this. I was going to give it to you anyway. You know you my ace boon coon.

★

I was at Mike's by 8:00, and at 8:30 we walked to the building. Carmen and Martin stood in the clearing, talking.

"How are you, my friends?" Each of my hands clasped theirs. Filipinos are great sentimentalists. They are also strict on procedures. A warm, comradely squeeze for Martin's hand. Carmen made no effort to withdraw her hand. I held on.

"Cigarette, Martin?" I said as I lit up.

"No, no. Keep them," I said. "I can get them for a nickel."

Mike spoke softly in Tagalog to Martin. They turned and went into the building.

Still holding Carmen's hand, I pulled her to the bush, reached into the canvas and handed her the leather, the awl, and the thread. Before she could speak, I piled the nylon high in her arms. She dropped the leather and whirled around, wrapping herself in the white, billowing, silky stuff.

"Is it for me? It's so beautiful—is it for me?" I had to smile watching this guerrilla, hardened by four long years of war, become a twenty-two-year-old woman, excited with being pretty.

"Sure, honey. It's all yours."

She dragged her treasure over to the coconut log and sat down.

"Now, I must give you something. What shall I give you? I have nothing."

"You got me!" As I reached to embrace her, she recoiled in mock fright.

"No touch Philippine girl, Joe." I must have looked a little bewildered. Laughing, she threw herself onto me and tried to squeeze me with her thin little arms.

As I hugged her, she wiggled and cuddled until she fit into and around all the depressions and bulges of my body. A little squeeze and she seemed to melt and disappear against me. She pressed lightly against the hardening bulge.

After a moment her arms slackened and, breathing heavily, we backed away from the fire. If anything was going to happen, it could not happen here. We used the two hours to talk about ourselves.

Her Chinese father was a lifelong Communist. Close and loving to his two children, he raised them in the spirit of the revolution. It was only natural that they should carry on his work. On December 5, 1941, he went to Manila to meet with Chinese Filipinos concerning ways to increase their support of China's revolution. The Japanese invasion stranded them there. They asked the government for arms to fight. These thirty-six Chinese-Filipino patriots, ranging in age from eighteen to fifty, made the Japanese pay for every engagement.

As she spoke of her father and wondered if he was still alive, she hugged my arm and turned her eyes toward the ground.

Her mother's family escaped the slaughter in Samar in the early 1900s when invading American troops indiscriminately and ruthlessly killed over half the island's population. They finally settled in Cebu, where Carmen's mother met her husband-to-be and joined him, first in the Socialist Party and then in the Communist International.

Guillermo entered the university at Panay in 1940. Carmen joined him in 1941. They both joined Communist student cells. When the war began they worked together to form a student resistance. The political wing of the united front needed Guillermo's talents and he left, unknown to her, for central Visayan. As the collaborators began to identify known Communists to the Japanese, she was sent to Mindanao.

She wanted to know all the details of the 1938 race riot against the Filipinos in Watsonville, California. I told her what I knew. Then I told her all about the Klan and Fascist gangs that dominated Watsonville politics and the politics of the valley for the growers. I told her about the Farm Workers Union the Filipinos were building in California. I told her about the Sharecroppers Union, about the cane cutters in Louisiana. About the Negro Youth Congress. About the YCL. About the Scottsboro Boys. About Spain. About the Farmer-Labor Party.

She held my hands in hers and I talked to keep from clutching her.

Martin and Mike returned with Guillermo. He offhandedly told me that Carmen was going to stay with him for awhile and help in the election.

There were *abrazos* all around. Was there the slightest touch of her pelvis against my thigh? I could hardly say good night.

I flagged down the convoy from the prophylactic station. Happy and singing to myself, I climbed onto the steel floor of the truck and greeted the drunken men, who were holding their peckers to ease the soreness of the rough syringe and the burning, prophylactic douche.

44

THE DIVISION STARTED liquidating its surplus equipment. That meant we would be going home soon. Some arms and equipment were to go to the Philippine Army on a contingency basis, but not much. It was more profitable for the armaments companies to equip it with new stuff from the States.

A directive allowed the Philippine elite to bid on some types of the surplus. The wealthy got entire lumber mills for one dollar. Huge generators, road-building equipment, various construction equipment, boats (including disarmed PTs), bridge-building equipment, tractors and all types of farm equipment—all were available with the right connections. What wasn't sold went to the bottom of the ocean.

Rifles, carbines, machine guns, mortars, artillery pieces by the thousands were counted, cataloged, and, with tons of ammunition, dumped into the sea.

The political situation unraveled. The big landlords began recruiting private armies to protect them from their serfs, who had received a taste of freedom under the protection of the Hukbalahap. These feudalists openly solicited arms.

Their serfs responded by going back into the hills. Too many guerrillas, believing the government or their leaders, had turned in their weapons. They were desperate for arms. Alongside the destruction of the means of war arose an insatiable demand for those means of war.

The Philippines were flooded with U.S.-backed pesos. Until then, there simply hadn't been anything to buy, although everyone had money. The American sense of enterprise moved into the vacuum.

A truck loaded with anything was worth six thousand dollars. An M1 rifle went for one hundred dollars. Ammunition, blankets, soap —all the materials of war and existence—suddenly were available for a price.

Fourteenth Corps gave the orders to Division Headquarters; Division passed them on to Regimental Headquarters. HQ 369 passed them to the battalions, and Major Akeley called me from the penny-ante tonk game to go with him to the staff meeting. At the meeting, the Negro officers smiled knowingly. When the major brought the sergeant to staff meetings, that meant the sergeant was going to do the work. Most of them had gotten their training that way.

Division quartermaster section needed to gain greater control of the matériel being gathered and dispersed. Too much of it had disappeared. The quartermaster and the operations section of the battalion staff divided the responsibilities. Quartermaster section would bring the matériel together. Operations section was responsible for routing the matériel to the docks or to the Philippine Sixth Division.

★

Sergeant Henson looked casually but carefully around the area. Satisfied that no one was within hearing, he began to speak softly.

"Nelson, your name was on the G-2 list again. Seems two white soldiers came to visit you. Somebody is keeping a close eye on you."

"Yeah, these guys came over to talk. Everybody saw them. Wanted me to help on 'Home by Christmas.' I wish they hadn't of come. But there's nothing illegal about some white guys coming by."

"You were in Intelligence and Reconnaissance long enough to

know that these people never go by any one thing. They build composites, just like combat intelligence. Your name was down last month talking about the guerrillas. This month it's there again—this time white soldiers, no insignia, just soldiers. They just might be building a composite of you in order to move on you."

"I know it don't look good. I'm really not into anything—but I am getting to know a lot of people."

"You know how this thing goes. First observation, then evaluation, then verification, then action. I've listened to them up at G-2. They still want to fry somebody about the Sabine River shit. They think there was a conspiracy to start a race war. They still think you were in on it. I think they're going to start watching you—especially now that the operations section is disposing of the surplus."

"Think you can take my name off one more time?"

Henson smiled. The graying mustache crinkled back, exposing the edges of a set of perfectly-cared-for teeth.

"I'm the only thing that stands between you and a court-martial. G-2 has ways of checking this list. They don't know I handle it—that's one way they'd find out. From now on, I can only warn you."

"Yeah. I know. I really appreciate what you've done. I'll be careful."

"We're going home soon. Nothing you do here is going to make a difference. Keep your nose clean; get home and fight it out on our own turf."

"I know you're right, man. I'll be careful."

"You'd better cut out before *my* name gets on their fuckin' list."

"Thanks, Henson. So long."

Henson frightened me. What if they had a tail on me already? What if we got nabbed? If they got to Jesus or Jose, the whole network inside the Sixth would be dead. I shuddered, thinking of the consequences. This is a war, man. There ain't no way to stop it now. Those comrades are soldiers. They know the score—they'll shoot it out—take a half dozen of those CIC motherfuckers to hell with them. I ain't no better than they are. Let her rip!

★

The fatigue detail stacked the boxes of weapons coming in from the line companies.

"These are carbines," I thought as I nervously directed the stacking of part of the arms and material to one side. "The average Filipino is too small for an M1. Put them over here. Ammo for carbines over there, too. 81 millimeter mortars? Shit man, the base plate weighs a hundred. Can't carry that in the jungle. Put those 60 millimeters with the carbines. Put all the surplus medical supplies there, too. Put the water-cooled machine guns over on the other pile. Put the air-cooled with the carbines. Boxes of belted ammo there, too. Bazookas and grenade launchers there, too. The Thompsons are too heavy and use too much ammo. Put them on the other pile. The rockets and the Cosmoline go with the carbines. The fragmentation grenades go there, too. The Composition C goes there. Jesus Christ—they'll never get all this on one truck."

I looked at my watch. It was just about time.

The driver swung the big six-by-six truck over to the pile of matériel I pointed toward. He stepped out of the truck, a new set of sergeant chevrons neatly sewn beneath the division insignia. The newly painted truck identification, HQ Co—4th Regt—6 Div—P.A., looked suspicious to me, but no one else seemed to notice.

The lieutenant, manifest papers in his hand, stepped out from the other side. The silver bars of a first lieutenant were new. I wanted to congratulate them both. I stepped up to the lieutenant and saluted smartly. He returned the salute.

"Sergeant Peery, 369th Infantry."

"Looking for a Captain Akeley. A consignment of weapons for the Philippine Sixth."

"He's gone for the moment, sir. I have the papers."

I stepped to the sergeant of the detail.

"Have the men load this pile on this truck. When you finish, you all will be dismissed."

"Off and on, men. Let's load her up and we can get out of this sun."

Some good-natured grumbling and they went to work.

I wanted to pitch in and help get them out of there. I glanced around. No one was looking in our direction. It was right before noon and everyone was waiting for lunchtime in the coolest place possible.

Finally, it was done. I gave the lieutenant the necessary papers. The sergeant locked the tailgate and secured the canvas covering.

His eyes met mine for a moment and shifted away. Salutes were exchanged with the lieutenant and he climbed into the truck. They pulled away. I watched as they stopped at the regimental checkpoint and signed out. My heart settled back into my chest and I took a deep, satisfying breath. The truck gathered speed and turned south onto the road that led to the hills of Misamis Oriental.

45

THE OPERATIONS SECTION was responsible for preparing the battalion to move to the replacement depot on Leyte. After that, the next stop would be home. Things were hectic. The days consisted of checking boxes of all sorts and going with the battalion commander on endless full field inspections. If I got a moment off, and got out of camp, chances are that Carmen had just caught a boat to any of the seven thousand islands.

After a week of near misses, I took off Sunday morning to talk with Mike and Guillermo and maybe look in on Daisy and Carie. Climbing the hill toward Mike's home, I heard Carmen calling my name.

She ran toward me, disregarding the aloof propriety a Filipino lady displays in public toward an American soldier. Smiling, arms outstretched, she ran between my open arms and laid her face against my chest as I enveloped her.

Haughty, elderly Filipino ladies who would speak only in Spanish tilted their noses a little higher as they passed the brazen little tart. A couple of white soldiers looked on enviously, and the slight shaking of their heads was asking, "What the hell's that black guy got that a white man ain't?" A black soldier, half drunk before noon on Sunday, maneuvered around us, mumbling, "You layin' down some righteously deep shit, man. Your shit is deep. Deep."

Carmen held on. She liked to hug and be hugged.

"I'm home," she mumbled into my shirt.

"Yeah. I'd almost given up hope."

She relaxed her arms and I released her. We clasped hands and turned toward Guillermo's home. I glanced at her. The skirt was made from a fatigue jacket. The shirt was cut down from a

khaki GI shirt and resewn to look a bit more feminine. The shoes
were wonderful: soft, thick, tan leather from the rifle scabbard cut
and sewn as Roman army sandals. The straps crisscrossed
halfway up, accenting her sturdy, shapely legs.

"They're very nice. I have a pair for Daisy and Carie. I know
you want them to have something, too."

Inside Guillermo's hut there were more *abrazos* and politics
took over.

After a short exchange of information on the elections, the
talk turned to the world revolution. It all looked so favorable for
us. Fascism was the last stand for imperialism. Social revolution
would have to take place. China was the key. It was only a matter
of time—a short time—before Chiang and the Kuomintang
would be defeated. Then India would go. The Vietminh were
already resisting the efforts of the French to take over again.

Guillermo excused himself and Carmen turned toward me.
We had so few serious political discussions. Everything was so
urgent and time so short. The discussions always ended with a
clash between my race man—Pan-Africanism, which had been
expanded to include all colored people—and her Marxism. Stim-
ulated by the discussion, she intended to carry it on. The discussion shifted from the international scene to ideology.

"So, where does this idea you have fit into the revolution?
You're really a Communist."

"I think the Communists are the only ones who understand
things. But I don't agree with everything they say—they're always
changing their line," I said.

"What don't you agree with?"

"Some of the things they say."

"What?"

"I don't know offhand," I answered. "They say so much."

"The basic thing we say is that the world is divided between
oppressed and oppressor nations. We say that all nations are
divided between exploiting and exploited classes. We say . . . "

"That's what I don't agree with. Just look. You can see
that the world is divided between white and colored. The white
people . . . "

"What do you mean, the white people?"

"Look, baby . . . "

"I'm no baby." Her black eyes were flashing danger signals.

"OK. You ain't no baby. That ain't what I meant anyway. I

mean, look, sweetheart . . . " Those eyes flashed again. "OK, comrade, then. But just listen to what I'm trying to say. The world is divided between two race groups. One group does nothing but make war on the other. The white exploits the colored and uses the money they take to build armies and organize for more war to take more money. They got the colored peoples' minds. White man's making new artillery while colored people are singing 'Ain't gonna study war no more.' They gotta stop talking that shit about peace and forgiveness. They gotta stop fightin' one another for the white man. They gotta stop begging and learn to stick together and fight."

"Why didn't you fight for Japan?"

"Japan? That's the shit we've got to get rid of. Why the hell were they fighting China?"

"Because they're an oppressor nation. An imperialist nation . . . "

"OK, Carmen. Let me finish. I'm about to make my point. Point is, we're nine-tenths of the world's population. They're one-tenth. One-tenth rules nine-tenths because one-tenth is united and armed while nine-tenths are disunited and praying. I'm only saying that we can get together and crush the damned imperialists once and for all."

I took a deep breath and waited for the tirade.

"We have to talk about the real world," she said. "Not something we're comfortable with . . . "

"I am talking about the real world. It's the world I live in."

"Let me finish . . . "

"I'm sorry." I wished that she would come to the States for about one week. Those hunkies would kick her cute little black ass around the block a few times and she'd understand.

". . . so people think what the economic system allows them to think," she said.

"I can't agree with that. These people create an economy to carry out their thinking." I didn't like being on the defensive.

"Oh. So first came slaves and then came cotton in your country."

I knew that the prewar schools in the Philippines used the same textbooks as in the States. College students tended to know more about the history of the U.S. than the history of the Philippines. I didn't want to get caught on that point.

"Well, you're right about that. The cotton had to come first."

"You're an idealist." She was slowly shaking her head. "The real world doesn't come from ideas."

"'Course I'm an idealist. I got ideals. That's why I'm a Communist. What's wrong with that?" I said, trying to find ground to defend.

She laughed. She wasn't really laughing at me. She just liked to laugh. She looked cute the way her face crinkled up and nearly closed her eyes. Her teeth were white against the velvet skin. I wanted to grab her and rub my lips across her face the way she did with the nylon. I knew better than to try that again when she was talking. Lawyerlike, she began to make her point. Those black eyes were looking steady-straight at me, unblinking, as if bore-sighting a rifle.

"A person would have to be crazy to think that the world is the result of his thinking. That would mean that there was a thought before there was a world." She spoke slowly, as if she absolutely had to convince me of this one.

"You know I didn't say that."

"That's what you said."

"I didn't say that. At least I didn't mean it that way."

"Your thoughts and actions aren't the same. Your actions are good . . ."

"That's not true. My thoughts and actions are exactly the same. I'm doing everything in my power to learn war and get the rest of our people to learn war and to unite all the colored people."

"You want to start with Japan? You fought the Japanese?"

"What kind of question is that? Of course I fought the fuckin' Japanese . . ."

"Why did you fight them?"

"Why? What do you mean, 'why'"?

"They're colored."

I felt the noose tightening.

"Sure they're colored. They don't act like it. They think they're white. They act white. Look what they did to China."

"Then you are fighting for colored China against colored Japan. Were you fighting for Russia? Why? They're white."

"They ain't thinking white. They ain't acting white."

"Are there Negro traitors in America?"

"The Negro mis-leader is the low-downist dog in the world. Sells cheap."

"Are they poor like most of the Negroes? Or is it class *and* race?"

"Of course, it's part class. I'm a Communist. I believe in class struggle. You Filipinos don't understand. You got a country. You got a nation. You got a flag. You got a language. You got an army. So some day you're gonna be free. Negro in America ain't got nothing. None of those things. All we got in common is misery and color. Shit, you're telling me we can't get together even on these things. We're saying the same thing, we're just using different words."

"I'm saying—learn from the Philippines. Our only hope is to unite with the workers and the oppressed people of the whole world, especially in America."

"I'm willing to get together as workers and oppressed people. It's the same thing and the same people."

The smile came back, and the face crinkled up.

"You are so stubborn."

"I ain't stubborn. You've been studying law with Guillermo."

"You've got a head like a coconut. Do you still love me?"

Her hand slid over my hand. Her eyes locked into mine and her breath deepened.

"You know I love you. I love you so much."

She nestled against me. My hand slid over her tiny, sculptured breast. Her cheek cuddled against my chest and she relaxed, sinking into the glowing warmth of her passion.

We could go no further. It was not the time, not the place, not the anything. We sat quietly embracing until we heard Guillermo's returning footsteps. We untangled ourselves.

"Martin is here. I have to go meet with the committee. Can you return?"

"Sure."

I hated that fucking committee. The committee giveth and the committee taketh away.

★

The four hours dragged by with tedious monotony. Each hour demanded its sixty minutes and each minute extracted sixty deliberate seconds. As the hands of the GI wristwatch made their painstaking way to 7:00, I started back to Guillermo's home.

She was a heart-stopping beauty in the new nylon Spanish dress. The flowing skirt and the tight-fitting bodice played different roles of accentuating or suggesting every curve and charm of her body. Thick black hair framed the dark, shining face and clashed with the brilliant white of the nylon.

She glanced into my eyes and knew I was adoring and devouring her. She partly turned to the right and then to the left and then, suddenly embarrassed, ran into my arms.

"God, you're so beautiful."

"I'm not beautiful. American girls are beautiful. Will you forget me when you go home?"

"Will you please shut up that talk."

"Will you forget me?"

"No. How could I forget you?"

"Will you forget the squadrons and the party?" She was suddenly becoming frighteningly serious.

"No, I won't forget them."

"Promise me."

"What's the matter, sweetheart?"

Now even more serious.

"Promise me."

"I promise. I could never forget you or the party or the squadrons."

She gave a little squeeze and released me.

"Señora Roa has opened a little restaurant in her home. Do you want to go there?"

It was only forty-five years since the ending of four hundred years of Spanish domination of the islands. Holding on to Spanish culture was an expression of anti-American defiance by the middle class. The highly educated Roa family had been a part of the political and cultural leadership of the town before the war. Refusal to cooperate with the Japanese cost them all their possessions, save their tastefully furnished, solidly built house. Serving meals to the soldiers was an effort to save it. They bore their demeaning burden with a grace characteristic of the Filipinos.

★

The elegant meal, which Carmen had ordered ahead of time, was graciously served by Señor Roa. I could not force myself to call him "Vicente," although we became friends before the evening ended. Throughout the dinner, and as we left the Roa house, Carmen and I talked of little things, agonizing through the certainty that the future of our relationship would have to be settled that night. Lost in our individual thoughts, we walked slowly past the docks and finally found a place to sit near the ocean and away from soldiers and civilians alike.

We sat silently for a few moments. It finally occurred to me that I would have to ask, and she would have to answer. It could not be the other way around. For the hundredth time that night I stared, memorizing that beautifully exotic, expressive face.

"Tell me." She tried to say it playfully.

"Do you know I love you?"

The moon sparkled on the whitecaps of the breaking tide. The shrill whistling of the nightbirds cut through the rustling of the palms. Her arms encircled my arm, and she nestled against it.

The plaintive "yes" gave voice to a terrible sadness that crept across her face. I knew I should back off. It was too late. There was no place to back to.

"I don't know how long I'll be here."

I struggled to say it so it made sense.

"I never talked about this because I know what it will mean—you being a member of the party—and Martin and Guillermo and everybody."

Her face was turned from me. She was looking into the sand and the black hair hid her eyes from me.

"I love you, and Jesus, I want you so much. I can't keep this up—hurtin' for you—scared to touch you or ask you."

She was silent. I paused so she could help me. I could feel the jumble of her thoughts and it frightened me.

"I've never really been in love." I said it as softly and sincerely as I could. "I was eighteen when I went to war."

I was afraid she was crying. I could already sense the answer. I had to go on.

"Do you love me enough to move in with me? I could fix a nice place. Down by the river. We could have each other." It was said.

The moment was anchored, fixed in time. The whitecaps, sparkling with moonlight, froze atop their cresting waves. The night birds hushed their shrill whistling. The rustle of the palms was stilled.

"Yes," she whispered. The world regained its life.

"Yes, I love you that much." Little-girl-like, she rubbed her fist across her eyes.

"I've never been in love, either," she said slowly. "I was also eighteen when I went to war."

I felt embarrassed—ashamed. Her war had been so much harder than mine.

"I wanted so much to love someone—and be loved, and to make love to him."

Her breathing became deep and regular as she regained control.

"We Filipino women," she finally looked up at me. "We're born in the tropics and our blood is hot."

The moon highlighted the little lines around her mouth and eyes at the beginnings of the smile.

"I remember when I first went to the university. There were a lot of women. At the end of the first year, half of them were pregnant and sent home. The Spanish used to say that Filipino women have their brains in their ovaries."

Her hand slid on top of mine.

"I wasn't going to be like that. I was going to study law with Guillermo. We were going to fight for the workers and peasants in the courts, where no one was fighting for them. I used to get mad at these women. All they talked about was love. All they sang about was love. They were all petty bourgeois. Guillermo and I— we had the party. We were revolutionaries.

"Then the Japanese came. At first it wasn't so bad. The combat soldiers had some discipline. Some of them really believed they were liberating the Philippines. They moved on to the Indies and New Guinea and the garrison troops came. They took our food. They raped us and beat us if we resisted. The landlords and the bourgeoisie believed the Japanese would win so they supported them. And the Japanese supported the landlords against the peasants. They began to kill all Communists. It was a people's war like China and Russia."

She glanced at me, realizing that she was talking politics.

"We formed our squadrons and went to the hills to hide and fight. At first we had only spears and knives. Sometimes a comrade would jump on a Japanese soldier and throw his shoulder against the bayonet to hold the rifle still and kill him with his knife. Dying, he would bring us the rifle so we could fight. Who could think of love?"

I pressed the olive-drab handkerchief into her hands and held her while the sobs racked her thin body. I wished to God I had never asked her.

"Carlos—I thought I loved him. I was only twenty. He always smiled and laughed through everything. Those times when we were discouraged and tired and hungry, he was our sunshine and laughter. When there was only a handful of food for ten of us, he would always share his with me. When I was barefoot, he risked his life to take the shoes from a Japanese soldier and bring them to me. When the Japanese sent troops to hunt us down and kill us, we would retreat far into the mountains and rest. Once or twice Carlos and I slipped away and made love. I was always ashamed. We were so foolish. We broke discipline. When we came near a Ou Sa Fee camp, he broke discipline again. He went and asked them for guns. The American officer told the Scouts to shoot him. I will always hate America for that."

She finally vomited it out. Slowly she realized that she had not answered me.

"You know I want to," she whispered. "The party opposes the emergency wife system."

Her gaze shifted out to the sea.

"I didn't mean it that way," I said.

She nestled against me again.

"You want to marry me?"

I had not even thought of it. The army did not allow the soldiers to marry. I said yes anyway.

Another deep breath of resignation.

"I can't leave my poor islands. I wanted to fill your heart with happiness. I only say no to you."

A slight shaking of her hair.

"I can't say no to the party and the squadrons."

She paused and breathed deeply again. As she struggled for composure, the words came out in phrases between the deep trembling breaths.

"We're going back to war."

Another trembling breath.

"I'm so afraid."

She struggled not to lose her composure.

"I can't leave the comrades."

I gathered her close to me and kissed the wetness of her eyes.

"Will you make love with me?" It sounded cold and selfish.

Her face was pressed into my shirt.

"If you ask me, I will. I'm a Filipino woman in love with you. Perhaps you will leave a baby in Mindanao, and a woman whose brains are in her ovaries."

She turned her face up to me. "You be the one."

I was not going to "be the one" to make that decision. It would be selfish. She would hate me for it. It would be . . . un-Communist. If we can't go forward, and there is no way to go back, what's going to happen to us? This isn't the way love affairs end. It can't be over. Sweetly, gently, lovingly—over.

We sat and embraced for a few moments. I felt relieved that it had been answered. A calm kind of emptiness set in. I took her hand. She rose and we walked back to Guillermo's.

"Tomorrow, I must leave with Martin."

Once again I etched her face into my memory. It was a terrible way to say good-bye. I was afraid and sure that it was good-bye.

"I'll always love you, Carmen."

"I love you, too. The world is not so big . . . "

I had to go, to get away. One more kiss, one more embrace.

"Good night, sweetheart. You'll be back. I'll see you then."

I had wanted to sound cheerful. Instead I sounded coldly nonchalant. There was nothing left to say.

★

I turned toward the prophylactic station where the convoy was assembling.

A group of white soldiers were finishing off a bottle of American whiskey. One of them handed the bottle to me. "Take a swig, sarge."

"Thanks—I need it." Old Log Cabin. A good gulp and the gasp for air.

"That's some good shit. Thanks."

The soldier took the bottle. Raising it above his head, he began singing the soldiers' parody of a popular song:

> *Fuck 'em all, fuck 'em all*
> *The long and the short and the tall*
> *Please give some nookie*
> *To the flatfooted rookie, and then,*
> *Fuck 'em all.*

Another soldier grabbed the bottle. "Home by next Christmas," he said and drained it.

The truck motors turned over and we climbed aboard.

46

A wish is too often the unappreciated father of the thought. The thought, expressing the wish, came to me in spurts. I didn't want to go back to America. Each year in America had been worse for me. I felt I could never again live with the segregation and discrimination. There was no end to it. Submit and kill your spirit or resist and get killed or simply leave. There were no other choices. I knew I could never again run from a white mob. I would fight and they would kill me, or I would kill some of them and then they would kill me. The only time in my life I felt like and was treated as an equal human being was in the East Indies and especially in the Philippines. I missed my parents and brothers, but I had been away from them since I was seventeen. In time I could go see them again.

Señor Roa had already suggested to me the sure, money-making scheme of getting a GI surplus generator and setting up a theater to show movies. The Filipinos loved movies and there was little other entertainment. Money was plentiful. I could simply melt into the millions of nameless, homeless refugees wandering the earth.

Each day of plotting to go over the hill strengthened my determination. I wouldn't allow myself to deal with the truth that I wanted to stay and fight the revolution here. I wanted to be with the comrades and near Carmen. War was my only trade and I was in love. These were the only things I had. I was afraid of losing them.

★

In the final stage of breaking camp and dissolving the division, we stored or shipped all the arms. The army issued new uniforms and personal items. Surprise inspections, held every day, found piles of grenades, trench knives, pistols, and submachine guns. The officers stripped us of any souvenir that was "the rightful property of the United States Government." They confiscated captured swords, daggers, and flags. Surprise "short arm" inspections discovered a few cases of the clap. The men, cursing their luck, were dragged off to the hospital.

I knew that whatever was to be done had to be planned quickly. The time to embark for Leyte was drawing near. The staff officers were relieved of their assignments and went ahead to arrange for our arrival and assignment to whatever ships were available to take us home. That left me alone in the operations section.

There were only two periods when I could get away and have enough time to hide out before I was missed. The first chance would be during the confusion just before embarkation for Leyte. The second would be in the confusion of the replacement depot on Leyte. I had no friends on Leyte and did not know the situation there. I decided that I would have to take my chances on Mindanao, where I would be missed sooner.

For me to get away, Sergeant Henson would have to cover for me if some directive came from regiment to our battalion. Bradley, acting as the first sergeant, could mark me present or accounted for and cover me for a day or so. I would have to talk to Mike and Guillermo. I needed a place to hide out. When the division embarked, I could head south into the hills and join up with the comrades. It all seemed so right and so simple.

Approaching Bradley was easy. As I spoke to him, his soft, fawnlike hazel eyes showed both sympathy and disapproval. When I had finished, he was silent for a moment, formulating his contradictory thoughts.

"I think you're wrong, man. You ain't no deserter. I don't mean from the army—fuck that. I mean our people. You done something important in this regiment. The guys respect what you tried to do. They ain't going to respect that you'd rather fight here than in Alabama. It's easy here. These people understand. They got their shit together. Marshall, Texas, ain't the nicest place on earth. But it's home and if it's going to get better, I got to do it. I'm goin' home."

"Yeah, I know what you're saying. I guess you might be right—but I don't know that kind of fighting. I know this. It's something I feel I got to do. Will you cover for me?"

"Sure. You know I will. You my road buddy, man. Remember how we used to talk about building a Negro people's liberation army? I knew it was just a dream, just an idea. But you stay here, an' I won't even have that."

Brad clapped his hand on my shoulder. There was no need to say anything else. We were buddies.

"It's just something I feel like I have to do."

"You're a fuckin' man. You're three times seven and you gotta do what ya gotta do."

★

Sergeant Henson wasn't so easy. Being from Saint Paul and thirty-eight years old, he felt sort of responsible for me. He listened to my plan with alternating looks of amazement and pain. He couldn't bear to wait until I finished.

"Nelson, Goddamn it, man," he protested. "You know you're talking some crazy shit. You desert and the United States Army will track you down and kill you if it costs a million and takes ten years. Last week I was looking at your 201 file. You know how they rate you? Combat efficiency: excellent. Personal efficiency: excellent. They wanted to send you to Officer's Candidate School. Major Akeley put his career on the line over that De Ritter shit. He's a Mississippi cracker. He went to bat for you. You're twenty-two years old. You've got the world in a jug and the cork in your hand. I'm not going to let you fuck up your life."

"Henson, this is something I've got to do. I'm going to do it. I just need your help."

"You know when I get back home, your mother and father are going to call and ask what happened. Your mother is going to say, 'Couldn't you have talked to him?' What the hell am I going to say? 'He's got a head like a rock?' Why do you want to do this?"

"I know how to fight. I believe in this fight. Beside that, you know I'm in love . . . "

"You're in love! You're twenty-two. You ain't been near a woman—you ain't been fucked since you were seventeen. You think you won't fall in love? You think it will last as long as that warrant for your arrest?"

His face was flushed. He thrust his head outward from his shoulders. The immaculate, wavy salt-and-pepper hair was becoming disheveled.

"Man!" he kept exclaiming, "Goddamn it! Shit. Hell no."

"I'm pretty sure you won't put me in prison," I said.

He ran his fingers through his hair, expressing his surrender.

"No, I won't. I just hoped that you'd come back to Minneapolis and get an education and take over that stupid fuckin' city."

"Thanks, Henson. I know what you're telling me. I appreciate what you feel."

"Sleep on it, man," he said. "It's an irreversible mistake."

＊

Mike came to the camp every day, making the most of our departure. Joking with the men, he sold them trinkets and gathered up the odds and ends that an army on the move must discard. They were things of value to the civilian population. I waited in the tent for him to make his way through his friends.

"Got to talk to you, Mike."

"Good. I have to talk to you, too."

Duffel bag of loot slung over his shoulder, he walked back to the road with me. I laid out my plan. As I made my points, his eyes would widen and he would mutter like a soldier of the Ninety-third, "Oh, Goddamn!"

"So. What do you think, Mike?"

"I think I better talk to the comrades."

"Yeah. I want you to. What were you going to tell me?"

"I was going to say you should talk to the comrades tonight. Jose and Jesus returned. Jose said he has some San Miguel ＊ for you."

"Good! Good! I'll be there. At the building? Seven?"

★

Half a mile beyond the building, I tapped on the window of the truck taking the men to Cagayan.

"Hey, man. Let me off."

"What the fuck you want to get off for? We ain't supposed to stop."

"What the hell you think I want to get off for? Lemme un-ass the Goddamn truck, man."

Tapping the brakes to warn the following truck, the driver slowed down and as I jumped, he yelped, "Hit it one time for me, sergeant."

★

Jose, Jesus, and Guillermo rose from their coconut log seat as I approached. I was surprised to see Martin.

Abrazos all around.

"Congratulations on the promotion, Jose. Congratulations, Jesus."

They smiled their thanks. I started to crack a joke about the truckload of weapons. Sosa seemed to sense it and his eyes narrowed. There was no need to talk about it, so why mention it?

"I guess Mike told you, I wanted to talk about something."

"Yes," Martin smiled. He was showing the strain of five years at war. He looked a little thinner than before. I imagined he must have had a difficult week. His eyes were bright and alert, but the lines in his face betrayed the weariness of the combat soldier. Even so, he still looked and spoke like a teacher.

"Yes," he repeated. "We were happy that an American soldier—a Communist soldier—would feel strong enough about our revolution to leave his family and country and come fight for us."

Sosa nodded in agreement. Guillermo looked softly but steadily into my face with inquisitive black eyes.

"We need you very much. It will be very difficult for us to win our revolution by ourselves. The military and political situation is becoming very difficult. Roxas, as chairman of the Senate, has taken over the Committee on Appointments. He has dismissed all of Osmeña's appointments and practically gained control of the government. Osmeña has compromised himself into an impossible position. Now, Roxas is fighting for a bill to outlaw the Communist Party, the Hukbalahap, and the Democratic Front. The elections are already a joke. Some Fascist army units along with some special U.S. Marine units are attacking our base camps and killing peasants who support us."

Martin paused for a moment to let the significance of his words sink in. I nodded in agreement and he went on.

"We can defeat the Philippine Army. If we do, the United States will invade again. China and Indochina have the advantage of friendly states on their borders. We have no common borders and could expect very little help. Our first effort must be to prevent intervention by the U.S. Army."

Martin paused again.

"How will you do that?" I asked. It was the opening Martin had waited for.

"We believe the people of the United States would support our struggle for national liberation if they only knew the truth. We are deeply grateful that you—and other soldiers, too—have offered to stay and fight. If you stay here, you will kill perhaps ten enemy soldiers before you are killed. If you went home and convinced ten Americans of our cause, it would be worth one hundred dead enemy soldiers."

I knew he was right.

Sosa, his smile full of comradely love and respect, picked up as Martin sat back.

"The strategic key to a revolution is to block the intervention. No matter how hard we fight, we cannot do this. Only the American people can do this. Only a Communist who has seen what you have seen can do this."

Jose paused for a moment. I thought I saw the glint of a tear in his eyes.

"Go back to America, comrade. Go back and fight for the revolution. Don't forget us in those hills," he nodded toward the south and then to the west and to the north. "In those hills will be comrades who will always love you and think of you." Jose blinked his eyes.

"It's more difficult in America than here," Guillermo said quietly.

"Here, we fight and win or die. There, the Communist has the job of closing the circle. When America goes Communist, the whole world will be free."

I had nothing to defend. I agreed with them. I'd go back and, Goddamn it to hell, I'd fight.

There were smiles and *abrazos*. Jose went into the building and came out with bottles of beer.

We made toasts to the revolution and to the party, to the American people and to the Philippines.

Halfway down the second bottle of San Miguel, I said to Guillermo, "Mike said you wanted to talk to me."

"Yes," he smiled. "We must meet tomorrow night. The comrades are not prepared to meet tonight. It will be a security meeting."

"Good." Perhaps, I thought, I'll meet with someone who will tell me how to go about this new assignment.

"Can you meet Jose just to the north of the Sixth Division at seven o'clock?"

"Sure thing."

We emptied the bottles and carefully put them away. There was plenty of beer but a shortage of bottles. The only guarantee of a full bottle was to return an empty one.

A few more moments of lighter talk and I said good night. They wanted to accompany me, but I thought it best that I go to the road alone and hitchhike back to the camp.

47

THE FOLLOWING EVENING I walked down near the Sixth Division area where it would appear that Sosa was simply picking up a hitchhiker. Within a few moments he pulled out of the camp and swung to the side of the road. I jumped in, acknowledging his hello grin, as he gunned the jeep down the road toward Cagayan.

Lieutenant Sosa slowed the jeep and swung off to the narrow dirt road that led from Mambajao to the sea. Then he left that and drove into a coconut grove. The tires spun and slid across broken palm branches, bumped over coconuts, and ground through the soft, sandy spots. He jammed it into four-wheel drive, weaving the jeep through the groves, up the sloping bluff and down the other side, toward a finger of the sea that jutted into the sandy beach of the ravine.

"Where the fuck you taking me, Jose?"

We were to ourselves and there was no need for military courtesy, just comradeship. He stopped the jeep and switched off the lights at the edge of the beach where the sand met the palm trees.

"I'm taking you to meet Mike." He grinned knowingly at me. The silver lieutenant's bar reflected the bright silver of the rising moon.

I had learned not to ask too many questions and to expect almost anything from my Philippine friends and comrades. I was not really surprised to catch a glimpse of Mike as he appeared and disappeared, making his way through the darkness and the palms and the underbrush. I suddenly wasn't so sure that they hadn't told me to get a pass in order to meet Mike at a hidden cove. He came to the jeep smiling—holding out that fingerless hand. I climbed down from the jeep to throw my arm around his thin shoulders.

"How you doin', Mike?"

"Good, good. You good too, huh?"

"What's happenin'? What we gonna do?"

He turned to look through the trees toward the beach and started to whistle softly. The first note sent my heart into my throat and the blood racing through my head, jostling the words around in my brain:

I'm waiting here to give you all my love,
That's my promise to the stars above.
I want to fill your heart with happiness—

Carmen came toward us, drifting through the darkness. The GI jacket, the Japanese pants, the carbine were gone. She wore a Spanish-style white blouse and colorful Philippine sarong wrapped around her hips. The moon, silver-white, and the huge bright stars of the Southern Cross had melted bronze into the dark of her face and arms. She walked toward us, lips parted, smiling "Hello, Comrade." I fought back the tears. I would have died for her to show how much I loved her.

I took her hand and apologized for staring.

Jose pulled a basket of food from the back of the jeep.

"Guillermo sends this to his comrade sister." Then he pulled the carbine from its scabbard and handed it to me, along with two clips of ammunition. "Better hang on to this—just in case." I was afraid to think what they had planned.

Mike climbed into the jeep.

"We'll be back later. You have a picnic now."

The jeep turned around, lights stabbing into the coconut grove. Jose pushed the accelerator. The red taillights bumped up the bluff behind a cloud of sand and disappeared over the crest.

I turned to her, wanting to say everything and unable to say anything. She leaned against me, relieved and happy to be a woman again. I enveloped her lithe body, half lifting her and holding the fifty-eight inches of Carmen against me, the marbled nipples hard against my chest. Embarrassed and perhaps a bit frightened, she pulled away. Something in the back of my brain was saying easy, baby; don't fuck this up. She's gonna do it.

I took her hand. She smiled up at me and nodded toward a clump of palm trees.

"Comrade Ruiz brought Mike and me here for a picnic. We have a blanket and fruit and Guillermo sends chicken and bread."

We both laughed and the tension was gone. We spread the blanket and devoured the food between forced talk and laughter. When it was over we kicked off our shoes and waded ankle-deep into the sea, splashing and washing our hands and faces. I followed her back across the beach and, afraid to speak, sat down beside her. She put her hand to my chest to still my heart and whispered something of how American women were beautiful with their big breasts and long legs. Her eyes were asking a lover's question as she unbuttoned her blouse and lay back with breasts bare and head pillowed in the mass of thick black hair.

Wiggling out of my shirt and supported on an elbow, I barely touched my chest to her breast and lowered my head to kiss her. Easy, baby, easy. I should have jerked off before I came here, but I didn't know. Don't hurry and don't come.

"I love you, Carmen."

Her thin arm went around my neck and the gentle pressure invited a deep, loving kiss. Unbuttoned pants were kicked away. Passion took over. Her breast tight against my chest, the rhythmical pressure of her crotch against my bare hip invited me to loosen her sarong. Her mouth, wet with sweet saliva, was glued to mine. Bent knees, inviting open legs—I knew if I touched her there I would lose control. I finally eased my mouth from hers and licked and kissed to her breast. She pulled me to slide on top of her.

I felt a wave of coolness not unlike what the infantryman feels watching the sergeant raise his arm and signal to begin the attack. Suddenly I was in control. I was a man in love with a woman. I didn't die in the war. I didn't go crazy, and Carmen brought me back to the revolution. Looking at her body, bronzed and black against the blanket, I knew I was going to love her and please her and, for tonight, we would forget the terror of war and starvation.

I remembered everything I had ever learned about sex. And remembered everything I had ever thought about sex. And remembered everything I had ever heard about sex for those four years in the barracks and bivouacs and foxholes.

★

I touched everything and held her still and kissed everything and when she whispered to me I was atop her, gasping—heart hammering.

Flag it to the East and flag it to the West
Oh God, Baby
Flag it to the North and flag it to the South
Oh Jesus, Sweet Baby
Do it like the rabbit
I love you so
Thrust like the dog
Sweet Carmen Sweet Love Carmen
Do the long steady stroke like the horse
Darling Baby Sweet Sweet Darling Baby
Jelly roll to the rhythm of the low-down Easy Ridin'
blues.
Oh God Yes HoneyLove Yes Sweet Heart Carmen

Her lips were wet against my ear, her moist breath whispering,

Iniibig kita   Te quiero   my love.

Dripping with sweat, spent, and exhausted yet unsatisfied, we lay side by side, clasped together as the hunger in my loins gave way to a creeping, leaden sleep. One arm relaxed its lover's grip and slowly stretched out onto the sand. A shoulder relaxed and, lying on my back, I saw the Southern Cross through half-closed eyes. Tiny and lovely, she crawled partly atop me. I felt the tears, gentle at first, then the sobbing and the flood of hot droplets on my chest. As I turned to hold her, I could not stop my tears, which fell upon her face and wet her hair.

Emotions damned and crushed by three years of war broke free. I held her close to ease my pain and soothe the sobs that wracked her thin body. Her tears fell for the thousands of Huks the Japanese had tortured to death. Tears for the raped and brutalized children. Tears for the comrades in Luzon and Leyte and Panay ambushed and killed by the marines and the Philippine Army. Tears for those betrayed by their leaders and murdered by the Americans. Tears for a love we knew we could never have.

★

The sobs subsided to little whimpers and, as she slept, I held her, her heart beating close to mine, warming and guarding her till dawn crept from the vast blackness of the Pacific, rising slowly, softly from the Philippine Sea.

The sun squinted above the horizon. Gulls took the air, hovering in the updraft of the sea. The birds of Mindanao began their day-long chatter. The sea slipped from the sandy beach, leaving flotsam markers. Surely, the world took note of what had happened last night. The gulls looked toward me with seeming envy. They, too, must know what love is. The tide gurgled and growled as it slipped from the beach and, after a moment's hesitation, roared back to claim the shore. How many lovers had that tide awakened?

I kissed her while she squirmed and stretched. For a sweet while she clung to me, unwilling to waken, suspended between dreams and daylight. I gathered her onto my lap and gently, slowly rocked and caressed her while the sun rose hot above the šea. As her arm went around my neck, she sleepily kissed me and whispered, "Te quiero—I love you so."

When she had woken enough to realize she was nude, she shook the thick hair, rubbed her face to awaken fully, slipped into the blouse, and wrapped the sarong around her hips. She knelt between my legs, eyes closed, cuddling her face against my chest, unwilling to leave our fragile little world for the one wakening to the sunshine.

As the earth awoke, I held her close until I heard the jeep that would take her back to a world that would claim her and take her from me.

48

I BARELY GOT back to camp when the order came to leave Mindanao. Bradley, thinking I was "over the hill," had already marked me accounted for. His thin, tan face broke into a wide smile when he saw me.

"Ya fuckin' nut. You going home?"

"Yeah. You ain't got rid of me yet."

By 9:00 A.M., the sun was hot. Drenched with sweat, we struck the last of the tents, folded them, and stacked them on the big six-by-six trucks. The bulldozers rumbled through the company area covering over the garbage pits, knocking down the fences and poles, and covering over the drainage ditches.

We lined up and stacked our duffel bags on the trucks. Then we spread out, policing the company area, picking up the last of the paper and trash. We were actually leaving. I looked down the road toward Cagayan and wished I had time to say good-bye to everyone.

The Sixth Division jeep left the road and swung into our area. It was Jesus and Mike. I walked over to meet them, happy they had come to say good-bye. When the handshakes and the *abrazos* were done, Mike handed me a folded paper. My heart skipped a beat. I knew what it was.

My Comrade, My Darling,

When you read these lines, do not cry as I am doing. I am sorry I had so little time to surrender my heart and my song. Remember your promise to me. If you do, then you will be true to our love. When you leave these poor Islands, take my broken heart back to America with you. If we win the victory, perhaps we will meet again. If not, the Philippines will be my tomb and there I shall love you forever.

Carmen

Both Mike and Jesus embraced me as I gave way to sobbing and tears.

I could hear Bradley calling out the company roll. As their names sounded, the men would shout a happy "Here!" and swing aboard the truck.

"I have to go, comrades." An arm around each of them, I pulled them close. I wiped my eyes and controlled myself for the walk back to the company.

"Adios, comrade."

"So long."

A trinket—a souvenir. She is so sentimental about these things. I almost forgot. I have nothing. My watch. I handed it to Mike. My dog tags. I pulled them over my head and pushed them into his hand.

"Give them to Carmen."

I couldn't say any more. I turned from them and walked back into the army.

★

The infantry landing craft lined up for half a mile along the beach. As each truck pulled into the designated area, we jumped down and lined up. Harold was looking anxiously at the little group of women who had come to say good-bye to their lovers and emergency husbands. He had brought his Javanese-looking "wife" up from Tawi-Tawi and had been with her almost three months. Her pregnancy was beginning to show. She saw him and stepped from the group. Harold looked at Brad, teary eyes begging permission to break ranks.

"Go ahead, man."

Lieutenant Hartsfield barely shook his head. How sad it was. The two stood apart from the company, embracing and sobbing.

Captain Christmas called the company to order. A platoon to each landing craft, Lieutenant Hartsfield led us aboard. Our craft was the last one of the battalion to back away from the beach. Harold pushed his way to the front and climbed the iron rings for a final look. He raised his hand in a pitiful gesture of "Good-bye, I love you."

Hartsfield looked at him for a moment and said, "For Christ's sake, be a man."

Then he turned his back on Harold.

"Sir?" Harold asked in disbelief.

"I said, be a man."

Lieutenant Hartsfield pushed his way to the rear of the landing craft. He did not want the responsibility of seeing it.

I reached into my pocket and gave Harold all the money I had. The soldiers nearby did the same. Pockets stuffed with pesos, he grabbed the battered trumpet case and swung over the side into the waist-deep water. The landing craft completed its turn to the open sea and made way for the ship that would take us to Leyte.

I closed my eyes and called her to me. First the smiling whole, then the sweet heartache of seeing each part: the short, even bangs across her forehead, framing her face; the thick jet-black hair falling alongside the feline, smiling eyes; the even white teeth; the perfect little conical breasts—I smiled, thinking how she would throw back her shoulders to make them appear larger; the slight swell of the "love belly" above the pubic bone, the soft, sparse hair beneath; the muscular thighs; the strong, straight legs ending in thin ankles and tiny, calloused feet.

I wished I was free, like Harold, to go over the side. I felt the note in my breast pocket and knew it could never be.

I did not know that Carmen had four years and ten months to live. In the spring of 1950, a retired Negro soldier in Manila decided to try for the fifty thousand dollars the government was offering for the location of the headquarters of the Hukbalahap. Coached by the CIA and relying on the trust the revolutionaries had in the American blacks, he slowly wormed his way upward until he was taken to their headquarters in the hills near the city. This black judas collected his money and the U.S. Army furnished the helicopters for the attack. As sometimes happens in war, the government accidently picked the perfect date for the assault. An enlarged central committee meeting was held on October 7, 1950, the day of the raid. A small group survived the initial assault from the air and attempted to fight their way out. They were surrounded by ground troops and systematically slaughtered. I wrote to the Philippine consul in San Francisco and asked for the papers covering that week. Carmen and a comrade who must have been her father were listed as those killed trying to break out.

That slaughter spelled the end of the Hukbalahap. Leaderless, the local squadrons fought on against the brutal, lopsided war of extermination until the rise of the New People's Army.

49

THE LITTLE ATTACK transport carrying our battalion home rolled and plunged, wallowed and plowed eastward through the choppy sea. Christmas eve morning, we embarked from Leyte and moved beneath a massive Pacific storm all the way to Hawaii. We celebrated Christmas 1945 with an official service and prayers led by Chaplain Watkins. The real prayer meetings were led by the two dozen jackleg preachers in the battalion. I pushed my way through and around the groups huddled below deck, listening to the preaching and the Christmas spirituals. The generations since slavery shielded and protected the taut emotion of the preaching and praying and the sweet sorrow of the spirituals. It was the glue of culture that held us together as a people.

I knew the most important phase of my becoming a man and a revolutionary was drawing to a close. In Wabasha and Minneapolis, I grew up and was educated around the fringes of my people and didn't really know them. At eighteen, I was thrown into the violent, loving conglomerate of eighteen thousand mainly Southern, mainly rural Negroes. They were the wellspring and the anchor of our culture and our sense of community. From Harlem, from the Black Belt, from New Orleans, from the violence of Texas, from Los Angeles we had come. Each brought his longings and beliefs and poetry and the common things that made us a people. We stood together and had gained a new pride and unity and understanding in the unending battle against an army that hated us, an America that despised and feared us, a white world that would rather be conquered and occupied by the Japanese or Germans than grant permission for us to enter their countries in order to defend them.

We grew strong-tempered in their forge, sharpened on their anvil, and hardened by their hammer. I knew that when the moment came—and it would come—these men were going to be the cutting edge of a movement that would change America.

★

On January 3, 1946, we stood along the rail, watching the mountains of California rise from the morning mist. By noon I could see the huge, white "A Grateful Nation Welcomes You Home" sign and the buildings along the Embarcadero.

The men were bitterly joking about the sign and coming home.

"I don't think things have changed. I think we're going to have to fight every inch of the way."

"Where there's life there's hope. But where there's trees there's rope."

Big Joe looked over the men and then out to America. Mostly to himself he said, "There's gonna be more lynchin' and beatin' and killin' us off. You kick a man's ass an' it gets tough. We's like that Louisiana mud. They gonna stomp us and we'll squish up 'tween their toes and finally we gonna stand up and walk like a natural man."

The loudspeaker drowned out further discussion.

"Now hear this: All army personnel report to the main deck."

We made our way as close as we could to where Chaplain Watkins stood on a platform. When the shuffling and mumbling died down, he held up his hands and said, "Men, we're almost home. Almost home to ring them shining bells." He smiled at his impromptu use of the spiritual.

"You've traveled a long, stony road. When you get home, never forget you are combat veterans of the greatest war in history and that you are citizens of the country you defended.

"Lift every voice and sing . . . "

The battalion joined in the familiar, beautiful if difficult, anthem:

> Lift every voice and sing
> Till earth and heaven ring,
> Ring with the harmonies of Liberty;
> Let our rejoicing rise
> High as the listening skies,
> Let it resound loud as the rolling sea.
>
> Sing a song full of the faith that the dark past has
>   taught us.
> Sing a song full of the hope that the present has
>   brought us.
> Facing the rising sun of our new day begun,
> Let us march on till victory is won.
>
> Stony the road we trod,
> Bitter the chastening rod,
> Felt in the days when hope unborn had died;
> Yet with a steady beat,
> Have not our weary feet
> Come to the place for which our fathers sighed?
> We have come over a way that with tears has been
>   watered,
> We have come, treading our path through the blood
>   of the slaughtered,
> Out from the gloomy past,
> Till now we stand at last
> Where the white gleam of our bright star is cast.

God of our weary years,
God of our silent tears,
Thou who was brought us thus far on the way;
Thou who hast by Thy might
Led us into the light,
Keep us forever in the path, we pray.
Lest our feet stray from the places, our God, where
    we meet Thee;
Lest our hearts, drunk with the wine of the world, we
    forget Thee;
Shadowed beneath Thy hand,
May we forever stand.
True to our God.
True to our native land.

Chaplain Watkins raised his hand to dismiss us. Someone started to applaud; a few picked it up. It spread and soon 850 men were applauding and whistling. It was from, to, and for us. We liked ourselves more than ever before in history and wanted the world to know.

The loudspeaker ordered us below to prepare to disembark. We felt the nudging of the tugs and finally the bump as the ship settled against the dock.

This time, Camp Stoneman was the first stop on our way home. German prisoners of war served us steak, freshly whipped potatoes, fresh bread, steamed vegetables, and frothy glasses of milk. When I went back for a second glass, the German said, "Das ist verboten, aber ich kriege ihn gern den Neger . . . "

I tried to leap over the railing, pulling at my trench knife, screaming, "You Nazi motherfucker, I'll kill you—"

An MP and two black soldiers wrestled me to the floor and got the knife away. After they released me, I got back to my feet.

"What the hell's the matter with you, soldier?" the MP said, as if trying to calm down a tantrum-prone child.

"You hear what that fuckin' German called me?"

"I heard what he said, and I know what you're thinking—that's why I ain't running you in. He said a second helping is against the rules, and he was tryin' to say but he'd get it for the black soldier."

Sheepishly turning to the two black soldiers, I said, "I thought he called me a nigger."

They grinned and I knew it had happened before.

I turned to the POW and held up my right hand in surrender. "Sorry, fella."

The German nodded and I went back to my table.

"I don't think you'll make it all the way home. The war's over, Road Buddy," Brad said.

★

We were youths in our teens and early twenties when we arrived at Fort Huachuca in 1942. For four years we had been molded by the army and the war. Socially disoriented, and as unsure of civilian life as we had been of army life four years before, we began the process of discharge from the army.

After lining up to have the Red Cross women sew the ruptured duck on our new jackets, we got our medals and combat infantry badges. Brad, Juicy, Lee, Joe, Hewitt, Jeff, Parker, Big Joe, and I stood together for a moment. Then we said our final good-byes.

Combat and the oppression of the army had held us together. It was gone with the war. Gone was the love and camaraderie that had sustained us through the years of loneliness. Gone with the hunger and foot-slogging exhaustion. Gone with the mud-slicked, jungle-canopied trails to terror in the phosphorous glow of Solomon nights. We could not admit that it was gone without admitting that it had been.

We exchanged addresses. We embraced and shook hands. We traded slaps on the back. This was really good-bye. We knew we would never see one another again.

We were going back to try and weave 1946 to 1942. We would try to reunite with old friends, wives, and lovers. We would try to bridge those four years. But we knew they would remain as a rampart, forever separating us from those who never served in the infantry.

A few of the soldiers from Louisiana and Mississippi cut the French blue helmet insignia from their jackets. It would be dangerous to wear it in some areas. Others stated they wore it fighting the Japanese, and they weren't backing down now.

We were happy, if apprehensive, as we separated into groups according to our home military areas. Our barrack bags, stuffed with new clothing, were hoisted onto our shoulders and we marched to the trains. A final surprise inspection and the army took back the grenades, tommy guns, and souvenirs of war that had been successfully hidden for the past month.

At Camp McCoy, Wisconsin, we went through the final health inspection, which consisted of a hurried short-arm exam. At the psychological examination, I admitted that I'd jacked off a few times during the war. I was judged healthy and sane. The adjutant handed me my discharge, a check for three hundred dollars, and a ticket home.

Minneapolis in January was chest-cramping, face-searing, gasping, bitter cold. The taxi pulled over in front of the house and stopped at a gap in the three-foot-high snowdrift. The front door still didn't have a lock. Kicking the snow off my boots, I pushed it open.

A younger brother was still in navy blue. Ben, in olive drab trousers and white civilian shirt, stood up grinning. He had been home from Italy for over a month. Mom, smiling with tears in her eyes, wiping her hands on the apron, came toward me. I embraced her. She seemed so small, weeping silently, her graying head against my shoulder. Her sailor was home from the seas. Her soldiers were home from the war. All her sons were home. It was a time for weeping.

As the moment became awkward, I released her saying, "We're home. What'cha crying about?"

She touched my face just to make sure, and stepped back smiling.

My six brothers came close for the embrace and the slug on the arm. God, how they had grown! The scuffling and wrestling that followed was the final ritual. I was really home.

We sat for an hour trying to talk, to catch up. It had been four years and it was difficult to say any but the most superficial things. We finally gave up. There would be time. We would have to learn again how to talk together. I put on the heavy olive drab overcoat and went to the corner.

The Dreamland was crowded. Mr. Cassius saw me and drew a large stein of beer, shouting, "Welcome home, Nelson. You're the last of the boys to get back."

The men standing at the bar turned toward me with welcoming smiles. It was then that I saw Pop. He looked me over, glancing at my left arm. The neatly sewn French blue helmet insignia of the Ninety-third Division, the staff sergeant chevrons, the hash marks and overseas stripes made an uninterrupted pattern the length of my jacket sleeve. His eyes shifted to the left chest, to the blue-and-silver combat infantry badge topping the two rows of awards and campaign ribbons. I think it was the only moment of my life when he approved of me. Pop rose, swaying a bit from the beer. I went to meet him. We embraced. He kissed me, for the first time in my life, I think, and then it was for the sake of the barroom audience as much as for me.

"I guess you're a Goddamn man now."

I released him, smiling.

"Glad to see you, Pop."

After exchanging a few words about the war with Pop's friends, I joined a group of vets on the cafe side. Dressed in combinations of civilian and military clothing, they'd been home for awhile. Some were guys I'd known for years; most of them had come to Minneapolis during the war. After the introductions, we sat down to exchange our stories.

We were all trying to find common ground—where we fit in. I was an uncomfortable stranger in my hometown. After a few pitchers of beer, the group left for the Elks Club. I sat for some time looking at the beer, watching the froth disintegrate.

One of Pop's friends, leaving the tavern, stopped at the booth.

"Got the postpartum blues, soldier?"

I looked up at him and smiled.

"I got something, I guess." No vet would dare say he missed the war and his rifle and his buddies.

"We all went through it after the last war. They said we were shell-shocked. But that wasn't it. I don't know if you ever get over it, but you'll learn to live with it." He smiled at me and left the tavern.

The weeks dragged by with visits to friends and relatives. Each night was spent with another group of vets—drinking, fighting off the new, indescribable loneliness, trying to find a place to fit in in a city that no longer felt like home.

★

Mac called on Saturday afternoon.

"The old gang is getting together for a real good party tonight. I'll pick you up about nine. OK?"

"Good deal, Mac. I'll be ready."

By the time we got there, the party was in full swing. Desperate to reenter civilian life, I joined in. The soft blue lights, the glass of bourbon someone pushed into my hand, the seemingly spine-less young brown body clinging tightly against me, writhing to the weepy, sensuous piano rhythm of Yancey's "How Long Blues" kindled the fire I thought dead for the past month.

The record ended. I gave her a little squeeze.

"Thanks—that's the first time I felt like I was out of the war."

It was then that I thought of Lonnie, of Herman, of Carmen and the others fighting on a handful of rice a day in the hills of Mindanao. The veteran feels a special kind of loneliness. It comes from his inability to communicate with the scores of people around him. He still thinks and speaks the language of the army and war. The loneliness deepened as I tried to drown it with bourbon and strangle it with laughter.

The blast of frigid air cut into the sweaty room. A few of the guys had gone out for more whiskey. They set a pint of bourbon on the table. I reached for it.

"You gonna have to get another bottle. I'm going to drink this one dry."

"You get one drink and pass it along."

"That's what I mean. I'm going to kill this one."

"You take it in one drink, you can have it."

I twisted off the cap.

Seeing I was serious, Mort said softly, "Don't try it, man. It will kill you."

"I got to drink a silent toast, Mort."

I lifted the bottle to my lips, threw my head back, and gulped the fire down. I set the empty bottle on the table and tried to walk to the door so I could puke the stuff out before it killed me.

It was thirty degrees below zero. The sweat froze on my face as I hung over the porch railing, vomiting thick brown fluid.

Someone steadied me, wiping my face with a towel.

"He's vomiting blood—we got to get him to the hospital."

We got into the car. Between the painful retching, I was alert enough to think about dying. It wasn't that I cared; I wondered if I had done it on purpose. As I was losing consciousness, it became clear to me: It doesn't make any difference. I no longer have a mission.

During the next two days, I would wake long enough to sip a little fluid and then sink back into the dark nothingness that enveloped me. Sometimes I was partly aware of the doctors examining me. I heard one of them say to the other, "I can't believe it. He must have the constitution of an ox."

The morning of the third day, I was suddenly fully awake. When the doctor came for the morning examination, I smiled as cheerfully as I could and asked to go home.

"You had a pretty close call, young man."

"I was throwing up blood. Is my stomach damaged?"

"It wasn't blood. It was liver bile. It started flowing the wrong way and probably saved your life." He looked seriously at me. "I'll discharge you, but I want you to tell me honestly: Did you try to commit suicide?"

"I don't think so. I just got drunk."

"How long have you been out of the service?"

"About three weeks."

"Where did you serve?"

"South Pacific—infantry."

"We get an abnormal number of cases of infantrymen who served in the Pacific. Automobile accidents, serious injuries from fights, accidental gunshot wounds. I think the war left a number of veterans suicidal. We list them as shell-shocked. I'm telling you this so if you feel such an urge again—come to the hospital."

I thanked the doctor. I wasn't going to come back. I'd had time to think. Out of the army, without guns, I didn't know how to carry on. I couldn't fight with guns anymore and didn't know any other way. I understood the problem.

Since my discharge from the army, Jesse Payne had been lynched near Tallahassee, Florida. Omar Bradley, the so-called GI's general, militantly reaffirmed segregation in the Veterans Hospitals. Negroes in the federal prison in New York—many of them veterans—struck against segregation. Black soldiers in Manila, Philippine Islands, rioted after the murder of one of their comrades by white MPs. Joe Louis, our greatest hero, was cursed and spit at when he entered a white waiting room in the bus station at Portsmouth, Virginia. One hundred brave Negro veterans—some from the Ninety-third—marched through downtown Birmingham, Alabama, demanding the right to vote. In New York City, a cop murdered a soldier and a civilian and critically wounded a sailor—all of them black. A Negro veteran was murdered by cops in Chicago; another was shot to death in Milwaukee.

A bloc of Republicans and southern Democrats defeated the Fair Employment Practice bill. When our petitions in support of the bill were presented, Louisiana's Senator Ellender said, "Negroes should be seen, not heard."

There was work to be done. I still had a mission—more difficult than the last one, and more urgent.

I made up my mind to go see Meridel Le Sueur, to talk to Sam Davis and Vickie. I would use the GI Bill of Rights and learn to fight another way.

I lay back on the pillows, feeling at peace for the first time since I left the Philippines. Without pain, or sense of loss, I thought of them: Those who gave their all, that we who lived might learn—and carry on.

★

Rest well, beloved comrades,
The fight will go on till we've won.